THE GREAT ROAD CLIMBS OF THE PYRENEES

Rapha

*To my beloved companion of the high places,
free spirit of the air and space beyond, for whom
the flat earth is a decided nuisance.*

© Rapha Racing Limited 2010
First published in Great Britain in 2008 by
Rapha Racing Limited, Imperial Works, Perren Street, London NW5 3ED
www.rapha.cc | +44 (0) 20 7485 5000

ISBN: 978-0-9558254-0-8
No part of this book may be reproduced or transmitted in any
form by any means without the written consent of the publisher.
Typeset in GaramontBQ

Creative Director: Luke Scheybeler
Design and Production: Jonathan Bacon
Illustrations: Ben Aquilina
Printing: The Manson Group

Special thanks to Will Webb for the original idea, Andrew Maxwell-Hyslop for editing, Mike Curtis for proof reading, Neil Wass for patience and all at Rapha for their help over two years.

THE RAPHA GUIDE TO

THE GREAT ROAD CLIMBS OF THE PYRENEES

by Graeme Fife
photography by Pete Drinkell

Rapha

Contents

Map	6
Introduction	8
Naming of the eight sectors	11
Geography	11
History	14
Riding the mountains	18
How to get there	21
Emergency numbers in france	21

Part 1 Eskuara — 22

Pico Gorromakil 1090m	39
Col d'Ispeguy 672m	40
Saint-Jean-Pied-de-Port	41
Col de Burdincurutcheta 1135m	45
Col de Bagargui 1327m	46
Abaurrea Alta 995m and Alto de Remendia 1047m	48
Paso Tapia 1340m	48
Port de Larrau 1585m and Col d'Erroimendy 1362m	49
Alto Laza 1129m	50

Part 2 Wild Peak — 52

Zuriza 1290m	71
Puyeta 1201m	72
Col de la Pierre Saint-Martin 1760m	73
Col d'Issarbe 1450m	75
Col de Soudet 1540m	76
Col de Bouézou 1009m and Col de Labays 1351m	78
Puyarron 1240m	82
Puerto de Oroel 1090m	83

Part 3 Lost Mountain — 84

Puerto de Cotefablo 1423m	103
Señor Banos 1400m	105
Puerto de Sarrablo 1291m	106
Vilas de Turbón 1300m	108
Collado de Fadas 1470m and Collado de Espina 1407m	109
Collado del Plano / Puerto de Bonansa 1380m	110
Collado de Perves 1350m	111
Puerto de Beret 1860m	112
Puerto de la Bonaigua 2072m	115
Collado del Canto 1725m	116
Collado de Faidella 1250m and Collado de Bóixols 1380m	117

Part 4 Circle of Death — 118

Col de Marie Blanque 1035m	145
Col d'Aubisque 1709m	149
Col de la Couraduque 1367m	155
Col de Spandelles 1378m	156
Col des Bordères 1156m	157
Lourdes-Hautacam 1535m (Col de Tramassel 1615m)	158
Luz-Ardiden 1720m	162
Col du Tourmalet 2114m	164
Col d'Aspin 1489m	169
Col de Beyrède 1417m	173
Hourquette d'Ancizan 1560m	174

PART 5 BEAR'S JAW 176

Col du Pourtalet 1794m 189
Cauterets 934m and Pont d'Espagne 1496m 191
Gavarnie 1365m / Port de Boucharo 2270m 194
Cirque de Troumouse 2100m 196
Piau Engaly 1870m 197
Pla d'Adet 1680m 200
Col d'Azet / Val Louron 1580m 202
Col de Peyresourde 1569m 203
Port de Bales 1755m 205
Col du Portillon 1293m 207
Superbagnères 1804m 208

PART 6 THE FOUR VALLEYS 210

Col de Menté 1349m 225
Col de Portet d'Aspet 1069m 229
Col de la Core 1395m 233
Col de Latrape 1111m and Guzet-Neige 1520m 236
Col de la Crouzette 1241m 238
Col d'Agnès 1570m 241
Col de Port 1249m 243
Col de Péguère 1375m 246
Port de Lers 1517m 246

PART 7 RAVINES AND HIGH WOODS 248

Plateau de Beille 1780m 259
Route des Corniches 262
Ax-les-Trois Domaines 1372m 264
Col de Chioula 1431m 266
Chateau de Monségur 1059m 269
Col de la Gargante 1352m and Col du Boum 1298m 271
Col du Pradel 1673m 272
Port de Pailhères 2001m 274
Col de Garavel 1256m and Col des Moulis 1099m 276
Col du Carcanet 1400m and Col de la Quillane 1713m .. 277
Col de la Llose 1866m 278
Col de Jau 1506m 279
Col de Creu 1712m 280
Col de Roque-Jalère 976m 281

PART 8 JUDGEMENT MOUNTAINS 282

Col de Puymorens 1920m 297
Col de Pradeilles 1983m 300
Font-Romeu 1800m 300
Collado de Jou 1480m 303
Coll de Pal 2080m 304
Coll de Creueta 1900m 305
Collado de Toses 308
Coll de Marolla 1090m 310
Col de Mantet 1761m 311
Col Palomère 1036m 312
Col Xatard 752m via Col Fourtou 646m 313
Coll/Collado d'Ares 1513m 314
Collado de Coubet 1010m, Coll de Canes 1120m,
Coll de Santigosa 1064m 315

ESSENTIAL REPAIR VOCABULARY 316
ACKNOWLEDGEMENTS 318
INDEX OF COLS 320

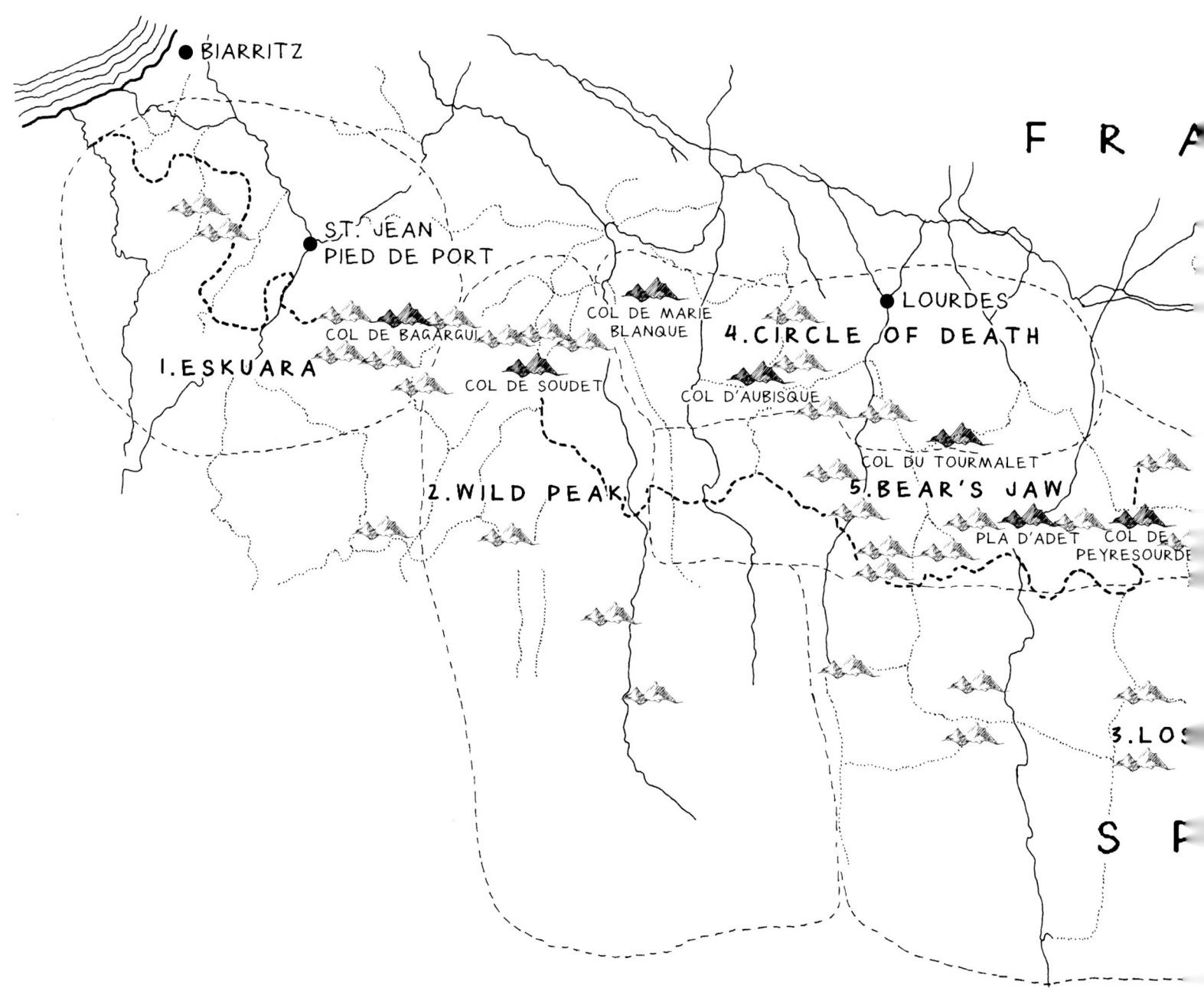

Map

- ST. GIRONS
- **6. THE FOUR VALLEYS**
- COL DE MENTE
- PUERTO DE BERET
- PUERTO DE BONAIGUA
- FOIX
- QUILLAN
- **7. RAVINES AND HIGH WOODS**
- AX-LES THERMES
- PLATEAU DE BEILLE
- PERPIGNAN
- COL DE PUYMORENS
- ANDORRA
- **8. JUDGEMENT MOUNTAINS**
- FIGUERES

FRANCE

SPAIN

Introduction

This is not a conventional guide book. Let me explain. In October 2005 I was in conversation with the patron of the bar-restaurant on top of the Aubisque, a man of that wisdom bred of living in a locale at once unforgiving in mood and beautiful in aspect, prey always to a chancy climate. I told him I was writing a book about the Pyrenees. (We had met before, albeit briefly, on a reconnaissance trip and on the two occasions I have ridden the Raid Pyrénéen – Hendaye on the Atlantic to Cerbère on the Mediterranean, 18 cols, 720 kilometres in a maximum of 4½ days.)[1] However this was the first time the patron and I had talked at length.

Hearing what I was about he smiled and nodded knowingly – and this was after he had plonked the bottle of Thirteen Fruit Cocktail on our table as a digestif, gratuit (digestif 'on the house') and said, 'It's not what it looks.' It was, in fact, the local Armagnac.

'I feel that such a book should not be two things,' he continued. 'It should not be exhaustive or objective.'

These were my thoughts entirely. I told him so and I repeat them here. For exhaustive, go to a conventional, bland, homogenised guide book; for objective, to a profile sketch and a map. That said, guidance is on offer of course, and thereto you will find in these pages the requisite factual information – neither compendious nor sketchy, but adequate – for a cycling exploration of these most beautiful mountains. Most important of all, you will also find accounts of climbs, those most famous and those less well known, together with a number of cols known only to a few nutters of the Ordre des Cols Durs (Order of Hard Cols) breed, accounts characterised by what in my view is the essential ingredient for any encounter with mountains: passion. The word comes from the Latin for 'suffering', the original narrow definition gradually expanding over time to embrace the metaphysical sense of intense feeling at both ends of the emotional scale, namely love and fury. Be prepared therefore for a combination

---

1   A col is the narrow neck between two upraised shoulders of mountain, and often the site of a mountain pass.

of both throughout this book. Passion is the handy abbreviation for a rather more complex experience than mere enthusiasm… which, incidentally and aptly, is Greek for 'being filled with a divine spirit'.

That great early explorer of the Pyrenees, Henry Russell, said that God is a palpable presence there, and in the imposing grandeur of the landscape and the unpredictable changes of weather – for instance sunshine swallowed up in swirling mist, a balmy day suddenly blitzed with rain and a bitter cold wind – there is much to corroborate such imagining. It is easy to believe that divine forces – not always benign, in fact frequently downright malign – are at work, lurking, ready to intervene, observing closely those fragile mortals who venture to gamble with Nature's caprices. You are always at risk, you must always be aware of the unpredictability of altitude.

Yet there is spiritual dynamic, too, not only in the majesty of the scenery but in the very business of surmounting the high cols, in the alchemies of physical and mental stress which accompany riding the bike up to and over them. It is not always a pleasant adventure at the time, but it is always a most glorious undertaking in the aftermath. Do not underrate satisfaction and do not forget, either, that all you can ever say of a mountain is that it did not defeat you on this occasion. Getting over the Tourmalet, say, gives you no licence to say you have conquered the Tourmalet for good and all. That is what makes riding the mountains such a rich, mysterious, and even spiritual, experience, whose very mystery is reflected in the sometimes opinionated commentary herein.

No-one can ride a mountain for you. The best that anyone who has ridden the Pyrenees can offer someone who has not, is the persuasive encouragement of their going back to ride them again. This I extend to all readers here. Above all, approach your adventure in the high cols with a certain humility and don't punish yourself any more than the kilometres and gradients will punish you. Be prepared to feel so tired you truly believe you cannot go on. Be ready to admit to fatigue and, yes, dejection. There is no such thing as an easy ride up a mountain so remember: all the climbs in this book have one characteristic in common, they all go uphill for considerable long distances. Riding them evokes a spectrum of emotions and those sensations will depend on where you are in the climb, what you are looking at as the mountainscape unfolds and the status of the col in the mythology. It will also depend on how you are feeling that day. Pro riders have the grisly experience of the jour sans, 'the day without', when nothing works, nothing flows. So will you. The totemic big cols of Tour legend will, perhaps, work a more powerful impression on you than some of those whose names you are reading here for the first time. But, they are all different, they all have their own difficulties and you must never be blasé. For, above all, this book and all the experience of which it speaks and from which it derives its own passion, will, I hope remind you that you go to the mountains to enjoy yourself, to drink in the glories of the so varied Pyrenean ranges. There may well be moments, passages of laborious time, when the very notion of 'enjoying yourself' seems mad if not surreal. But, that is part of what mountains will do to you, part of the unexceptionable satisfaction of getting up there on this one day. Having done it once, you can never say it is done for all time. No. But you will have done it. Therefore, keep your eyes and ears peeled for all that there is to see and hear as you ride and an open mind for all that there is to learn about yourself.

Rapha's guide to the Pyrenees is firmly rooted in two things: firstly, exalting the love of and passion for the beautiful machine together with the whole gamut of feelings it excites, from the zenith of joy to the nadir of fatigue and, yes, not uncommonly, the spontaneous resentment at what the wretched bike has put you through on a particular day; and secondly, celebrating the terrain which has so often been the ultimate duelling ground of the Tour de France since the Pyrenees were first included in 1910. Here, as a cyclist, you will get closest to the epic endurance test which is stage racing, closest to the core of the peculiar essence of ultimate cycling. As Henri Desgrange put it, the true champion needs head *and* legs. I have aimed to probe the appeal of the mountains to both, to the utmost demands they make on the legs, indeed the whole body, and to the gruelling test of mind, willpower, and dogged tenacity. All that and the exquisite thrill of being there, of doing it, of coming back down having done it… jingling the names of the cols that resonate, all matched herein to the vibrant reality of tarmac, gradient and hairpin, together with the glorious panorama and sheer stark natural grandeur of the Pyrenees.

Graeme Fife 2008

Naming of the eight sectors

The Pyrenees divide readily north and south, French and Spanish side but, without further subdivision, a survey of the whole range would be unwieldy. Besides, there has been enough to and fro violence across this frontier line of mountains already without Rapha fomenting any further Franco-Hispanic stand-off. West, West-central, Central etc would be horribly dull: we looked to the map. We settled on eight distinctive 'sectors'.

Three of the sectors already show geographical or cultural distinctness: the Basque cols at the western end (Iskuara), the Pays de Sault (Woods and High Ravines) to the east and the Couserans (The Four Valleys) of the Ariège department is a region of ancient date and name. The Circle of Death, containing that monstrous ring of cols in the centre, is famous in Tour de France legend. Each of the remaining four sectors takes its name from a feature on the map and, thereby, boasts some local resonance, but the boundaries are ours: Bear's Jaw is for the long Ossau gorge, Wild Peak for the prominence called Tête Sauvage near the frontier pass of La Pierre Saint-Martin. Lost Mountain centres on the Monte Perdido national park and Judgement Mountain nods at the Sierra del Cadi. The cadí was a civil judge in Moorish Spain. Aptly enough – the French call the high mountains 'arbitration (civil) judges', juges de paix, because on any one day they decide which rider is the strongest.

Geography

The Pyrenees extend for approximately 384 kilometres from the Atlantic to the Mediterranean, let us say from Hendaye to Cape Cerbère, south of Perpignan, the route followed by the Raid Pyrénéen. The altitude diminishes gradually westward in a long slide down to the sea. Eastwards, the mean elevation remains steady, apart from one break in the Ariège, till the sudden drop from the ridge of the Albères Mountains to the coast. Between 96 and 128 kilometres broad, only around a quarter to a third of the range lies in France. In consequence there is a marked topographical contrast between north and south; the distance between plain and high peaks on the French side is never much more than 24 or 32 kilometres, making the slopes much steeper, whereas on the Spanish side the mountains stretch for up to 96 kilometres from the frontier, dipping and soaring from high peak to high peak. The asymmetry in the mountains' overall topographical form also extends to the scale of their catchments – the basins which collect rainfall. The northern approaches have steeper slopes and lower minimum elevations than their southern counterparts, since glaciation in the northern catchments reached lower altitudes than in the south and the rates at which earth was washed away to expose bare rock varied considerably between the two sides.

The Pyrenees were formed when the European and Iberian tectonic plates collided, pressing massive amounts of sediment together and thrusting it up in folds. In the process, the Iberian plate rotated a little and caused the eastern parts to be more folded than those in the west. (The southern part remained active for longer which explains the difference in rock type between north and south.) The result is series of mountainous chains crossing the watershed at an oblique angle, and almost all the earliest formations of the range continue diagonally on the Spanish side. So, the central ridge extends in a pattern of wrinkles or folds, north-west to south-east. Less pronounced wrinkles intersect, south-west to north-east and this interleaving gives the Pyrenees its distinctive irregular crest.

The central massif and most of the higher summits are composed of primary rocks and granite; to either side, north and south, there is limestone where the rock has a covering of cretaceous deposits due to prehistoric submersion under the sea. The precipitation of rain and snow is generally heavier in the west and there are glaciers only on the northern slopes of the central massif, although they do not extend far down the valleys.

On the French side, the rivers tend to flow north as most of the east-west, i.e. longitudinal, valleys have disappeared, except at the eastern end where the Têt plunges down towards Perpignan and, a short way south, the Tech courses below the ridge of the Albères. By contrast, in Spain, after cutting through the highest part of the range at right angles, the principal streams then swing along the direction of longitudinal folds to spill into the flatter lands much further on.

The scenery has five main characteristics:

1. An absence of major lakes as in the Alps.
2. The rarity and elevation of the passes.
3. Cirques: these dead-end, glacier-formed amphitheatre walls of rock at the upper end of the valleys are a distinctly Pyrenean feature.[2]
4. A large number of mountain torrents, in French 'gaves', often in the form of waterfalls taller than any in Europe bar those in Scandinavia. The loftiest, at 505m, is the Gavarnie cascade off the famous cirque at the head of the Gave de Pau.
5. The dry gulches and craggy ravines commonly found on the Spanish side.

There are low passes only at the extremities of the range; these littoral passages are wider at the western end where the Roncesvalles corridor and the route through the Baztan valley south of Ainhoa are relatively low. The gentle Col du Perthus gives easy access through the eastern corridor. Otherwise, the principle roadways cross the Franco-Spanish border at only two high points: the Col du Pourtalet and the original traverse, built by the Romans, the Col de Somport (Latin summus portus, 'highest entrance'). The modern Bielsa and Vielha tunnels add alternative routes for motorists but not cyclists.

Mineral springs abound, most notably the hot sulphurous sources at high altitude near the margins of the granite, for example at Bagnères-de-Luchon, Eaux Bonnes and Eaux Chaudes. The lower springs, such as at Bagnères-de-Bigorre, are mostly selenitic (impregnated with sulphate of lime) and not very warm.

[2] Cirque comes from Latin 'circus', origin also of circle, circus, arena

The lower flanks of the mountains in the extreme west are very well wooded but the extent of the forest rapidly dwindles the further east one goes on the French side, with the exception of the Pays de Sault [see part 7]. The granite massifs of the central and oriental Pyrenees are peculiarly wild and naked. The Spanish ranges, tend to show more wood cover. The Port de Boucharo for example, bare of vegetation on the French side, is so named for the trees and bushes on the Spanish side, 'bouch' being a Languedoc word derived from late Latin boscum (bush, wood), hence 'bosky' a word you will find in later pages.

The flora and fauna changes along the range as well: in the west closer to that of central Europe, in the east more Mediterranean. For instance, cacti, oranges and bougainvillea are plentiful in the Tech valley.

History

Northern Celts swarmed over both ends of the Pyrenees early in prehistory, first in a series of invasions of peoples drawn by sun, fertile soil, and, who knows, the comforting barrier of the mountains whose shallow passes had given them access. They fused with the indigenous population and are known as Celtiberians, famous for their metal-working. Greek traders, nosing round the northern Mediterranean coast, arrived on the coast of Catalunya in the mid-5th century BC and set up shop in the broad natural bay off Roses. Another mercantile people, the Carthaginians from North Africa, crossed over to Spain in the late years of the 3rd century BC and it was from Carthago Nova (modern Cartagena) in April 218 BC that their great general Hannibal set out for Rome up the eastern corridor, through Catalunya, with his elephants. After his final defeat in 202 BC, the Romans came to the Iberian Peninsula and, by 133 BC, had crushed all resistance. Around then they adopted the double-edged Spanish sword developed by the Celtiberian smiths that became standard legionary issue: the stabbing gladius. The Roman conquerors built a vast latticework of roads across Spain and many of those on either side of the Pyrenees today follow the line of the old Roman highways including the famous Via Domitia linking the Rhône valley and Spain. They traversed the mountains at four points: Roncesvalles, Somport, Perche (near their town of Julia Libyca, modern Llívia) and the Perthus.

With the decline of Rome, Spain suffered a succession of invasions by various Germanic tribes,: Franks, Suevi (Swabians), Alans and Vandals, until the Visigoths, who had migrated from the Baltic into south-eastern Europe, established their kingdom with capitals in Toulouse and Barcelona in the late 6th century AD. This lasted until 711 when the Moors, with their light cavalry and slashing swords of Damascene steel, flooded across the Straits of Gibraltar (Pillars of Hercules) and moved northwards across the Pyrenees, until the heavy infantry phalanxes of the Frankish warlord Charles Martel, 'the Hammer', crushed them between Tours and Poitiers deep in France in 732, and they retreated south.

His grandson Charlemagne, Holy Roman Emperor and King of all the Franks, extended his empire south of the mountain chain and built defensive forts along its line at vulnerable points. This advance marked the start of the long Reconquista by Catholic princes of the Moorish holdings in Spain; by the mid-eleventh century for example, the frontier between Christian and Muslim Spain ran roughly from south of Barcelona to northern Portugal. Gradually the Moors were pushed further and further south, their territories eventually confined to the southern region which they called Al-Andalus, (modern Andalucia), the old Roman province of Baetica. This Arab name is probably derived from their hearing of Vandalicia, its name under the Vandals.

Miscegenation between Moors and Spanish was not uncommon but frowned on by the hidalgos who boasted of their pure breeding, uncontaminated by dusky Moorish, Jewish or other foreign admixture, as proven in the blue-black cord of the veins showing against their pale skin. This sangre azul is the 'blue blood' of the true, inordinately proud, Castilian aristocracy.

The Reconquista was concluded by the conquest of Granada in 1492 by armies fighting for King Ferdinand of Aragón and Queen Isabella of Castille whose marriage in 1469 had imposed unity on Christian Spain. Their daughter, the unfortunately monikered Joanna the Mad, (she became totally insane early in life, but had the blue blood in her veins) married Philip the Fair of Burgundy, and their son, the future Holy Roman Emperor, the Habsburg Charles V, brought a new solidity to the kingdom south of the Pyrenees. (He famously said that he spoke Spanish to God, Italian to women, French to men and 'German to my horse.') His son, Philip II, he of the Armada, ushered in the dawn of Spain's Golden Age as wealth from the South American conquests poured into the country.

His contemporary, the protestant prince Henri III of Béarn and Navarre, converted to Rome, became King of France in 1589 – 'Paris is worth a Mass,' he remarked – and consolidated the Pyrenean territories, part of his own fealty, for France.

Philip II's death, in 1598, left Spain to his son Philip III and his favourite, the rapacious Count Lerma, 'the greatest thief in Spain'. Lerma's expulsion of the Moors in 1610 stripped Spain of an intelligent, commercially astute community, while foreign wars – principally with France in the Netherlands, a Habsburg territory – exhausted an already impoverished, and depredated, country.

The Treaty of the Pyrenees in 1659 ended the Franco-Spanish War that had begun in 1648. Negotiated in Llívia, it ceded whole tracts of the mountain territories to France, and Louis XIV, the Sun King, announced: 'Les Pyrénées n'existent plus.' (The Pyrenees no longer exist). By the end of the century, there was even a French king on the Spanish throne: Charles II, last of the Spanish Habsburgs, almost imbecile from birth, willed the succession to Louis XIV's grandson Philip of Anjou who, from 1701, ruled as Philip V. Charles' idiocy was imputed to sorcery rather than the palpable cause – years of Habsburg in-breeding – hence his nickname Carlos the Bewitched (El Hechizado). Exorcism seems not to have helped.

The Emperor Napoleon, seeking to close down Portuguese trade with Britain during his European war, crossed the Pyrenees in 1808 and, by force majeure, secured the right to march through Spain and to establish military garrisons. He also compelled the French incumbent of the Spanish throne, Charles IV, and his brother Ferdinand to abdicate in favour of his own brother, Joseph. His projects to construct crossings up the Marcadau valley south of the Pont d'Espagne as well as over the Boucharo pass came to nothing but he did establish military hospitals at a number of spa towns on the French side.

Finally, however, the Spanish had had enough of the French interlopers. A popular uprising led to British military intervention and at the conclusion of the Peninsular War (1808-14), the victory of Wellington's army at Vitoria southwest of Pamplona in June 1813 liberated Spain. Wellington pushed on across the Pyrenees, and near Orthez in the northern foothills on 27 February 1814 defeated Marshall Soult, sustaining his first war wound in the process. The war was effectively over, and after the battle the Iron Duke's veterans took a long repose in Pau. From there they marched on north and captured Toulouse.

For the next 120 years, Spain was subject to incessant internal conflicts, between the liberal, republican, anti-religionists exaltados and the monarchist, Catholic moderatos, the Carlist supporters of the legitimate descendants of Charles IV. In September 1923 the Captain-General of Barcelona, Primo de Rivera, headed a military putsch and, in agreement with the king Alfonso XIII, established a military dictatorship. He managed the government as a civilian prime minister, resigned in 1930, and died a month or so later in exile in Paris. The Republicans won the communal elections in 1931 and Alfonso quit Spain without renouncing his rights to the throne. During the Second Republic, first Catalunya (1931) and then the Basque region (1936) were granted autonomy, but greater tensions were racking the embattled state. A military uprising in 1936 backed by the Carlists and the Fascist Falange – (literally 'phalanx') – founded by the dictator de Rivera's son in 1933, ignited the Spanish Civil War (1936-39). Hitler's Luftwaffe supplied the Nationalist armies of Franco – El Caudillo, (the Leader) – with Stuka dive bombers on trial. Picasso's painting of the obliteration of Guernica was shown at the 1937 World's Fair in Paris; later, when asked by a German officer visiting his studio in Paris, 'Did you do that?' he replied, 'No, you did.'

The Pyrenees played their most significant role in modern times during the Second World War. Franco's Spain – Catalunyan and Basque autonomy summarily suppressed – remained neutral, albeit a tacit ally of Germany, and the men who escaped over the passes, led by mountain men, shepherds and herders, faced an uncertain reception if they did manage to evade the German patrols and make it into Spain. They were duly imprisoned and detained, without specific charge, in Spanish gaols for long periods; ill fed in unsanitary conditions, their fellow inmates included prisoners from the Civil War, many of whom were serving sentences of up to a hundred years.

The stories are legion, the Pyrenees a backdrop for the unsung heroism of many: you will find a few of them mentioned in the following pages. Salute their memory.

Riding in the Mountains

French guides proffer an incredibly complex statistical analysis of gearing, average speed, wind resistance, body-weight ratio to machine, a welter of contributory factors vis à vis riding a bike in the mountains. Go to them and get calibrating if you will. My inclination, when it comes to navigating inclines on two wheels, is less scientific but, I hope, rooted in practicalities. My intention is to inspire you to go to these lovely mountains and ride them as I have done. That philosophy lies at the heart – and soul – of this Rapha guide.[3]

Nowhere in the Pyrenees, with rare exceptions, notably out of Saint-Jean-Pied-de-Port in the Basque region, will you encounter gradients harsher than the worst confronting you at home. However, the climbs are almost without exception much, much longer than any you will find on home shores. You must be prepared for up to two hours in the saddle, if not more, for some of the weightier challenges. As to gearing, this is, of course, a matter of personal choice but, taking a cue from the professionals, the common sense is to reduce

---

[3] With one exception, the rule for inclusion of cols here is that they should top 1000 metres. This rules out a lovely climb in the Six Valleys, the Col du Serailler, which has five approaches. Make it your task, therefore, to clamour for its instatement.

the physical stress to a minimum. Gear low and go for high cadence; pushing a big gear is both wasteful of energy and punishingly hard on the muscles. Lucien Van Impe, six-times winner of the Mountains Prize and overall winner of the 1976 Tour, advises: 'You must regulate your breathing right at the start [of a climb], concentrate on it above everything else... to do this you must start the climb in a low gear, lower than you think you need. That allows you to concentrate on breathing deeply and effectively... and on getting a lot of power from smooth pedal revolutions, don't push and pull.' Thus economy of movement, a steady rhythm of breathing and pedalling, with as little strain as possible.

My advice is to fit a gear which gives you maximum comfort on any hills you know at home and then ride a lot of them in preparation for your foray onto the big climbs. Don't try to match the professionals: they do nothing but ride a bike all year round, they get paid to waste themselves in races and they are very good at their job. No contest.

For a day's riding, you should carry all you would carry on a club run or long ride, bearing in mind that the weather can deteriorate rapidly in the Pyrenees. Therefore, take warm and waterproof gear, arm and leg warmers, gloves, hat, energy bars or gels, two water bottles (bidons), spare tubes, levers, chain-link remover, allen keys, pump, phone numbers.

As to the terrain itself, like Shakespeare's Cleopatra, it can boast 'infinite variety'. The hills of Eskuara, for the most part lower and more accessible, apart from the extreme lifts of the roads clustered east of Saint-Jean-Pied-de-Port, are wooded and smooth, dotted with hillside farms, the gateway between the Atlantic shore and the central chines (narrow ravines). Wild Peak, straddling the border, has a marked frontier feel, a stony neutral zone sliced through by two big crossings. This is bandit and pilgrim country, an evocative collision of morality in a landscape where the resolve essential to both activities – evading the law and tramping long distances for faith – somehow leaves morality aside. The Circle of Death probably best incarnates the appeal of riding these mountains as a way of trying to get close to the mystique of the Tour de France. The Tour pioneered the Pyrenees from 1910 on and the giants of the central massif represent all that is most formidable and magnificent in cycling: stupendous height, intimidating aspect, gaunt profiles, mythic names. Bear's Jaw, although it contains two passes famous in Tour history, is a region of spectacular high dead-ends, where the roads lead south into the impassable bleak frontier rock wall up deep, lush gorges hemmed in by trees. Adjacent to it, Lost Mountain, dominated by the peak of that name, typifies the nature of the Spanish Pyrenees where the mountains fall away in slow increment to the valley floors. A narrow circuitry of roads threads through remote and inhospitable but fascinating country. Abandoned villages lurk everywhere, testimony to the harsh nature of the land, but also to the irresistible lure of going where few go. The Four Valleys rather mocks the official geographers' appellation of Lower Pyrenees. What these climbs lack in height – not much, in truth – they make up for in gradient (some of the tightest you will encounter) and integrity. This is a region, wooded and exposed by turns, which offers some of the loveliest views in the mountains, perspectives which open out round corner after corner. Ravines and High Woods has a glorious mix of landscapes: barren plateaux, thickly afforested ridges, lush valleys. Nowhere, apart from the west, where the Camino de Santiago symbolises the long association with intrepid travellers, is the history of the mountains so writ large as in this region. Here the outlawed Cathars found refuge and the intimate privacy of the roads speak eloquently of them still. Judgement Mountains joins the long chain to the Mediterranean and the Vermilion Coast, sun-baked slopes falling away from the major crossing at the Puymorens into the byways of northern Catalunya. Tranquil routes link up with more frequented roads in a region which has a distinct friendliness about it. Here in the old kingdom of Aragón, the French and Spanish mingle in closer blend than anywhere else.

How to get there

There are regular international flights to Biarritz, Pau, Perpignan and Carcassonne in France and Girona in Spain, from each of which there are relatively easy transitions into the mountains.

Flights to Lourdes tend to be quite expensive and their passenger complement overlayered with the odour of sanctity.

Major airlines fly to Barcelona from where you can take the train into the city, alight at Plaça Catalunya and there board the train north to Puigcerda. Either stop off at Ripoll or Ribes de Ferrer and ride the Collado de Toses or stay on the train and enjoy a delightful ride up, into, and across the mountains, changing trains at Puigcerda because the French and Spanish railway gauges are different; simply walk along the platform over the frontier to the French station at Latour-de-Carol. There's also a good café/restaurant on the French side. From here, the line continues across the mountains alongside the Col du Puymorens, at the foot of which lies Bourg-Madame, to Ax-les-Thermes and Foix, in the Ariège.

Emergency numbers in France

Pompiers (First Aid): 18
Police: 17
SAMU (Services d'Aide Médicale): 15
Weather (Sp. Météo): 3250 (mobiles only)

1. Eskuara

The western end of the chain splays out onto the Atlantic coastal strip. These Basque cols are generally of lower altitude than further east, the valleys shallower but very beautiful, the flanks of the hills often folded like ruched velvet, the countryside more populous, the vegetation more lush. A region sculpted by seaborne winds and rain.

The Basques call their language Eskuara, its precise meaning undetermined but possibly something like 'clear speaking'; entirely apt, somehow, such a contradiction. For the language itself, a conglomerate of eight distinct dialects, amply studded with the letters x, k and z, has no connections with other European linguistic families and underpins the combative sense of independence for which the Basques themselves, French and Spanish, are noted. Neil Stephens, the Aussie ex-pro, speaks the lingo – his wife is Basque – but it's a notoriously difficult skill to acquire.

The region, at the southerly angle of the Bay of Biscay, extends south-west along the valley of the Bidassoa River, which marks the Franco-Spanish border. This is ripe smuggling country, if you know the terrain and the mountains' moods. The Basques were always famous contrebandiers (smugglers), padding the mountain tracks in their espadrilles, humping wax-clothed bales of Lyon silk, caskets of silver chains, beads and watches down to nocturnal punts across the Bidassoa, dodging the revenue patrols, to the receiving houses in Spanish Basque territory.[1] Contraband signified much more than money; it was a defiant act of liberty. Overrun so many times – Romans, Goths, Vandals, Visigoths, Moors, Gascons, English – all the Pyrenean mountain people have a deep and atavistic sense of identity begrudging any wider patriotism. They tend to say: 'Town first, region second but nation?… If you insist.'

Everywhere you will see the curious Basque script, a florid variant on the Roman

---

[1] Pierre Loti's Ramuntcho is a Basque smuggling tale, written by him in the Hôtel de la Rhune in Ascain, Lower Pyrenees.

character, and tall-gabled, half-timbered houses with white plaster and woodwork painted in the traditional Basque pimento red. Indeed, red peppers are a staple of the local cuisine as is fish: anchovies, salt cod, mixed sea-food, assiettes de fruits de mer and a Basque version of bouillabaisse. Black cherries are a speciality and the little town of Itxassou is famous for them.[2] Charcuterie and a diversity of sausages feature highly as, too, does sheep's milk cheese, named after the Forêt d'Iraty. Eat it with membrillo quince gel often served in restaurants in a triangular sachet. The celebrated piquant Basque condiment sauce is worth a try as well.

Espelette, some 20 kilometres south-east of Biarritz, is the great centre for the growing of pimento and in late summer the houses are adorned with garlands of red peppers drying in the sun. The annual Pimento Festival takes place in the first week of September – lots of wine drunk and food consumed, principally a veal stew called axoa (pronounced 'hachua'). Basque conviviality is justly celebrated and they are a cheery, unruly bunch to be around, the violent separatists of ETA apart.

Every community has its fronton, the big back wall of the pelota court, for the playing of the Basque national game, fast and furious, the players dressed in traditional white shirts and red neckerchiefs.

Griffon vultures are common, so keep moving, and there is a regular indaba of them up on the Pico Gorromakil, which makes the ride up worth the effort.

---

2 The Hôtel Paradis there – original name Iguzkian, 'In the Sun' – is cyclist friendly and a good place to stay. It's near the Pas de Roland, in which a large boulder above the river has a hole in it kicked out, so legend has it, by Roland's horse.

P25 The road south below the *Port de Larrau* into Spain

P26 Woods in the remote highlands east of *Saint-Jean-Pied-de-Port*

P28 The road south below the *Port de Larrau* into Spain

P30 The tunnel just beyond the col line of the *Port de Larrau*

P32 A fine hairpin on the southerly flank of the *Port de Larrau*

P34 The Madonna lending her friendly presence to the pilgrims crossing near the *Arnostéguy* en route for *Santiago de Compostela*

P36 A lovely pleating of hills below the *Arnostéguy*

P38 Out of France, the *col d'Eroimendy*, and the road continuing round the mountainside towards the *Port de Larrau*

Pico Gorromakil 1090m

From Puerto de Otxondo

LENGTH: 10KM
HEIGHT GAIN: 520M
MAXIMUM GRADIENT: 10%

Of this Pico, David Millar, former resident of Biarritz, for whom the Basque cols were his principal training ground, says: 'It's horrible.' What better recommendation could you ask for?

The Puerto de Otxondo lies on the N121B, 11.5 kilometres south of the small border town of Dancharia.[3] Apart from a middle section of between 5 and 7%, the Otxondo is a steady climb of around 4% out of the valley of the Rio de Olavidea. Turn left at the *puerto* away from a fine prospect of the valley sides cloaked with pine and deciduous trees. An avenue of poplars to the right; while ceps grow abundantly under poplar and beech, conifers change the acidity of the soil and the fungus does not like that.

Through gates over a cattle grid on the NA2655 past a sentinel line of pines, Gorramendi signed at 10km. (The Basque word *gorri* means 'red', *makil* is a baton or cross and *mendi* a mountain. The soil hereabouts is the red of raspberry fool.) A small stele indicates Santio Bidea…Camino Santiago, the pilgrim route which begins in Paris and leads to the shrine of Saint James in Compostela.

There is a long view of the radio masts on the Pico from what rapidly becomes a narrow, corniche road at around 6-7% for the first 2.5 kilometres before crossing a yoke of ground into a snaking descent. It is partly the breaks in rhythm – losing height you have just won and having to win it back – which make the climb hard, as the gradients are not over-taxing.

At 3km, the road is a sort of causeway crossing open heathland with views to both sides; to the left, a board with information (in Basque) for Camino walkers picking their way through outcrops of rock.

At 4km the climb restarts, winding up through trees, a good surface, though recently re-laid so a bit granular until it's endured more wear from cars and campervans. (There's quite a lot of wild camping up here.) At 4.8km down you plunge once more along another causeway for a short distance onto another gentle rise and a very twisty section of road to an exposed crest. Look out for the sturdy Basque mountain ponies – *pottok* (pronounced 'potchok') grazing on the hillside. Once the pit pony of choice in England, they are now bred for riding or their meat.

Then another steep plunge at 5.9km and a flat ride from around 6.5km.

The final kilometres assert themselves and from 8km the gradient stiffens doling out the one short stretch of 10% on a road which narrows and makes a ledge cut into the side of the mountain. Round a big sweeping left-hand bend, the bare dome of the Pico looms away to the left and vultures gather to eye the pickings. Far to the right, across the Vallée des Aldudes, the mountains recede as in an Italian quattrocento landscape in folds of paler and paler perspective.

There is no sign at the top, only the abrupt cessation of the tarmac – the road continues unmade – and the radio mast and buildings of the old military installation up to the left. A French cyclist with whom I talked was full of praise for this climb – not as hard as the Aubisque, but a great test for the legs. The descent? Twisty, tricky, yet view-laden, the ups and downs very much a part of the attraction.

---

3 In Spain both cols and mountain passes are called Port (Catalan) or Puerto (Castilian).

Col d'Ispeguy *(ispegi in basque)* 672m

Western approach

LENGTH: 9KM
HEIGHT GAIN: 387M
MAXIMUM GRADIENT: 7%

Eastern approach

LENGTH: 9KM
HEIGHT GAIN: 510M
MAXIMUM GRADIENT: 8%

(About 4.5 kilometres further south from the Otxondo, to the left, a café/bar/restaurant run by an American who left the States when he was 18. Bilingual, of course – a good place for lunch.)

The Ispegi is included as a transitional pass between France and Spain. It happens to be a beautiful ride too, and though of no great difficulty from the Spanish side, the eastern approach from Saint-Etienne-de Baïgorry (162m) is harder and more spectacular.

From Erratzu (285m), a small town with typically narrow streets, the western approach along the NA2600 makes a classic frontier crossing, the col seen from some distance away as a V between two shoulders of mountain… a delightful 9 kilometres of nothing more severe than 6%, in and out of trees, through lush green farmland, with a slight kick of the gradient in the final kilometre.

There is a restaurant with a booze and souvenir shop attached just below the col itself – run by Spaniards so that the menu del dia goes on long past 2pm, but closed on Mondays – and an abandoned border post at the very top. I enjoyed the sight of four French cyclists from a Bayonne club peeling out after a hearty lunch, one of them wearing a Festina cap, backwards, under his helmet, dark shades and a large cigar stub clenched between his teeth, hailing one of his mates: 'Vous déconnez, là' (You're talking bollocks.)

The view from the top is fine; a deep valley and the road cut into the mountainside swishing away down, down, down into the re-entrant – the cleft in a mountainside formed by a stream or torrent, flanked by two projecting salients or spurs. As a climb this poses no great difficulty – a gain of 510m in 9 kilometres – but it's an interesting ascent: fluid bends, intermittent shade from trees, the distance marked by faded old kilometre *bornes* (markers) and, from 3 kilometres below the col, the pass hoves into view, beckoning you towards it in the friendliest manner.

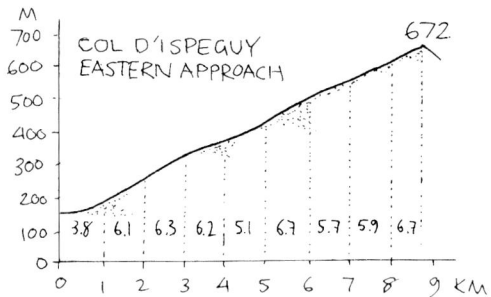

Saint-Jean-Pied-de-Port

Circuit I, three main cols

COLS DE LANDERRE 1072M
APHANIZE 1044M
AHUSQUY 1072M

LENGTH: 45KM
HEIGHT GAIN: OVER 1500M IN TOTAL
MAXIMUM GRADIENT: 12%

This is one of two extremely difficult but rewarding excursions across the plateau overlooking Saint-Jean. The town sits on a confluence of rivers – the Nive, the Bidouze and the Laurhibar – which join as the Nive to flow into the Pau and thence the sea near Bayonne. It has been an important stopover for pilgrims heading for Santiago since the Middle Ages and remains so. They enter the town through the Porte Saint Jacques and leave by the Porte d'Espagne, trudging on towards the Puerto de Ibañeta. The 'foot of the pass' soubriquet signposts what was, for centuries, one of the main, (because the lowest), crossing points between France and Spain, past either Roncevaux in French or Roncesvalles, Spanish.

There is an excellent bike shop at *Saint-Jean-le-Vieux*: workshop, bikes, clothing and spare parts, also altimeters, ammo for the shotgun in case of bears, designer shades and annoying mountain walkers who can't remember where they put their wallet and have to unpack the entire rucksack before they remember it's in their bum bag…

The D933 leads directly east from Saint-Jean Pied-de-Port (165m) for 4.5 kilometres to Saint-Jean-le-Vieux (210m). Turn right along the D18 towards Mendive and at Bastida (6km) take the left-hand fork, D417, for Béhorléguy (9.2km) where the trouble starts. An overpowering nastiness for 6.3 kilometres, never much less than 10% and mostly rather more than 11%. The road is narrow, not badly surfaced, kinked as hell and very, very steep, but of a most beautiful savagery.

It evens out onto the flatter skirts of the high plateau over the Col de Landerre at 17km, the Col d'Aphanize at 18km and round the rim of the Pic de Béhorléguy past the Gouffre d'Aphanize, at 525m the deepest vertical shaft in France. It doesn't look much, rather neglected in fact, but a board alongside informs the cyclist who stops for a breather about the local long-haired sheep: the Manech, tête noire and tête rousse (black- or red-headed) and the Basco-Béarnaise (good milkers) who stroll about these ranges looking shaggily over-dressed.

Past a crossroads (D417 to the right, 20.2km) on over the Ahusquy – an agreeable auberge, café/bar off to the left up a short, sharp incline – and a most beautiful descent, 23.5 kilometres to Mauléon-Licharre (141m), left at another fork, or 16.6 kilometres to Tardets-Sorholus (217m), right. The left-hand fork eventually plunges down a fine

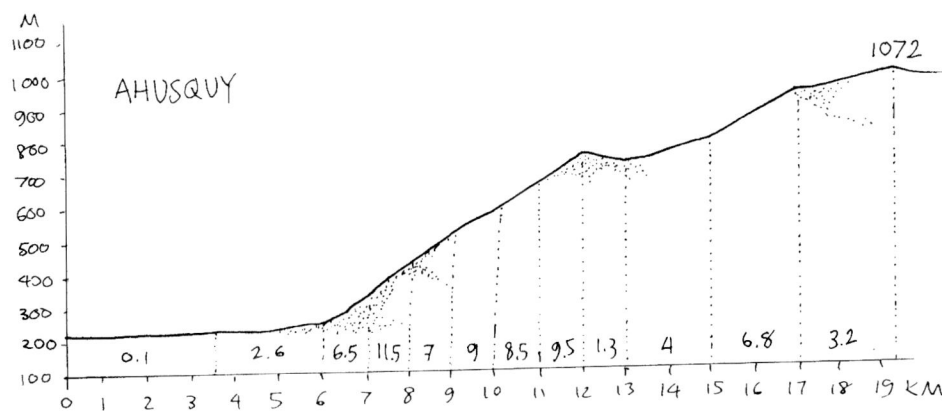

sinuous course through trees, in a grove of which, on the lowers slopes to the left, stands an open burial chamber, some 1500 years old: the Dolmen d'Ithe which would originally have had a stone cap. The grove is usually spangled with flowers, the purple-blue gentian prominent.

The climb up from Mauléon is rather gentler – an easy ride into the wilder pockets of the area and, a couple of kilometres out of Aussurucq (210m, 19km: note a small but rather fine château), 4 kilometres of around 9 and 10%, made marginally less taxing, somehow, by the friendly screening of trees.

From the Tardets direction, the climb kicks in a kilometre out of Alçay (6km, 305m). Five kilometres of very steep riding, oscillating around 12% for the first ramp and settling into between 7 and 10%. In both these cases, after the severe lift up to the plateau's edge the going is a lot easier, and the sense of wildness at the top is worth every shred of the nerves to get there.

Eastern approach to the Col d'Ahusquy

LENGTH: 18KM

HEIGHT GAIN: 852M

MAXIMUM GRADIENT: 11%

The D247 west goes through Alos and Alçay (220m) to the D117, right. Neat gardens, palm trees, hay fields, a long empty road. The minor D117 gets the first punches in, around 9% past another palm tree and a fronton and hardly lets up for 3 kilometres into rustic isolation – 10 and 11% – until you are riding high on a narrow strip of tarmac (not a very good surface) above the valley in company with stunted trees. High to the left, trees cling to the flank of the rock like climbers on pitons. This is a lonely, steep road that might be going nowhere, despite the rural gîte at 6km, spindly arbours of parched dwarf oak, some dead, like stands of firewood, but… this is the comfort of this Rapha guide: the steadying hand on your saddle, the voice of encouragement in your ear, the shared knowledge.

At 7km the road levels towards what looks like a summit and, bingo, it is: the Col de Lecharria, (832m – also called Arangaïtz). You know what's coming, of course: a steep plunge away from the joys of altitude to the junction with the D147 and a lone farmhouse which the map calls Potto (775m). A potto – English and French – is the West African lemur, more commonly known as a sloth, but there is probably no connection.

A flat, valley-bottom road ambles past a concrete sheep-fold, a small grove of conifers, almost certainly a witches' coven rendezvous, and then climbs up to the intermediate Col Ibarburia (966m, 16.4km) and a junction, left, with a track which goes up to the Bagargui. Two hundred metres on, round a cliff-side road the Ahusquy announces itself, somewhat mutely. A kilometre of plateau later, the Col Inharpu (1029m) appears, 18 kilometres from Tardets, at the junction with the D417 which descends into Mendive, where you will enjoy a fine lunch stop at the Relais d'Iraty.

Circuit II, a loop from Saint-Jean-Pied-de-Port

COL D'ARNOSTÉGUY 1236M
COL D'ELHURSARO 1145M

LENGTH: 45.7KM
HEIGHT GAIN: OVER 1500M IN TOTAL
MAXIMUM GRADIENT: 14%

Clockwise: take the D301 south out of town towards Estérençuby via Saint Michel following the river. A quiet and gentle loosener of a road. At a fork (305m, 9.2km) the D301 shoots off up a steep ramp to the left.[4] Take the fork (D428, not marked) which falls away to the right, direction: Source de la Nive. A kilometre on, into the Fôret d'Orion, the climb begins in earnest – upwards of 9 and 10% most of the way for 9 kilometres. There will be some who do not see the attraction of such a climb, because it carries no celebrity. Who has heard of the Arnostéguy? One is tempted to riposte: you have heard of it now, your friends have heard of it, the gods of the high places, too… not a bad audience.

The landscape around here is glorious: grassy hillsides scattered with farms, velvety tapestries of shrub and trees cloaking another mountain flank, craggy wind-sculpted outcrops of bleached rock and woodlands of slim trees filtering the sun through their high bonnets of leaves. The crest profiles of the Basque Pyrenees have the look of what you might get if you gave a child giant some modelling clay and asked for a range of mountains; dints and pokes of fingers, and moulding and squeezing, nudging, bashing, smoothing… a wonderful hotchpotch of shapes: sharp peaks, jagged, rounded, flat, humped, in shallow crests; fretted ridges, rutted, folded, furrowed, hound-toothed, pleated, corrugated, striated and smooth. One ridge, crowned with a tiara of ribbed stone, catches the eye. Or else, (as I mused on the outline of one Basque range) the sort of graph line you'd get on a cardiogram monitoring your reaction as you ride up, say, the Arnostéguy.

At 20km and 985m, as the road noses out of the tree cover and just before the torture stops for a while, a road off to the left goes to the Col d'Orgambide (988m) but it leads nowhere that you would want to take a racing machine. Two more kilometres of around 9% take you to the more exposed corniche and the milder run-in to the col at 27km.

---

4 This road offers an alternative, very tough approach to the Lac d'Iraty [see Bagargui]: from 305m, 9 kilometres of nothing less than 9% and most of the way around 12% on a narrow, twisting, steep climb over the Col d'Arthe (937m, 5.9km) to the Col d'Arthabaru (1115m, 8km) where it gets much nicer in temper and gives a rollercoaster ride down to the start of the Bagargui. Very rustic, very impressive and very, very hard.

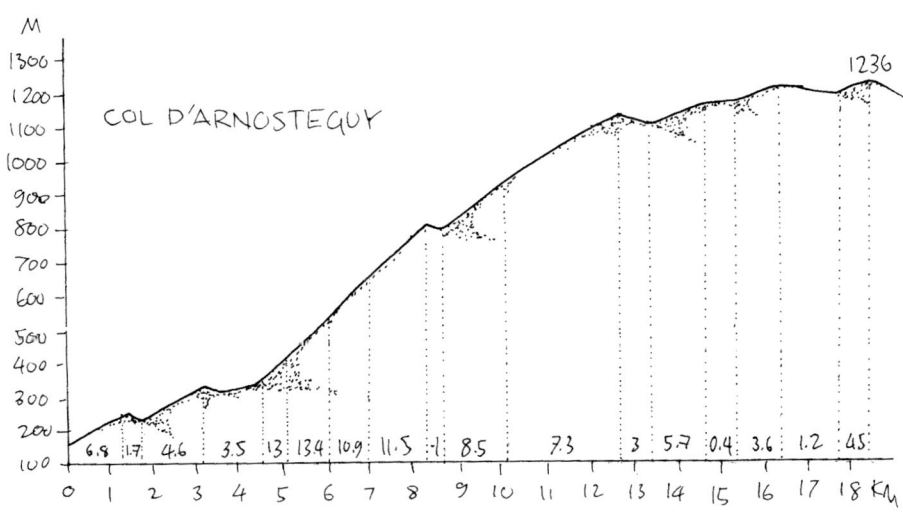

Rejoice. You are now on the Camino Santiago… Chemin de Saint Jacques, a few metres away from the frontier line. Up to the north-east on a peak at 1419m stands the Tour d'Urculu, the remains of a Roman outpost (or mausoleum). The views are breathtaking, 360° of sublime Pyrenean majesty. This is the Arnostéguy.

The road swings round the bare hillside in a big right-hander for 4 kilometres towards the Elhursaro where the D128 tips off down a wickedly steep descent round viciously tight hairpins – 9 kilometres and up to 14% in places, but a fabulous view – towards Arnéguy. The D428 continues along the pilgrim route past the Vierge d'Orisson where the faithful stop for spiritual uplift and pious and impious alike loiter for panoramas and picnics. I encountered two cyclists on this climb heading for Santiago on faith, energy bars and triple chainwheel.

The cathedral in Santiago de Compostela houses a gilded bust of Saint James the Apostle, Jesus' brother, whose martyred body was brought from Palestine to Galicia for burial, although history does not relate quite why. (Sant'Iago is Spanish for Saint James.) The original pilgrims' route began in Paris at the Tour Saint Jacques, reached down to the south-west of France, crossed the Pyrenees at the Ibañeta and continued across northern Spain. Mediaeval pilgrims wore a scallop shell (Saint James' symbol) as a badge – it still identifies the route markers. When they arrived at the 11th-century cathedral, they planted the fingers of one hand in the five dints worn in the stone. I watched an elderly pilgrim fumble confusedly for the hollows and then, having located the dints, he suddenly relaxed, his entire body flooded with the relief of getting there.

The statue of the Orisson Madonna stands atop a large natural cairn of stone, looking across the road up which her people have struggled to commune with her. Troupes of Manechs are her other constant attendants and there is a sign claiming this as the Col de Bentarte, unrecorded elsewhere. Nearby are the remnants of the ancient redoubt of the Château Pignon built in 1512 by Ferdinand of Aragón as a border fort during his annexation of Navarre.

A sign warns against the shooting of rabbits. Outcrops of split and layered rock.

The narrow descent carves its way off the bare mountainside through woodlands, through which there's a fine prospect of farmland in the bowl of the valley, down slopes of varying gradient – as little as 5%, as stiff as the 13.5 kilometre drop from the hamlet of Honto, 6 kilometres from the bottom. (The anti-clockwise loop is quite as tough as the clockwise, but rather more exposed.)

Just before Honto, note the Refuge/Auberge d'Orisson, as for the most part this loop offers nothing in the way of sustenance, apart from a dip in the river. Lower down there are watering holes: the Hôtel/Restaurant de la Source de la Nive by the river at Béthérobie, for example, while in Estérençuby the Hôtel Andreinia 'proposes you its rooms'.

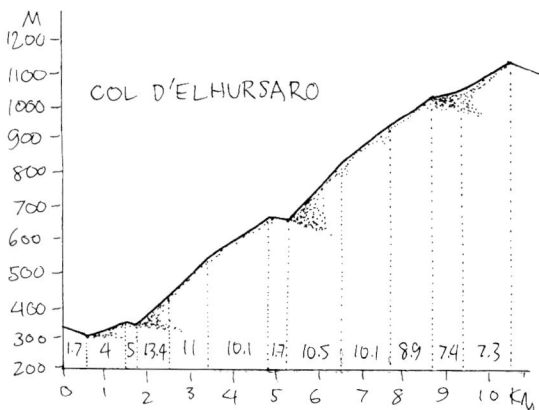

Col de Burdincurutcheta 1135m

From Saint-Jean-le-Vieux

LENGTH: 19.2KM
HEIGHT GAIN: 950M
MAXIMUM GRADIENT: 12%

This also covers the northern approach to the Col de Bagargui. A short way past the bike shop in Saint-Jean-le-Vieux (210m), turn right off the D933 onto the D18 towards Mendive where the road forks – left goes on to the Ahusquy.

A short distance beyond the fork, as the road follows the river through Bassaburua (320m, 10km) a marker indicates: Col d'Iraty (1327m, 17.5km – otherwise known as the Bagargui) and every kilometre is posted from here. The first two of them are shockers – a double whammy of 11%, as if the Burdincurutcheta, reduced to the humbler status of intermediate col, is really angry about not getting a mention in the advertising. The road, broad and well-surfaced, winds through trees for much of the way, the hairpins are deep and the views of the valley very fine. Kilometres 3 and 4 relax a tad to around 10.5%, big deal. A flattish section delivers a swift come-uppance on a half-kilometre stretch of very steep corniche, the valley abyss yawning below, and round a hard left onto more corniche.

Suddenly the col's coltish hissy fit peters out over the minor Col d'Haltza, 782m at just over 14km, and past a cordon of trees to the left the road spills onto a small plateau: to the right a long view of the valley, ahead the undulating road, the drop, the corner and, beyond it, the next metres of rise. Three kilometres of around 8% ensue. A ring of rocky chines stands off to the right as the road becomes a ledge cut into the flank of the mountain and on through alleys of bushy poplars which grow denser. A large right-hand bend clear of trees, as if the wind had blown them off the corner, and back into cover.

The final 3 kilometres are peaceful: around 7% to clear the tree line, snaky bends, a downhill to the marker for the penultimate kilometre which bucks and rollocks along to the Burdincurutcheta, which still gets no recognition. There follows a fast drop of 2.5 kilometres round easy bends, for the most part, to the Lac d'Iraty at 1030m. There's a friendly and cheap bar/restaurant off the road, by the river, Le Kaiolar Iraty.

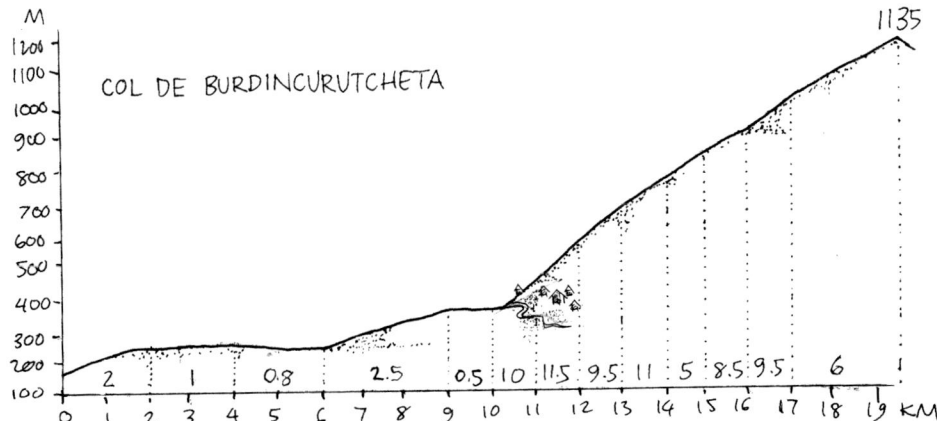

Col de Bagargui (les chalets d'iraty) 1327m

Eastern approach from Larrau

LENGTH: 12.2KM

HEIGHT GAIN: 700M

MAXIMUM GRADIENT: 12.5%

The approach to Larrau itself is by no means insignificant: a mild-enough ride along the valley until 3 kilometres out of the village when the gradient kicks up nastily, between 7 and 10%, followed by a long drop to 515m at the foot of the Bagargui, 10 kilometres away. A plaque in Larrau celebrates 'the road of fraternity' linking the valleys of the Soule, the Socurs de Roncal and Salazar, inaugurated in 1970.

There is absolutely no relief on this climb after the first 2 kilometres of a relatively easy swing through trees along the banks of the river to a second bridge, the Pont d'Aguerborda, at 630m. From here the gradient is merciless, as anyone who did the Etape in 2003 will confirm. They christened it 'the Bugger-me', possibly musing – in their delirium of effort – on the fact that the town to which they were headed, Bayonne, gave its name to a sharp weapon fastened to the end of a gun.

The road soon breaks out of the trees and continues at the back-breaking toll of never less than 9% and, most of the way, a cruel 10-12.5%, round long, buckled hairpins. (The view of them from the top is one of the more impelling sights in the cols – the steeple-pinnacled graph of suffering writ large.) There are kilometre and altitude signs all the way – only one missing, 4 kilometres to go.

The surface on these last kilometres is generally not too good, gouged and scarred, and the cover scant. At around 2 kilometres from the top, the road divides round a central eyot, for reasons undiscovered, and just beyond it, written on the road: '*OURS EN LIBERTE CHARGEONS LES FUSILS*' (Bears at liberty, let's load the rifles). The bears have been reintroduced – brought in from Slovenia – and the farmers are (literally) up in arms. Sheep are found disembowelled or decapitated. The worst times are when the animals emerge from hibernation and are starving or else in the mating season when the frustrated male bears, in particular, are in a frenzy. Timid beasts, they rarely return to the same killing spot twice, but farmers are fly to this: they put out pots of honey laced with glass. Other comminations read: 'Bears out, hikers (*randonneurs*) in danger' and 'Bears, the death of the Pyrenees'.

Suddenly, there is a most welcome sight: a sign reads 'Dernier kilomètre: 7.5%'. The road narrows as if squeezing the last drop of willpower and energy out of you and then, you are there. I spoke to a French cyclist on the col – he had just ridden up this brute and was suffering from a nose bleed.

Western approach

LENGTH: 7KM

HEIGHT GAIN: 293M

MAXIMUM GRADIENT: 6%

An up-and-down climb along the course of a river, which earns its low gradient averages with flats and drops and sudden surges. The first 4 kilometres are very hard, largely because of the abrupt changes of rhythm, but there follow plenty of opportunities to recuperate. The route is scenic and varied, the road winds happily through trees, past a lake with a large sluice to manage the flow of water from melted snows, camping chalets to the right in the Fôret d'Iraty and on through a lonelier wooded section to the Chalets d'Iraty, a centre for cross-country skiing. There's a bar/restaurant and a terrace from which to look out over the panorama eastwards of the peaks which line the frontier, somewhere among them the Port de Larrau.

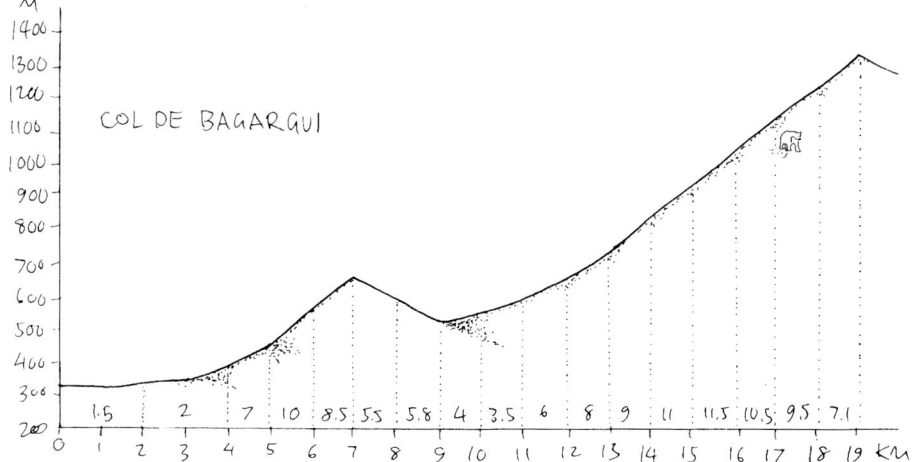

TOUR DE FRANCE 2003 STAGE 16

Hamilton's mental strength

In a disastrous pile-up at the end of stage 1, Tyler Hamilton sustained two hairline fractures in his right collarbone and decided to ride on. 'I'm not doing this for the team,' he said, 'I'm doing it for me.'

His team osteopath Ole Kaare, a charismatic Dane, was sanguine about Hamilton's chances of survival and bandaged the injured shoulder firmly. His mechanic bound the bars with rolls of tape – as for the Paris-Roubaix, to reduce jarring – further padded with strips of gel and raised them to make braking and changing gear easier, as well as lowering the pressure in his tyres. He finished the second stage 'white as linen' from the pain and even mere survival seemed unlikely. But, two weeks later he was still there.

Caught off the back on the Côte des Crêts when the peloton exploded, Hamilton had to be ridden back on by five of his team mates.

'I made a terrible error,' he said. 'It was my fault. I wanted to win this stage for them.'

He joined an escape at the foot of the Col du Soudet, 145 kilometres from home, and at the foot of this brutal climb of the Bagargui, 50 kilometres on, he went alone. Quite a place to attack; by the summit of the giant of the Basque cols he had an advance of 2min 10sec on his immediate pursuer. The yellow jersey group were at 4 minutes. Hamilton had just over 76 kilometres to ride. The images of him riding into the outskirts of Bayonne are unforgettable: his face grimacing with pain, his tongue lolling, his body heaving with effort, his legs visibly wilting. As the finish line came into view, Hamilton sat up, waited for his manager Bjarne Rijs in the car behind him to draw alongside and held out his hand, in thanks.

There are moments in this beautiful sport which touch the heart.

Rijs said that the team's great strength was their mental attitude and 'Hamilton is the living proof.'

Abaurrea Alta 995m and Alto de Remendia 1047m

Into the Basque region

LENGTH: 5KM
HEIGHT GAIN: OVER 800M IN TOTAL
MAXIMUM GRADIENT: 8%

These two relatively unimposing summits form part of the route which leads further east into the Spanish Basque region. The NA140 is well-made, not overloaded with traffic, wide and pleasant to ride. It crosses the river Irati in Aribe (690m) over a fine old packhorse bridge with side bulges for laden animals passing. There is no bar here, nor yet in Garaioa (740m). The gradient begins to lift a few kilometres on but it's smooth and easy pedalling to the wide sweep of the first main height. Three kilometres or so of descent into farmland and light tree cover, over the river Zatoya (950m) and an 8% climb over the last kilometre up to the Alto de Remendia.

There is, at last, a bar in Jaurrieta and, one bright sunny morning at 10.45am, I watched two old guys tucking into huge cooked ham rolls washed down with a bottle of *vino rosado*.

Ochagavia, left at the junction with the NA 178, straddles the river Salazar; fine cobbled streets in the old quarter, restaurants, bars, church bells. Hostal Orialde is recommended – in what looks and feels like an old priory.

Paso Tapia 1340m

A beautiful detour

LENGTH: 37KM
HEIGHT GAIN: 610M
MAXIMUM GRADIENT: 8%

If you are happy to add some 20 kilometres of most pleasant forest trail on a packed-earth forest track round a lake and along the course of a small stream, this route will lead you back to the minor road following the Salazar into Aribe. If not, the clearing by the small Ermita de Nuestra Señora de las Nieves (Our Lady of the Snows) below the Paso Tapia makes a most agreeable picnic spot as a break in what is a fine there-and-back ride. From a small bridge crossing into Ochagavia (730m), the minor road snakes north along the flat course of the river Zatoya past a beautiful old stone bridge and a roofed-over woodstack for 4 kilometres to a drop onto more open ground, a tiny house with a barn and a second barn (5km and 810m). Flat agreeable pedalling and, with that new sensitivity imbued in you by this Rapha guide, as the road swings to the right you feel the start of a climb coming on, a barely perceptible 3% to the uninitiated.

Soon you are on an open mountain road, the slopes around 6-8%, the valley falling away below, buzzards wheeling overhead. At 8km, beetling cliffs of dimpled rock sprouting more of those abseiling trees; at 9km, 1040m, the road flattens onto a shelf with a fine view over the valley and continues into a recess of the mountain, as if shouldered by a giant making his drunken way home in the dark. So, on through an overhang of large bushy poplars and a sweet sight of the road just travelled.

Eleven kilometres gives us 1150m, the way easy on a good surface. At around 12.8km, an open, treeless hillside, a big expanse of country away to the left, and at 13.4km, 1340m, comes the Paso, which is unmarked, and the Mirador de Goñiburu, which is. A *mirador* (viewpoint) plan picks out the jumble of mountain peaks to the south.

The drop to the picnic area, 6.5 kilometres, rolls down hairpins on an exposed re-entrant and into trees at around 3 kilometres. Full cover, readable bends, steady slope to the bottom (830m), the river to cool off in, picnic tables, forest glade, the track disappearing off into the forest most invitingly.

My path was crossed this day by a pine marten: barred tail, sleek body, swift, slinky action. There is probably folklore attached.

The return descent from the Paso is glorious, swooping round long bends through air and sky into landscape.

Port de Larrau 1585m and Col d'Erroimendy 1362m

From the south

LENGTH: 19.3KM

HEIGHT GAIN: 850M

MAXIMUM GRADIENT: 8%

NA140 from Ochagavia to the junction at 8.5km where the road continues to France as D26. At 18.7km there is an unlit tunnel about 150m long, with cattle grids at either end. No problem with light, however. A tarmac graffito reads: 'MATAR LOS OSOS' (Kill the Bears).[5]

The road is wide and well-surfaced, with a steady lift of around 7% most of the way but for a snarl of around 8% some 3 kilometres from the junction. Sweeping bends, the view dominated by conifers, a Centro de Esqui Nordico at about 14km where the climb is settling into its own prevailing rhythm of around 7% – probably the standard tempo for this guide's second-category grading. This eases a tad round the final long hairpins over exposed ground, a majestic progress over the final acres of Navarre with Spain slipping away behind you. And with a run-in of no more than 4% to the col, the sense of satisfaction is deep. Finally, from the balcony of the Larrau opens out one of the finest panoramas in these most beautiful mountains: a huge perspective of distant ranges, north and east. Revel in it. This is what you have come to see. This is what informs every stroke of the pedals and every ache in your limbs and back.

Any frontier crossing has a double potency and the Larrau does the envoi in real style, marking the transition into the new territory with a stern reminder of the days when crossing these passes was for the very intrepid few.

The first short section of the descent towards the Erroimendi is ropey indeed – the road littered with shale, broken stone and gravel washed off the mountainside. And it's steep, a nasty 11.5% for just over a kilometre and then a flattish cirque road clinging to the curved flank of the rock. This lends more sobriety to what is already quite a sombre forlorn aspect, a sort of stony-faced No-Man's Land. The terrain leading to the Erroymendi and the col itself, a broad bald wind-blasted plateau, home to sheep and a scattering of hides defines the French word *sauvage*: wild, inhospitable, remote. Whether the hides are for watching birds or shooting them is a point, the French keen either to torment the wild life or eat it. If you can combine both, so much the better.

Northern approach

LENGTH: 12.3KM

HEIGHT GAIN: 958M

MAXIMUM GRADIENT: 12%

The pull up from Larrau out of the Larrau gorge on the D26 is haughty, tough, implacable. It gives not an inch... although metricated elsewhere, English still demurs on 'give not a centimetre'. The surface is rough at the edges in places. Two kilometres on the road enters the trees and begins to swing, but there is no letting up in the gradient – a relatively mild start at 6 and then 8.5% before the gloves come off and you are on 6 kilometres worth of 10... 10.5... 11... until 2 kilometres from the top, the trees go, the road becomes a shelf, cliff to the left, precipice to the right, and so onto the barest of bare mountains. '*OURS MORT DES PYRENEES*' (Bears, death of the Pyrenees) greets you. Topping the Erroymendi gives you a chance to breathe before the grim last kilometre of 12% in parts.

The broad scallop shape of the tunnel entrance grins at you, rather, at the start of what is a grand descent off the Larrau into Spain and Navarre – long straights between bends before entering the trees past an installation kitted out with large solar panels.

5 'Graffito' is the singular of the plural 'graffiti'.

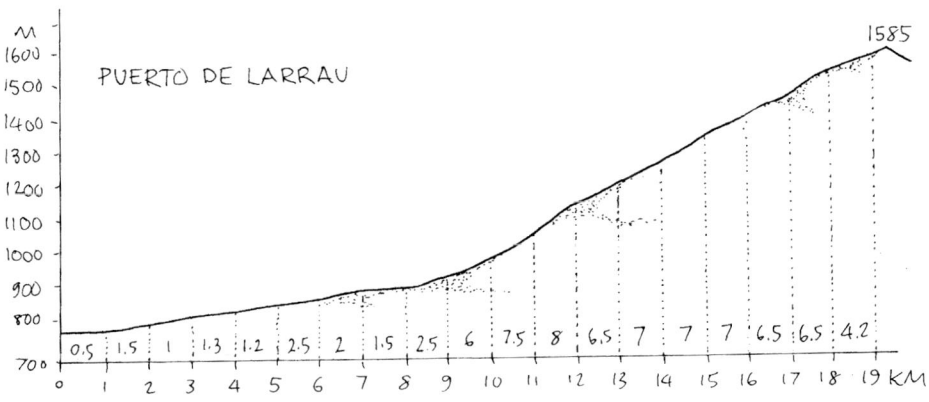

Alto Laza 1129m

Western approach

LENGTH:	11.5KM
HEIGHT GAIN:	399M
MAXIMUM GRADIENT:	10%

Another transition climb, a good route into the Lost Mountain region through lovely countryside.

From Ochagavia, the NA140 heads for France, sidling along the course of the river Anduña which rises in the rock below the Port de Larrau, the frontier pass. At 8km, 900m, it swings right at a junction towards Isaba, where the frontier road continues as the D26. A smooth carpet of tarmac leads straight into a hairpin and climbs quite sharply for a kilometre through spindly poplars. Larches and pines join as the gradient slackens to around 7% but the pines crowd out their droopier-fronded cousins and at the Alto Laza, they dominate. The descent is fine, down the course of the Barranco (gorge) de Ustárroz, an initial drop of 5% into the small town of Ustárroz itself where it evens out along the valley.

Isaba makes a good base and the Hostal-Restaurante Lola, at the end of a longish courtyard off the road in the centre of town, is recommended as cyclist-friendly. On my second visit, I met two English cyclists staying there, exploring the region. They found the climb of the next col, from the French side, 'the hardest climb we have ever done.' It is undoubtedly very hard, but they had not done either the Tourmalet or the Marie Blanque. Nevertheless, such opinion sits well in this guide's rationale, which is that there is no such thing as absolute judgement. Contexts vary, different factors prevail; all that one can say is that on a particular day a climb did not defeat you.

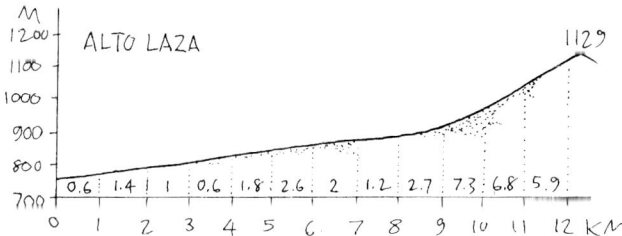

50 THE RAPHA GUIDE

TOUR DE FRANCE 1996 STAGE 17

Eclipse in the Pyrenees

On stage 16, Bjarne Rijs, in yellow since his victory at Sestrières, had confirmed his dominance over the incumbent champion, Miguel Induraín, with a show of strength on Hautacam. Now the race headed for the Basque region, Induraín's home turf. Had this stage not been planned for him, a crowning moment? The route was a killer: the Col du Soulor, 20 kilometres from the start, followed by Aubisque, Marie-Blanque, Soudet and Port de Larrau, these latter two included for the first time, and then the Remendia and Abuarrea.

Richard Virenque, col-bagging for his third polka-dot jersey, claimed the Larrau, but it was on the Soudet that the decisive break came. As one French commentator put it, 'pitiless but superb'. Rijs and Laurent Dufaux went clear and raced together onto the Avenida Pio XII in Pamplona. Dufaux took the stage, but Rijs had no need of it. Eight and a half minutes ticked by before Induraín, the local hero, five Tours de France, two Giri d'Italia, three Tours of Catalonia, two Paris-Nice, two Dauphinés Libérés… trailed in, thoroughly beaten and, in this race, outclassed. The reception the crowd gave him was so loaded with emotion, that the Tour organisers invited him to join Rijs on the podium. The Dane handed over his bouquet as a mark of esteem and condolence. In the suburbs of Pamplona, Induraín had stopped to kiss his wife and son at the side of the road – this private salutation in a rider's village, town or city, is an old and respected Tour tradition. Now he faced a huge crowd applauding him, cheering him in his eclipse. He could barely speak.

'This has been a great stage,' he said 'but it was for the strong men, and I wasn't one of them…'

2. Wild Peak

Bounded to the west by the Roncal valley and to the east by the valley of the Aspe, Wild Peak is named for the craggy Tête Sauvage which overlooks the main crossing of the range at the Col de la Pierre Saint Martin. It incorporates the inland extremity of the Basque region. The historian Josephus records a legend that after the Flood one of Noah's sons, Japhet, left Armenia and pitched up in Uesca, the Aragónese name for the Roncal valley, and from his seed came the Basque peoples. The Roncalais have a proud history. In the early 8th century, a local anchorite (hermit) called a meeting of 300 local Basque fighting men to organise resistance to the invading Moors. They voted one of their number, García Ximenes, chief and it was the men of the Roncal valley who formed the backbone of his army which won a series of bloody battles with the Moors, notably at Ainsa, the ancient capital of the Sobrarbe, a county in northern Huesca (ancient Uesca) part of the old kingdom of Aragón. The Moors had fortified the town strongly: Garcia opted for a night attack. The Moors had the upper hand when suddenly the Christians saw a sign in heaven: an old oak tree against a field of gold. Inspired, they drove the attack home and took Ainsa. Garcia made it his capital. (Sobrarbe is from Latin super arborem – on top of a tree, an example of legend explaining etymology, not the other way round.) The reputation, well-deserved, of Basque physical fortitude was born.

    The valley on the Spanish side ends in a broad bowl of pasture confined by a massive semicircle of rock over which runs the road to the Pierre Saint-Martin. Here the landscape changes dramatically to the barren limestone desert known as karst – named after the classic Kras or Carso Plateau linking south-west Slovenia and north-east Italy.

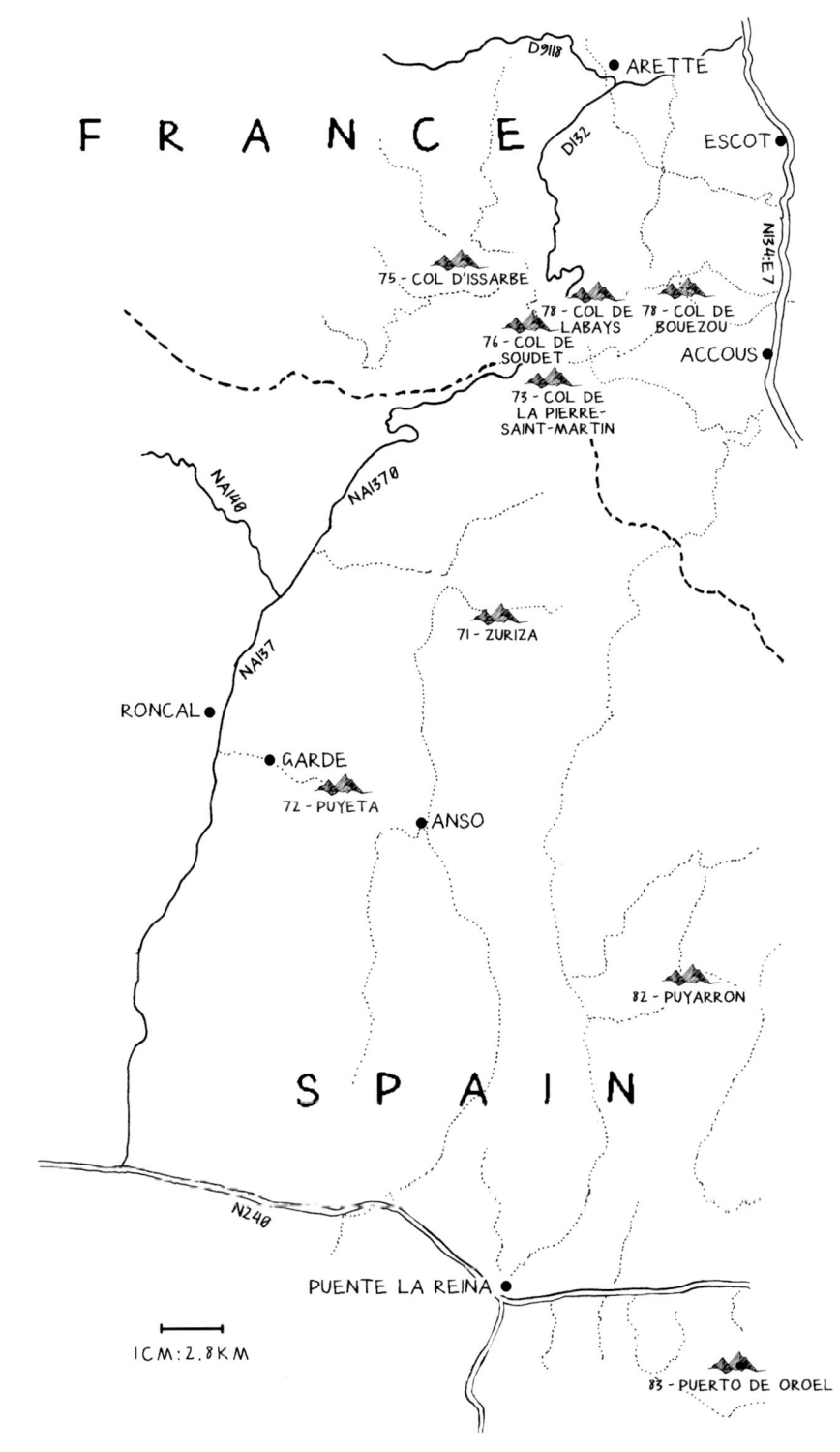

The distinctive rock sculpture – ribbed, grooved, torn, hacked, fretted – called lapiaz in French and Spanish (Latin lapis is 'stone') results from the erosion of the bare limestone (a compound of skeletal remains of fish and marine shells), initially by glaciers and then by wind and rain, sun and ice, on the surface and, underground, by spring water. Cliff faces are lined with ledges where softer limestone cracks along fault lines, contracting and expanding through the action of heat and cold.

The tiny village of Sainte Engrâce, patron saint of the Basques – they invoke her against bad weather, drought and headaches – is a focal point of the region. It sits at the foot of the famous Gorges de Kakuetta, below the Pierre Saint-Martin and for a long time outsiders considered the crossing from here to be impassable; that intrepid mountaineer Hilaire Belloc tried twice without success. The Roncalais, many of them shepherds – day job – and noted smugglers – night job – surely had their ways. Visit the church; it's a gem.

This is wild territory, dry gulch borderlands. It is also dotted with hermitages – small, secluded refuges for men and women who, like the anchorite already mentioned, turned their back on the world to commune in solitary peace with God. The first Christian hermits sought their tranquillity in the Sinai desert in Egypt. The barren rock deserts of the Pyrenees proved just as attractive to these lone contemplatives, their feet planted firmly on the living hard-rock base substance of God's creation.

The famous gâteau Basque is good cyclist tuck, up there with toasted tea cakes: a large roundel of pâté sable (sable is French for 'sand' and this is a crumbly, cookie-like crust used for dessert tarts) with almond crème pâtissière and cherry preserve, sometimes made at the side of the road on portable ovens by determined picnickers. Basque men, traditionally, reign in the kitchens.

P55 One kilometre to go… a cheerful sight

P56 The view south along the valley into Spain as the road climbs northwards to the *Pierre Saint-Martin* and France

P58 Nearing the *Pierre-Saint-Martin*, Spain to the left, France to the right.

P60 The fretted cliffs of the *Cirque de Lescun*

P62 The rocky yoke of mountains straddling the border near the *Col de la Pierre Saint-Martin*

P64 Bandit country… the gorge valley road leading from *Anso* to the *Zuriza*

P66 River near *Zuriza*

P68 Gorge and high rock bluffs beyond *Zuriza*

P70 Ovine sentinel patrols the heights near *Lescun*, ramparts leading towards the *Pic du Midi d'Ossau* in the background

Zuriza 1290m

A Gastronomic Loop

LENGTH: 14KM

HEIGHT GAIN: 450M

MAXIMUM GRADIENT: 8%

The valley road leads north out of the old town of Ansó along the course of the river Veral. Narrow, ill-surfaced to begin with, it winds through an impressive, low barranco (gorge) and is included here for that reason alone. There are also three restaurants en route offering local fare – cocina tradicional and comida típica – Borda Changale (4km, 860m), Borda Arracona (7km, 900m) and Borda Chiquín (9km, 950m), by a bridge.

The ride is not hard but it is beautiful: the waters of the Veral babbling, overhanging rock, dwarf and full-growth conifers and, further up, beech trees which shade the route agreeably. There are frequent rock falls, obstacles to the unwary cyclist, and the road is rarely much more than a car's width. At around 10km, 1000m, a new bridge, built within the past year, has replaced the old traverse which collapsed into the river and prevented me from proceeding to the head of the valley on my first visit. Beyond it the gradient begins to crank up steadily, and there is a brand new surface which the cars are wearing in nicely.

Zuriza itself stands at 1227m in a verdant plain overlooked by the big peaks which form part of the frontier wall to the east. Horses graze, there is a large campsite and the road to the 1290m mark is shocking: gouged, pitted, very rough but manageable. Should you wish to approach it from the west and ride back down the gorge, the NA2000 joins the main NA131 up the Roncal valley.

Western approach

LENGTH: 12KM

HEIGHT GAIN: 480M

MAXIMUM GRADIENT: 8%

From the junction, the road climbs quite steeply – 8% – through woods for just over 2 kilometres to 1000m and then drops down into pastureland along a flat river basin. At 6km, 1040m, it begins to climb again, between 6 and 7%, to the high point and then bumps over the scrambler's track to Zuriza.

Puyeta 1201m

Western approach

LENGTH: 11.5 KM
HEIGHT GAIN: 600 M
MAXIMUM GRADIENT: 10%

From the junction on the NA137 4.5 kilometres south of Roncal, the NA176 follows the Barranco de Gardalar, a placid, easy 3 kilometres of not more than 4% on a good surface through the village of Garde. On the wall behind the counter of a friendly bar opposite the fronton, hangs a wooden plaque inscribed with what are reputedly the first words ever to be written in Eskuara from the Monasterio de Suso in the 10th century:

"Izloqui dugu guec ajulu ez dugu."
'We have seen the light, we need no other help.'

This is the declaration of the hermit – illumination through silent dwelling on the central and internal mystery of human existence caught up in the awesome majesty of divine creation. Somewhat more exalted a purpose, maybe, than the inner mental toil of the cyclist grappling with the curious quadratics of gradient, physical stress, satisfaction and the irresistible force of geology amongst other things but, well, it's a start. And as the patron of the bar/restaurant on the Aubisque said: 'The first mistake a man can make is to think it's someone else's fault.' There is, you see, philosophical gold in them thar hills…

Further on the road flattens and dips, the valley closes in and, after a slight roughness, the good surface resumes over a bridge. The last 4 kilometres to the col, which also marks the border between the old kingdoms of Navarra and Aragón (Huesca province), delivers gradients of 6–8%, with one short section at between 9 and 10%. The surface deteriorates in parts but trees shade the route, and from just below the col up to the right appears the small, rectangular white building which is the Ermita de Puyeta. There is a marked difference in surface quality between the poor of Navarra and the good of Aragón.

Eastern approach

LENGTH: 5.5 KM
HEIGHT GAIN: 361 M
MAXIMUM GRADIENT: 9%

A short haul up from the well of the valley, after the road dips out of town to a bridge and then swings round a left-hand bend onto the climb through barren terrain – exposed strata of rock, dwarf conifers, a good view back over Ansó, past a road left to Fago. The hermitage sits high on the ridge up to the left and the final kilometre-and-a-half eases to a manageable 4 or 5% on what is a pretty good surface all the way.

This climb and the circuit to Zuriza spin off the main road to the frontier crossing at the Col de la Pierre Saint Martin.

Col de la Pierre Saint-Martin 1201m

There are actually four approaches to this major col, but because they incorporate other intermediate cols, only the main southern and northern approaches are treated here in detail.

Southern approach, Spain into France

LENGTH:	27 KM
HEIGHT GAIN:	945 M
MAXIMUM GRADIENT:	8%

The first 12 kilometres from Isaba ramble along the floor of the Belagua ('fine water') valley as it narrows towards the frontier wall at no more than 1.5–3%. The trees crowd in to begin with but gradually thin out as the road edges into a more open landscape of meadow and pastureland, scattered farmhouses, mountain spurs projecting south from the big sierra to either side, their slopes wearing a stubble of trees. The road makes for the closing curtain wall of the border, like a runway, straight as an arrow flight.

At 12.5km, 1000m the road traverses a bridge and makes a big left-hand turn onto the long first ramp cut into the side of the mountain, clearly visible during the approach ride. The change of gradient is marked – from the 4% just after the bridge to a sudden 7.5%. This settles into a steady rhythm for 7 kilometres of long, tree-lined straights which, periodically, lean round languid hairpins. There's a glorious view back along the throat of the valley and down to the hairpins just travelled, and away to the left a stegosaurus spine of rock.

The hairpins begin to tighten though the gradient remains fairly constant, and at around 16.7km they unfold onto a corniche roving round the upper rim of the chasm. To the left stands the Refugio de Belagua, now a military establishment patrolled by armed sentries, and to the right the fine prospect of the peaks topping the border ranges, among them the Tête Sauvage, begins to open out. Riding the line of the frontier, the road, with barely a bend in it, looks down to the right on a Gothic ski chalet with a tent-shaped extension at one end and a chimney stack in the form of the simple, open belfry characteristic of many churches in this region – a standing slab of wall with embrasures in which hang the bells. Next to it, a solar panel station. Here the gradient tails away to a mere 4%.

This is a splendid ride. The summit of the Portillo de Eraice (1578m – there is no altitude sign) looms way ahead on the bleak top. The road dips for a short distance as if, like you, it is tired of climbing, oppressed by the close proximity of the frontier, and then recovers its pluck to climb gently again, but at no great rush to a border stone with an elegantly engraved E for España.

The plateau is a mixture of rock and hard place, swathes of it covered with a bristle of sheep-munched scrub grass: unwelcoming, exposed, affirming the hostility which for so long characterised relations between the two nations whose division it heralds. When I first rode up here, the Spanish road – wonderfully smooth, thanks to EU subsidies and symbolic of the emergence of a new Spain from the suspicions and alienation of the Franco era – merged at the frontier line with a ramshackle tarmac French piste (track). Things have improved since.

The road drops to a short tunnel with a lid of flat rock and a bushy brow of trees, and continues to drop beyond it to the start of the final climb to the high point on the French side. The scenery on either side is landmark Wild Peak: rock outcrops, tumbled boulders as if from a giants' stone-throwing fight, withered shrubs and trees scratching for purchase in blisters of the thinnest of soil, more mature conifers with dark needle foliage. When the sun is broiling, this is a most inhospitable place: unforgiving as a goblin's heart.

The final 3 kilometres swing round a big loop under cordons of pine perched on low ramparts of riven stone and then snaps back at around 5.5 to 6%. Another drop and flat for a way to a big left-hand bend and open tarmac to a blue and white sign registering 'Dernier kilomètre 1733m, 3% sur 1 km' (3% for 1km) up to the border stone (broken) and the col (1765m). Thus, between the Spanish border stone and the French, there is a hesitant passage where road and frontier run conterminously in a sort of unidentifiable nowhere, as if either side were saying, in echo, 'You can have it, we're not bothered… there's nothing there anyway, only… just keep your distance.'

The vista of mountains beyond into France is majestic. The gallimaufry of chalets, restaurants, residential high-rise buildings, shopping tower blocks and ski-lift gantries which make up the winter resort of Pierre Saint-Martin is most decidedly not majestic. However, there is food and drink on offer all year round in at least one fairly seedy establishment in the bowels of the main snow-holidaymaker complex.

Northern approach

LENGTH:	25.8 KM
HEIGHT GAIN:	1440 M
MAXIMUM GRADIENT:	15%

The first 8 kilometres of the D132 from Arette along the bosky valley floor to La Mouline are simple enough, 2.5% maximum. It's leafy, pleasant, generally quite free of traffic, though often in summer host to herds of cows lolloping along to the mellow sound of their throat bells, flocks of sheep, goats, all at leisurely pace and blithely indifferent to other forms of traffic, even, (shockingly) the environment-friendly bicycle and its devotees.

At 0.4km out of town, the D341 leads off left

to the Col de Lie (601m) and at 0.8km a roadside crucifixion stands by the junction with a much smaller side road, left. Two kilometres beyond La Mouline (453m) there is an abrupt change of mood: a right-hand hairpin initiates a vicious section at 15%, like a 'Welcome' mat overlaid with blazing coals. It's a horror but mercifully quite short, and the slope relaxes to a mere 9–11% for another 8 kilometres up through trees, past wood piles left by local lumbermen in clearings of roadside grass. It eases briefly like a smile just after 14km across the Plateau de Chousse, where the hairpins kick sweet temper back down the hill and there is another section of very steep road, teetering on 11–12%, albeit well-shaded and on a good surface. It's wide as well, which always seems to increase the difficulty, giving the illusion, perhaps, that you have not only to ride a long way up but a long way round, too. Okay, so all is, in the long run, illusion, depending how extreme your existentialism and hard-nosed attitude to reality. As you ride these climbs, with the Rapha guide descriptions of them lodged somewhere in your memory, but faced now with the inescapable actuality of tarmac, heat, weariness and gradient, do you perhaps say with Horace:

"auditis an me ludit amabilis insania?"
'Do you hear me, or is some crazy illusion toying with me?'

This Rapha guide's shell-like ear is ready for your messages and comments – anytime. Accuracy and passion invited. No bullshit.

At 17.7km, 1351m, the road slackens its grip dramatically (around 2.5%) towards a junction, left, with the tiny forest road winding up from the north-east via the Col de Bouézou. This meeting of roads sits on the intermediate Col de Labays. Such staging-post cols are not uncommon in these mountains and the Labays deserves separate status more than most. From here to the big crossing the road is considerably easier and the Labays itself is a very agreeable spot: it has the character of a forest clearing, a quiet glade, a sweet confluence of cycle routes, grass on which to sit and loll and contemplate the ardours of the journey and the promise of the destination, those two essential ingredients in the complex equation of satisfaction. The naming of these lower heights comes from the ancient past when the network of mountain tracks, familiar to shepherds, defined the topography as much as did the unattainable high peaks, often named for their shape, their aspect and their proximity to more accessible locales.

Two kilometres on, at a steady 5–6%, comes another named height, the Pas (or Pic) de Guilhers (1436m, 19.7km). The road has broken clear of the trees and the wind-blasted rockscape of the Pierre Saint-Martin imposes itself. As if in response, the gradient sharpens and flings some 8.5% at you to get to the next hump, the Col de Soudet, (1540m, 21.9km) and a joining road from Sainte-Engrâce to the right. The breezes swirl, the bare stone and dirt first soak in and then pulse out the heat, the long, long view of ranges to the northwest is inspiring and the final 2 kilometres to the (slight) anti-climax of the border col are, after the torture of the lower slopes, easy-peasy… 5–6.5%.

Col d'Issarbe 1450m

From Lannes-en-Barétous 315m

LENGTH: 18.3 KM
HEIGHT GAIN: 1135 M
MAXIMUM GRADIENT: 11%

This is undoubtedly an old foot track which has been metalled to serve the cross-country ski station near the Issarbe whose identity seems to be somewhat in contention, indeed not recognised by some aficionados as a col. However, it makes an interesting alternative to the more celebrated approaches to the high plateau of Wild Peak.

A short way west of Lannes-en-Barétous, the narrow D632 turns south off the D918, the old coach road. It ambles along the course of the Vert de Barlanes sedately enough for 5 kilometres into the eponymous village of Barlanes (385m) with one fractious growl of steepness halfway. Two kilometres beyond, at the Pont de Blancou (463m) – and in these regions blanco (white) almost invariably refers to the characteristic limestone – the climb digs in. This is hard going, 11 kilometres of unremitting gradient, close hairpins, with sudden pitches of added steepness, strictly for the enthusiast.

A significant feature of the Pyrenees is the variability of their gradient. Because many – indeed, most – of the roads follow the ancient tracks which were worn into the natural contours of the mountains, negotiable by men and animals with no great concern for gradations of steepness, the natural changes of rhythm have been preserved in the tarmac. No great concern? They could not change the contours so they got on with them. For pure climbers in the Tour de France, this unevenness offers an advantage. They have the flexibility, the lightness, the conditioning to cope with changes of rhythm whereas the bigger men, the power climbers, are not so easily adapted. Out-of-the-saddle, true climbers twirling low gears revel in uneven gradients which allow, nay, encourage, bursts of acceleration which the steady-state bum-in-the-saddle riders cannot readily match. Consider the contests between Armstrong – who made himself as close to a pure climber as he could get – and Ullrich, whose big-gear mentality never had an answer to the devastating spurts which the American delivered. Charly Gaul, the Angel of the Mountains, rarely got out of the saddle, it is true, but he rode at an exceptionally high cadence. French for out of the saddle – en danseuse (like a dancer) is expressive indeed.

At around 11km, 880m, the gradient dips a barely perceptible touch, and there's another wicked stretch of the horribles as the hairpins begin to open out near 16km, 1305m. The road creeps round a rock sidewall; to the right yawns the great chasm of the gorge. The surface is good, the road narrow and, above the tree line, no more than a ribbon of tarmac threading across open, sloping moorland.

To say that the final 2 kilometres are, by comparison with the early passage, light entertainment would be missing the point, but topping out onto the crown of the climb combined with the curvaceous 4.6 kilometre descent to the Col de Suscousse are undiluted pleasure. Tilt the head to the right and there below lies the green-sloped re-entrant of the Uhaitxa.

Col de Soudet 1540m

From Tardets-Sorholus

LENGTH: 34 KM
HEIGHT GAIN: 1323 M
MAXIMUM GRADIENT: 11%

From Tardets-Sorholus (217m), a pleasant Basque village with a part-colonnaded square, (a bar there is a checkpoint for the first day of the Raid Pyrénéen), the D26 heads south for the Port de Larrau crossing into Spain. After 8.5 kilometres of doddling gradient, the D113 turns south-east towards Sainte-Engrâce up the exceptionally beautiful verdant lush valley of the Uhaitxa. The mountain slopes are clad in trees, the long pleats of the rock like opposed knuckles. The way is not demanding either, no harder than 3% ambling along to the tiny village of La Caserne – French for 'barracks', derived from Latin quaterna (of four) – but in the 17th century specifically defining an outpost for four soldiers of the revenue garde.

Such men, like the Guardia Civil of Franco's Spain latterly, were cordially detested by the local population on whom they had been quartered – another link with the Latin quaterna. Not known in the area – so there would be no problem of loyalty clashes – they were ill-paid, often illiterate, incompetent, brutish and expected to supplement their wages from what they took in tolls. Not permitted to carry muskets, they toted only pistols, but officially empowered only to warn anyone they caught hunting – illegal in pre-Revolutionary France – they frequently confiscated, and then used, any musket they could get their hands on.

The slope tightens fractionally, now, to around 3.5%, past the celebrated Gorges de Kakouetta, left. The principal gorge is dark and very moist, conditions which produce a temperate rainforest micro-climate.

At around 5–5.5%, the road winds in and out of the valley's curves past hay meadows and pastureland, skirting the Gorges d'Ujarre, into Sainte-Engrâce (727m, 19.5km). This village at the head of the valley floor was, until some 20 years ago, reckoned by locals to be journey's end. There was no road up over the high ridge which lowers above it. Here is where French Basque country dwindled to an abrupt full stop. Beautiful, glorious rural solitude, balmy in summer; oppressed, dark and cold in winter, and nowhere to go beyond it, save for the most intrepid or the ingrained larcenous. The presence of the garde lower down –ancestors of the hated local milice (militia) – indicates that smugglers certainly negotiated the hidden paths, the tortuous tracks up to and over the heights. In 1987 the road

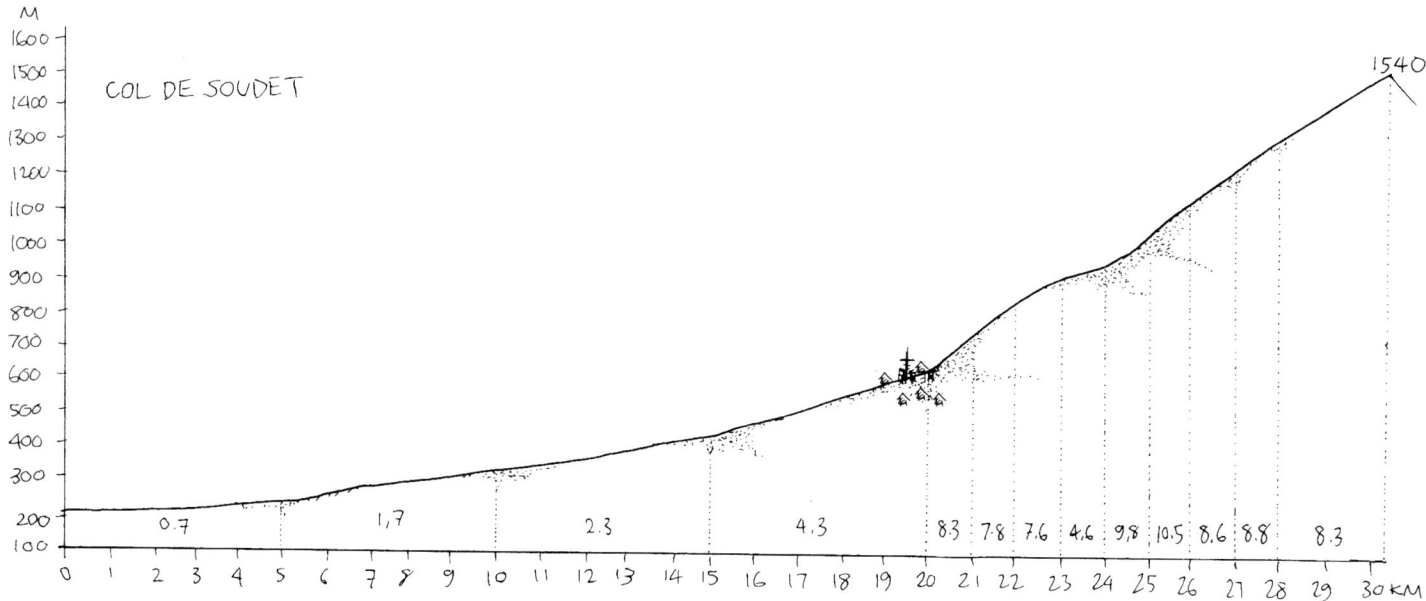

was extended up to the col but not much motorised traffic uses this route: it's still too damned narrow for most car drivers, so rejoice that it is.

The 11th-century Romanesque church has an unusual, awning-like sloping ceiling over the nave, a pitch-roofed square belfry and a graveyard dotted with Basque headstones that's crowned with a disc, reminiscent of the Celtic cross. The view down the valley is fine. Next door is a small gîte.

A bit further up the valley, a pleasant restaurant/auberge: Chez Berreix, 'last house' in Basque… last chance saloon.

The way now begins to get very tough: five kilometres of varying steepness, up to 10% on a surface of middling quality; there's a short breather halfway where the road crosses a bridge (970m), and then two vicious ramps of unremitting 10%+ to the Col de Suscousse (1216m, 26.3km) and the road, left, up to the Col d'Issarbe. There is, here, a feeling if not of danger then assuredly of brooding disquiet, of suspicion, as if the road's temerity in penetrating these high acres after having been for so long denied entry has disturbed the local sylvan spirits and the ghosts of the men who did flit through the shadows on their nefarious business, wary of the hated garde.

The road swings right onto a long ramp overhung with trees, an evil surface, and, even in hot conditions beyond the cover, generally damp, cold and inhospitable. By now the legs are complaining, the head trying to match perceived experience with statistical fact, and the offer of the Col de Soudet, crossed by the Tour de France five times only, (most recently in 2006), an object of wary disbelief.

Four kilometres of around 9%. Forest, dappled with sunlight. Lonely road. Then the tarmac breaks clear of trees onto the bleak Wild Peak and, round the bare slope, the final approach hits the full glare of the sun or else slithers into the clammy, swirling, inspissated [thick] mist of the Pyrenean mer de nuages (sea of clouds). As in Dr Johnson: 'In the description of night in Macbeth, the beetle and the bat detract from the general idea of darkness – inspissated gloom.' It was up here that I first witnessed this amazing phenomenon. The dense cloud swims up from the valley bowels like fog or steam in a cauldron to hang in the cooler air round the high peaks which then protrude above the clouds. On that occasion over the Pierre Saint-Martin, the evening sun cast a roseate glow over the vast, smoky grey sea of clouds, the high peaks protruding like islands. A ravishing sight, but not so good to ride into from underneath.

The Col de Soudet announces itself on the bare rock and immediately remembers its place, duly subordinate to the imperious border pass.

Col de Bouézou 1009m and Col de Labays 1351m

From Bedous

LENGTH: 20.9 KM

HEIGHT GAIN: 941M

MAXIMUM GRADIENT: 10%

There are five approaches to the Labays, none of them easy: here is perhaps the most picturesque and most interesting, historically, that through the Forêt d'Issaux.

Should you choose to have lunch in Bedous, do check out Chez Michel on the main drag: the translations in the menu are improbably comical. Herewith some samples of 'English as she is spoke':

Faux filet grillé sauce vin…
'Wrong grilled net wipes wine'

Ris de veau braisé sauce Madère…
'Laugh at braised calf wipes Madère'

Filet mignon de porc aux pruneaux…
'Pork cute net in prunes'

Pâtisserie ou entremet maison…
'Patisserie or ice mediates houses'

Omelette plate à l'espagnole…
'Flat omelette has the Spanish'

Tranche d'agneau…
'Lamb's edge'

On a more sombre note, just north of Bedous towards the Marie-Blanque turn-off, a roadside plaque (left) commemorates the men who escaped from France into Spain and the passeurs (guides) who helped them 'at peril of their lives', as the inscription reads. 'They chose the dangerous venture of crossing the Pyrenees for the honour of serving their country'.

At the cross-roads in the centre of Bedous, take the D442 to Osse-en-Aspe and then the D441 south through Athas (450m, 1.6km) and into the Forêt d'Issaux. These forests provided the French royal (and then republican) navy with much of the wood required for its fittings: beech for oars, box for pulleys, slow-growing pines – strong and tall – for masts. When supplies of pine from the Baltic were cut off during Louis XIV's foreign wars, his military engineers cut the chemin de la mâture (the 'masting' road), a hollow ledge, out of the sheer cliff face between the valleys of the Aspe and the broader Ossau. A spectacular and precarious folie de grandeur. (Find it south of Bedous to Etsaut and Pont de Sebers, then up the Gorges du Pont d'Enfer… Hell's Bridge. There are several such in these mountains.) The masts were carted across, their final destination being the shipyards in Brest, Britanny. Athas itself later became a naval base when the Lourdios gorge was rendered deep enough to allow the passage of wood made into rafts all the way to the Aspe River and thence to Bayonne.

Reflecting this long-established 'rhythm of constant passage' the forest is preserved by incessant renewal – replanting, cutting, clearing, nurturing. As a notice further up says, heralding this world of pastoralism and forest: 'Here the shepherd and the forester and the fauna live together in mutual respect. The shepherd and the forester need the tracks, the wild animals need tranquillity. In deference to their living in harmony, be discreet'.

The first kilometres are nicely shaded by the overhanging trees, a steepish haul of around 7% out of Athas and a gentler kilometre to follow through the forest, bend following bend, bluffs of rock and plenteous arboriculture. The gradient varies markedly – from 4.5% to the maximum 10% nearing the Col de Bouézou, a twist and dip in the road with no obvious ceremony about it except that, weary of its own exertions, the ascent suddenly flops and tips away for just over 4 kilometres, losing over 100m. This is galling: you know you have it all to do again.

At 6 kilometres from the col (now the blue and white signs give altitude and distance) the road passes through a sort of stone gate – two projections of rock either side of the road – into a long umbrageous arcade of trees. The gradient is marked as 7.5–9% but actually feels a lot tighter on the legs, due perhaps to the aspect of the narrow road, the remoteness, the silence. Very few cars venture this way which makes it doubly attractive and for sure it is beautiful anyway, one of those hidden paths to cycling bliss on which to pounce, like a rediscovered lost precious object.

The final kilometre – gratifyingly signposted – is, after the withering steepness of the lower slopes, a balmy 6.5% only, very narrow but with an expansive breath, a happy mood, bidding you welcome. The arrival at the Col de Labays, scented with pine resin, is most agreeable. I discussed the merits and hardness of the climb with a French cyclist who, having just ridden up, lounged on the grass in spring sunshine with his wife (driver of the car), his bike propped against a tree. He vouchsafed that he would rather ride the Marie-Blanque, which is eloquent testimony indeed, and glossed this preference by adding that whereas the Marie-Blanque is a curse for only 4 kilometres or so, the Labays by this route is relentless.

His wife also remarked, and it is valuable advice:

"In the mountains one must be humble
– everything can change in the blink of an eye."

An alternative: The northern loop up to the Bouézou takes the D442 north out of Osse-en-Aspe and is open pretty well all the way, through pasturage smooth as a billiard table with fine views back down the valley and across to the thickly-clustered trees sheltering the route more fully described above. At 5km, 620m – as a connoisseur of the genre – my eyes fell appreciatively on an exceptionally fine wood stack, packed with infinite care and precision, a veritable geometrical art installation, far too handsome ever to be dismantled for the mundane purpose of fuelling a fire.

An excursion to Labérouat

LENGTH: 6 KM

HEIGHT GAIN: 750 M

MAXIMUM GRADIENT: 16%

On the N134 heading south from Bedous along the Vallée d'Aspe towards the frontier on the Col de Somport, through the towering bluffs which form the jaws of the gorge, the D239 turns right for Lescun, just beyond a large hydro-electric station (500m). Three torrents flow down into the Aspe here and the road swings wide and easy for 5.5 kilometres up to the tiny mountain village. It's largely a ghost town; narrow, paved streets, houses either abandoned or owned in absentia, but the shop/post office well stocked to supply the walkers who throng here drawn by the Cirque de Lescun, the main reason for riding up to the mountain refuge at Labérouat.

The choice of road is straightforward; there's only one. It heads through neatly tonsured farmland into the bowl of the Cirque with commanding views all round. It's narrow, tranquil, well-surfaced and the gradients are severe. All the way. Worse over the second half. Beautiful.

The girding rocks of the Cirque loom into view – in particular a ridge of white limestone standing up to the right like a Jacobean ruff from the lower edge of which tumbles a cascade of grey-white scree. At the very top – the road crossing a large clearing to the somewhat shabby and neglected chalet building which hosts groups walking the area in summer – the views repay every curse and recrimination you have unleashed in attaining them. Why, even the sheep stop to stare periodically.

The Cirque is an assortment of pyramidal bosses rearing out of the landscape like spokesmen for the encircling audience of ridges behind them, some smooth-backed, some notched and broken-toothed along their spine. The scale is more manageable than the titanic scale of the big cirques further east, the lower slopes of the rock draped in trees so that this might be uninhabited islands of stone swimming in a sea of vegetation. The whole experience of the Lescun is exquisite, enchanting, unmissable.

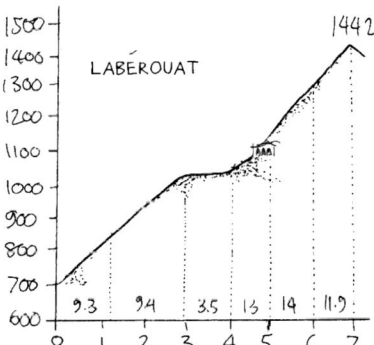

VUELTA A ESPAÑA 1998 STAGE 12

The green climbers on the attack

The rivalry between two big Spanish teams – Abraham Olano's Banestos and Kelme led by Fernando Escartín – animated the 1998 Vuelta in high style. The race turned into a classic encounter of specialist climbers scrapping for the final golden jersey. Heading for the Pyrenees, the Kelmes, a team brimful of climbing talent – Roberto Heras, José-Luis Rubiera and Escartín himself – got ready to hit the Banestos hard. The aim was to grind Olano down, now in the amarillo (yellow) jersey, but the strategy had its flaws: unless their attacks were decisive, they would be doing little more than giving the opportunist Banesto support riders as well as Olano himself free tows to three mountain-top finishes: the Ordino in Andorra, the Pico de Cerler ski station and the long haul up to Canfranc, below the Somport Pass into France. That, at any rate, was the original published route. That third finish crossed the frontier and added what might have been kilometres and gradient to the stage.

However, the Festina affair[6] on that summer's Tour de France had put the Spanish and French Federations sorely at odds. The Spaniards had been summarily expelled and Manolo Saíz, the director of the Spanish ONCE team, had fulminated at the Tour organisation for not standing up for the riders in the face of extremely heavy-handed police treatment. The luckless Alex Zülle of ONCE had been stripped naked, deprived of his glasses – without which he could not see – and confined to a police cell. The Vuelta organisation decided, in a gesture of defiance, to boycott France.

The Festina team came to the Vuelta and were given a demonstratively warm reception from the side of the road. Another planned stage, which was to have taken in the Pourtalet and the Marie Blanque, was replaced by a circuit round Sabinanigo, over a mere third category climb, the Navasa.

Further, the second Pyrenean stage to the Pico de Cerler, had also been trimmed of its topmost kilometres because the road surface was so bad. This was another

---

6 The Spanish Festina team was found to be following a routine and systematised programme of illegal doping.

blow to the Kelme attritional tactics. On the etapa reina[7] nevertheless, 200 kilometres from the plains of Catalunya to the steep roof of Andorra, across three first-category passes in the final 60 kilometres, they launched their offensive. Three of their mountain men, Escartín, Heras and Marcos Serrano, escaped on the final climb to the Ordino but they could not shake off Jimenéz who took the sprint for stage victory. The Kelme gain on Olano was just a minute: a lot of work for such a paltry advantage.

Jiménez did exactly the same next day, on the shortened ascent to Cerler, and ridiculed the futile effort of the Kelmes. 'I won,' he said, 'almost without trying.' The Kelme strong man Serrano had punctured earlier on the stage and been lost to the attack.

With but one climbing stage left, the Kelme strategy had seemed to be blown. They were simply riding their rivals to victory. Escartín had climbed to 3rd on GC overall at 51 seconds, but Jiménez was hot on his heels. In the event the finish at Jaca, down the valley from Canfranc, taken by Gianni Bugno, pretty well neutralised the Kelme challenge for the leader's jersey. In this, his last year as a professional rider, Bugno showed his cunning and class by a timely attack out of a break of four riders. He opened up a 90 second gap that took him to the stage win on the outskirts of Jaca, in lone pomp. He had been close to Miguel Induraín's father, who'd recently died, and dedicated his win to the old man.

Olano had survived the Pyrenees though he had looked extremely vulnerable, suffering badly on the climbs under the attacks of the green climbers.

---

7 *Etapa* (stage) *reina* (queen) thus 'queen of stages' i.e. the hardest in the race.

Puyarron 1240m

Transition to the lost mountain

LENGTH: 18.5 KM
HEIGHT GAIN: 900 M
MAXIMUM GRADIENT: 12%

Included here principally as a transition from Wild Peak to Lost Mountain. From Ansó [see Zuriza and Puyeta] head east up over the sierra towards Hecho and its valley, along which flows the river Aragón Subordán, boundary of the Basque territory. The Puerto de Ansó isn't marked, but the road cuts boldly through bare-rock canyons, twisting and climbing for 2.5 kilometres or so, through an ancient tunnel early on, to descend onto the main valley road, the A176 (on maps, marked as HU2131), just south of Hecho. Seven kilometres on – a fast run down – the A2065 (formerly HU212) turns east towards Jasa at a hermitage dedicated to Santa Isabel, daughter of the King of Aragón, born 1271.

Married to King Denis of Portugal at the age of 12, Isabel had a rough time domestically, although reading between the lines she probably gave as good as she got. It's the familiar story of dynastic marriage: he, adulterous, domineering, strong leader, king; she, sanctimonious, long-suffering, manipulative, princess up-graded to queen. When their son Alfonso led an armed revolt against Denis – and what kind of name is that for a monarch? – no wonder he overreacted. Isabel, it is said, 'worked hard for reconciliation', although probably aiding and abetting young Alfie to begin with… or else she kept mum, so to speak, as things started to get a bit more than routinely tetchy between old wolf and young wolf. When the belligerent sprog eventually succeeded to the throne, he set out to prove his new credentials by leading his army against his half brother, in exile in Castile… another Alfonso. One can't help speculating that royal family dysfunction may just be rooted in a certain lack of imagination when it comes to nomenclature, betraying an abnormal degree of egocentricity and possessiveness. Louis in France… Carlos in Spain… Henry (hoo-ray) in England…

Anyway, Alfonso was followed onto the battlefield against Alfonso by his ever-loving mama in her self-appointed peace-keeping role. 'Mother,' you can hear the pugnacious siblings shrilling, 'get off my back. Our back. This is men's stuff.' Well, history records that she did indeed get them to kiss and make up, albeit the emotional stress of the effort killed her.

Back in the present, 7 kilometres of flat and undulating road along the riverbanks of the Osia and a punishingly steep climb lead into the tiny hill village of Jasa – up to 12%. Cobbles take over from tarmac. Through the square, head for the church; the tarmac resumes and there is a short drop before the climb to the Puerto de Puyarron. Good surface, tight hairpins and onto a narrow shelf of a road which leads to the descent towards Aisa and glorious views north of the big ranges. The Somport is up there on the skyline, atop the road first cut by the Romans and used by the Moors when they pushed north into France in 732.

Aisa, a neat and trim stone village stuck in the middle of a rustic nowhere, shows a jumble of roofs, a church with a pointy-hat roof mimicking the penitential cone caps of Spanish Holy Week, a hostal and restaurants. Out of town, the road crosses a bridge and splays into a very broad section of new highway, soon to be worn in. Lombardy poplars and riverbank meadows, a right-hand bend on a narrow bridge back over the river and from here on an exuberantly fast descent into Jaca, with occasional undulations but no sharp bends, the river to the left for 9 kilometres. When the road does swing away from the course of the river, it climbs for a short distance before evening out again. The asphalt is smooth and Jaca announces itself at the end of a double avenue of trees enclosing a central ramblas (avenue).

Jaca gave welcome rest to footsore Santiago pilgrims who chose the Somport crossing. They could then press on along the main westerly route out of town over a mediaeval bridge, the Puente de San Miguel, heading for the more popular crossing at Roncesvalles.

Puerto de Oroel 1090m

Eastern loop

LENGTH:	33 KM
HEIGHT GAIN:	550 M
MAXIMUM GRADIENT:	10%

Continuing the transition and taking in the quite remarkable Monasterio de San Juan de la Peña, a 33 kilometre loop from the Pamplona road (N240) 11 kilometres west of Jaca or, if you follow the Hecho valley road, 10 kilometres east of Puente la Reina de Jaca. [All intermediate altitude readings are from an altimeter and, therefore, approximate.]

From 600m at the junction, the road ambles without any real exertion for 5 kilometres to Santa Cruz de la Serós (740m). The big Romanesque church once formed part of a Benedictine convent and the Serós is a corruption of Latin sorores (sisters, nuns). This is a decidedly pious neighbourhood in a markedly religiose area.

Right out of Santa Cruz (Holy Cross), the surface gets lumpy – a penitential road, forsooth – and winds along under high bluffs that resemble rampart walls. A kilometre on (800m) with the penance done, the surface gets smooth; sentinel pines line the left verge, and there's a perceptible increase in the gradient, around 10%, up to 7km. At 7.5km there is a broad patch of sun-baked earth to the left, a car pull-in with a Spanish picnic shop. This is grandly termed an 'area recreativa'. Do you need a translation?

Cliff walls hug the road on either side as it noses left towards a breach, a natural gateway, at 9km, 1010m. It might be a door leading from a dark corridor to a secret room full of light, for on the far side a glorious panorama opens to the left and the road becomes a long and narrow viewing platform. Around 8% for a kilometre to 1090m before dropping to 1060m at 11.5km: an Información cabin and a sign indicating 'Monasterio 150m'. That's for walkers. In fact, it's at 12km, 1090m, and what a marvel.

Beneath the overhang of a towering cliff, it dates from the 9th century: towers, belfry, chapel, refectory, cloisters open to the sky under the beetling rock of the cliff, the church on an upper storey… Occupied by Benedictine monks sent there from their main house, Cluny in Burgundy, it has a signal place in history as the first religious house in Spain to switch from the ancient Spanish Mozarabic form of the mass to the Roman in 1070. The Mozarabs (in Arabic 'would-be arabs') were those Christians under Moorish rule who, on condition of owning allegiance to the Moorish king, were allowed to practise their religion.

Whether the monastery's unique place in theological history is what drew them or not, a conventicle of local Spanish women bikers roared up on Kawasaki Classic, Harley Davidson and Honda Shadow even as I contemplated the religious house under the cliff. (The Harley Davidson company was founded in 1903, first year of the Tour de France. So there.) With petrol-yellow hair, sealskin leathers, flamboyant silk neckerchiefs, very un-flamenco boots and stacks of attitude, they injected a heady shot of sex-cular overtone into the prevailing conventual sobriety. They were later spotted lounging at a bar in Jaca with glasses of chilled lager – lager of the singing not the fighting variety – leather jackets nicely slung on chair backs, white t-shirts tightly to the fore.

Two kilometres on (1120m), stands the late 17th-century annexe of the ancient monastery, a huge establishment with an imposing Baroque façade. There is a mirador (viewing point) nearby. The road moves through a copse of tall trees to broach wild country dotted with shrivelled shrubs like bonsai bushes run to seed, a rockery garden, and views down into a valley basin carpeted with olive green. On round a flat ledge (1090m) into the easy-flowing descent, open country and a wide perspective, a blaze of toffee orange on the far mountain slopes, like painted fire.

This drop lasts for around 4 kilometres to 900m but it rolls and dips so the climb it offers is taxing. A high bluff of rock, striated in wide bands which make it look scaly, rears over the road and the climb to the Puerto is an easy lift of around 4–5%. The actual sign reads 'Puerto de Oroel 1080m' but 1 kilometre on the trusty altimeter shows 1100m. Perhaps this is a Spanish thing: absent-mindedness. The 6 kilometre drop back to the main road threads through the same stony landscape.

3. Lost Mountain

The first real taste of a markedly rugged grandeur in the Spanish Pyrenees is provided by the massifs of the Monte Perdido National Park – inaugurated in 1918 – that form the south-westerly extension of the huge line of impenetrable battlements in the centre. This region, all in Spain, and south of the great French Cirques, contains the three highest Pyrenean peaks: the Aneto (3404m) to the east, the Posets (3375m) in the centre and Monte Perdido, actually the highest limestone mountain in Europe at 3355m, to the west. The Vignemale, the fourth highest (3298m), stands on the border but its glacier is unequivocally French. The ascription of Lost Mountain conjures, aptly, the vast upshoots of grey, cream and white limestone which dominate the landscape. Golden eagles, lammergeier,[8] griffon and Egyptian vultures wheel overhead, the valleys are verdant with beech trees and higher up, as the soil thins, mountain and Scots pine and silver fir take over. Isards (Pyrenean mountain goats), roe deer, wild boar, and the mole-like desmans abound but the last ibex died in 2000. The Grotte Casteret on Monte Perdido is the highest ice cave in the world known to contain ice permanently. It was named after the celebrated speleologist, Norbert Casterets (1897–1987) who discovered it with his wife Elisabeth in 1926.

Probably the best way to approach the cols of the Lost Mountain is as on a thread from either direction, an exploration of these lonely roads, now generally well-surfaced, offering an excursion through a lovely part of northern Spain below the lofty gazebos of the frontier. Not so long ago many of the larger towns were still no bigger than villages, and some of that sense of being way out on a limb of the modern world still persists. A photograph of Pont de Suert, taken in 1903, for instance, shows a tiny community lodged precariously on an

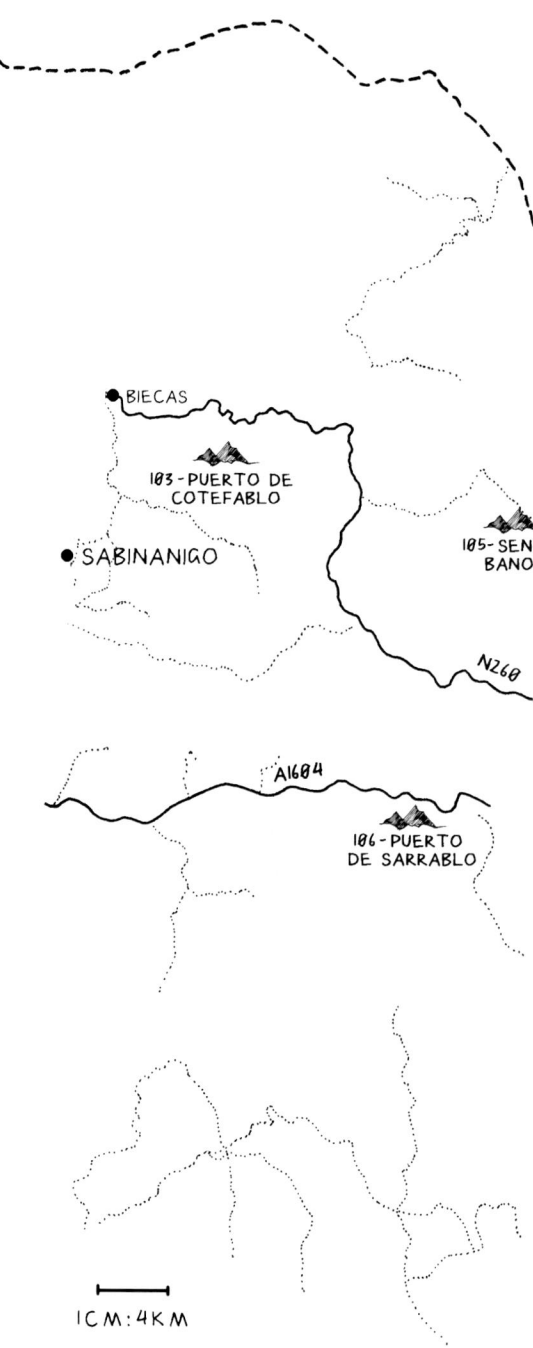

---

8 The 'bearded vulture' (Europe's largest bird of prey) sports a wing-span of 9 to 10ft and black feathers below the bill – thus its name.

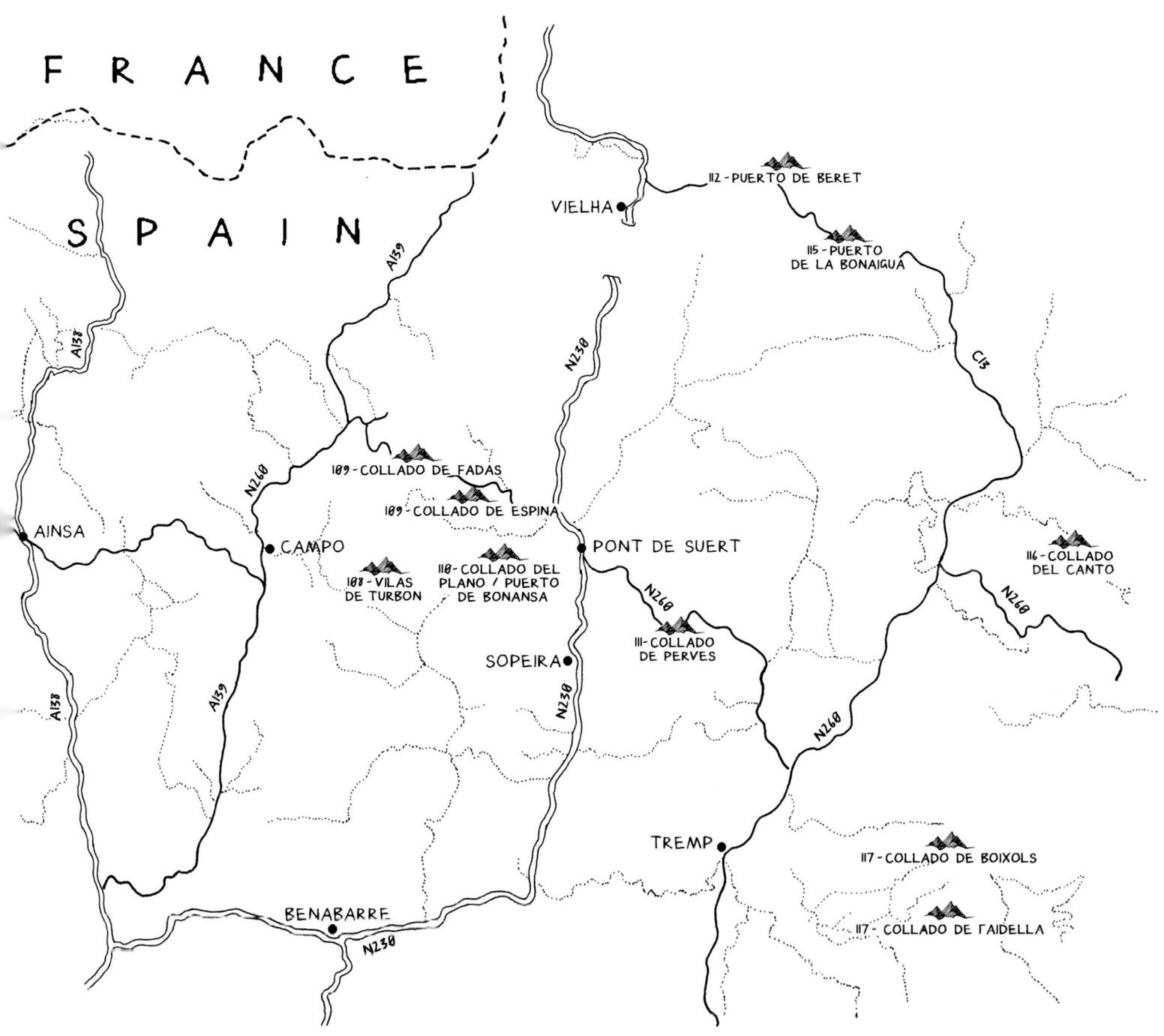

eyot in the expanding flow of the wide Noguera Ribagorçana River flowing along the line of what is now one of the arterial routes linking France and Spain. The town has grown since, but the tiny old enclosed square (no cars) in the centre of the old quarter gives an idea of what it once was. In this Plaça Major, the Hotel Mestre, with its tiers of window boxes, is recommended and in the lobby you will see the photograph of old Pont.

At the region's other end, Aínsa – a very fine hilltop old town with an arcaded Plaça Major – is a reminder that in wilder days people built high up and behind ramparts. Town squares in Spain tend to be either d'España or the more neutral Major.

Seek out the Catalan bouillonade, a local mixed fish stew and cargolade, snails barbecued on a fire of vine branches. Pan amb tomaquét or pan amb oli is a common snack, or amuse-bouche: a goodly chunk of fresh bread rubbed with olive oil onto which is then crushed fresh tomato. The rivers are well populated with trout and they are offered as a local speciality, often liberally smeared with honey before cooking. Crema Catalá is a must for pudding: a light custard in a shallow dish topped with caramelised sugar. And café cremat: a small coffee with a coffee bean in the bottom of the cup and laced with flaming rum or the toffee-flavoured Spanish brandy… hence the cremat, or 'burnt'.

P87	Chapel sanctuary to the mountain spirits
P88	*Bonaigua*, the descent towards *Esterri*
P90	The valley of the *Bonaigua*
P92	Some fine looped hairpins on the descent of the *Bonaigua* towards *Esterri*
P94	A lonely gorge road in the heart of Lost Mountain, destination *Plan*
P96	Lake south of *Esterri de Aneu*, eastern end of the *Bonaigua*
P98	Bluffs tower above the trees and scrub of the *Monte Perdido* national park
P100	The descent into the empty interior from the *Canto*
P102	Mountain ponies on the trot: make way…they won't

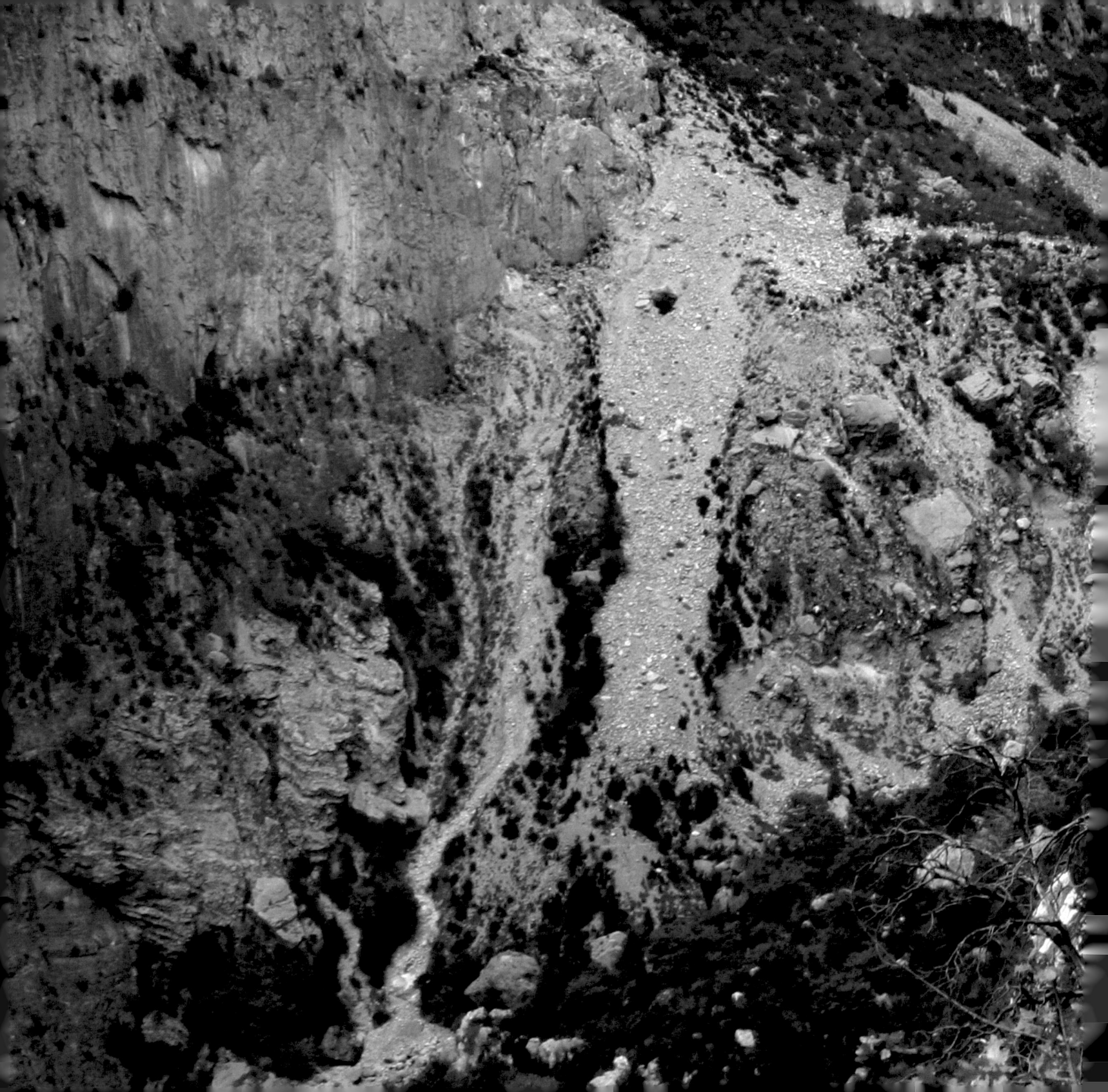

Puerto de Cotefablo 1423m

From Biescas

LENGTH: 14 km
HEIGHT GAIN: 523 m
MAXIMUM GRADIENT: 9 %

At Biescas (900m) on the road south from the Pourtalet [see page 189], the N260 heads east for Gavin and Yésero. Like many of the Spanish side roads, it is lonely, small-scale, attractive, tree-lined but without shade, well-surfaced. Spain's entry into the European Community in 1986, eleven years after General Franco's death, hastened the modernisation of a country which El Caudillo had resolutely resisted. He insisted that 'The Spanish are different' and had no interest in changing that. Suspicion of strangers was a feature of the old Spain. In his delightful book Both Sides of the Pyrenees (1952), Bernard Newman records how when he arrived – by bike – in Linas de Broto, having crossed the Cotefablo, an innkeeper refused to serve him. And many of the roads he crossed were very beaten-up. But most of them have been resurfaced quite recently and they are a joy to ride.

For 3 kilometres the gradient mounts steadily into Gavin (990m) – hotel, bars, restaurant – and beyond it, 5% or so, to where a deep gorge opens up to the right below the road. A long descent pitches into a tunnel about 200m long, unlit but straight so you can see daylight at the far end. Still slightly downhill and then flat between 6km and 7km (1010m) past Yésero perched up on the heights across the barranco (ravine) to the right. The gorge is called El Infierno (The Inferno)... incorrigibly religiose, these Spanish. A cooling torrent tumbles over the rock at 8km, still only 1010m, but this is a deceptive up and down. A kilometre on, there is some welcome light shade from the conifers and a bouquet-like clump of pink saxifrage growing out of the roadside rock wall. Pine trees hold sway and I watched two Guardia Civil motorcyclists roar past out of the saddle like a couple of stunt riders, or just cooling their arses.

The rock is layered hereabouts, long slabs of stone sandwiching strata of earth and pebbles. The col sign precedes a second tunnel – it's about 500m long, but lit and the far end is just visible – so the Cotefablo passes rather without ceremony, almost a notional high point. The descent is very mild, fields to either side enclosed by drystone walls and at 18km Linas de Broto (1280m) offers hotels, bars, a church with an open belfry, while at 20km the village of Viu (1250m) has a supermercado.

Dwarf oaks begin to take over from the conifers and, as the descent gathers pace, the town of Broto hoves into view way below in the valley. Just south of it, up a rough side road, the village of Buesa, 'balcón Pirineo', gives a taste of the old, very rustic Spain.

VUELTA A ESPAÑA 1996

The Champion bows out

The Cotefablo lay on the route of the 17th stage to the ski station at Cerler but by then the race was notable for the absence of one of cycling's greats, Miguel Induraín. Spanish champions have often had a difficult relationship with their national tour. Ocaña, winner in 1969, said that winning the Tour de France in 1973 had been much easier because the weight of home expectation was stifling. Bahamontes never did win the Vuelta and, for a long time, Induraín preferred to ride the Giro, as a warm-up for the Tour. (Until 1994, the Vuelta was run in April.) He came to the Vuelta in 1996 having lost the Tour de France. As an article in El País put it: 'In the end, it was all a matter of faith, of wanting to believe that what happened in the Tour was no more than a temporary loss of form, that if he, the Almighty Induraín, so wished it, the mountains would turn to valleys as he passed through them…'

On stage 14, when Rominger, the man whom he had overshadowed for so long in the French Tour, launched a vicious attack on a first-category climb, Big Mig buckled and, by the summit, he was four minutes down having already waved his team car through and told his team mates to ride on. He pedalled the short distance to where the road turned off to the finish at the Covadonga ski station and wheeled his bike into a hotel lobby. He was done with the Vuelta, he was done with cycling.

Next day, the headlines carried not a word about Laurent Jalabert's victory – no news, this – only the piercing lament: 'Induraín abandons Vuelta in etapa reina' (…on its hardest stage).

Señor Banos 1400m

From Sarvise

LENGTH: 11.5 KM
HEIGHT GAIN: 500M
MAXIMUM GRADIENT: 9%

If Sergio Leone didn't send his location scouts this way, he missed a trick. It's bushwhack country. Wheeling buzzard country. Lonesome pine, hole-in-the-wall gang, hear them coyotes howling, country. Maybe the local tourist-board wallahs have sent work details round to clear up the sun-bleached skulls littering the roads because there are none on view but they were there, you had better believe it, they were there. No drink for miles, no sign of habitation, no folks… No matter, win your pioneer spurs.

From Sarvise (900m) 4 kilometres south of Broto, (hotels and restaurant), an even narrower, more remote road heads east into the southern reaches of the Ordesa National Park. Old-style yellow-capped white kilometre stones dot the distance. There's not much of a rise for 4 kilometres and the surface is good, but after the bridge over the Barranco de Chate the road gets much narrower and is pitted with holes and scabs, littered with loose gravel and at 5.8km, 1040m, a rock fall has damaged the entire stretch quite badly. This means 20 metres or so of quite careful riding. At 7km, 1080m, a sign bids you 'Bienvenido al Valle de Vió' and this really does feel like a lost valley, bare rock, deserted, unvisited, Monte Perdido earning its sobriquet. The road is rough, the sort of stuff that Sean Yates and Paul Sherwen would revel in.

Beyond a new bridge at 8km, 1110m, the surface is still hacked and scraped up to a flattish section where the road becomes a leaning shelf, at a gradient of around 9%, for some 3 kilometres to the unmarked summit (1400m) on new gritstone and tarmac. The short diversion at 11.5km up a side-road to the right to the tiny village of Fanlo adds some 30 metres of altitude, and the Bar las Eras, on a small rise of grass with fine long views, makes a handy stop. Fanlo has the air of a holiday-home settlement, although the Gothic church, dedicated to the Canilla de los Dolores, clearly belongs to its previous incarnation as the vicinity's main shopping, gathering and worship centre.

The drop into the canyon, 2 kilometres and stretches of 10%, negotiates some tight hairpins to a bridge where it flattens out above the dry-bed arroyo (stream). High bluffs line the canyon to the north, bare rock and scrubby trees provide no shelter in what is designated a coto deportiva de caza (hunting area)… just some good ol' hunting boys out with they's rifles for a bit of backwoods fun.

The fairly new Hotel Palazio at Nerín, 2 kilometres off to the left, serves a decent menu del día. On the sachets of sugar (which I don't take) that come with the coffee there is an assurance that 'We cater for every sort of adventure activity, winter or summer – ask us' and there is plainly a big government/provincial initiative in train to open up the national park for tourism. What makes this patch of country so attractive is its very lack of habitation: a few scattered, isolated communities and in between, emptiness – no land to be worked, nothing to live on, the feeling that this territory is lost, in the sense of being, for centuries, unclaimed.

At 18km, 1090m the road forks right to Buerba and becomes one-way – in fact, the left fork is the route up the canyon – and the climb is steep, as bad as 9%, to top the rise. A strange concrete blockhouse presides on a slight rise above the 1290m mark and from there the road falls away into an arid, partial desert of scrub, dry earth and boulder into Buerba (1200m, 22km). The Casa Lisa offers bar, terraza and rooms.

The remaining 12 kilometres down the verge cycle lane loses 510m at a steady slide to the main road.

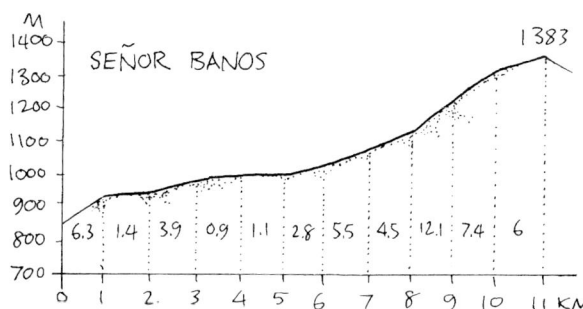

Puerto de Sarrablo 1291m

Eastern approach

LENGTH:	13.5 KM
HEIGHT GAIN:	691M
MAXIMUM GRADIENT:	8%

The A1604 joins the N260 – heading north-west from Ainsa – just beyond Boltaña. This begins as another canyon road, narrow, rough and of a wild, raw beauty. The La Ferrera viaduct spans the torrente at 1.9km, a single-arched bridge follows and at 3km, 790m, the road begins to cut through high walls of rock to either side. A steep kilometre, 8%, and lots of tarmac graffiti on the road encouraging one Sergio – who he? At 5.5km the chasm narrows still further, enclosing the road like a helter-skelter. Blind corners inhibit an easy descent; trees and rock press in, but gradually the road emerges onto a vague plateau. At 7km, 1030m, Campodobe, a tiny community of three or four houses and a church, pops out of the landscape. What happens there? The terrain is arid, bare, inhospitable. A dessicated valley lies panting in the heat off to the left. The isolated road has an obdurate 'I know I'm going somewhere but I neither know nor am bothered about exactly where' feel about it. At 9.3km, 1115m, a sizeable grange stands alone in its demesne at the end of a cobbled causeway drive; an imposing dwelling place indeed, but where do they do their shopping?

The gradients hover at 5% past another minuscule community, that of Las Bellostas, at 11km, 1190m, where, as if the discouragement of intruders were not blatant enough already, the surface of the road deteriorates too. The Latin word paganus, from which pagan derives, means 'country-dweller' and, early Christianity being very much an urban thing, the countrymen tended not to be Christians. Hence the derivation. The churches up here, therefore, have a distinct air of insurance value. This is a road out of mediaeval Spain when hobgoblins roamed, or so they thought and feared: all that's changed is the layer of tarmac except that – shocking intrusion of modernity – a radio mast towers over the Puerto de Sarrablo (1291m, 13.5km) and the view is, well, wild.

VUELTA A ESPAÑA 1988 STAGE 13

Total domination

This was the 'etapa reina' crossing three puertos: Sarrablo 1291m, Cotefablo (1st category), Foradada (2nd category) to finish at the ski station in Cerler 2409m (hors catégorie – unclassified).

The race was overshadowed by the announcement that Pedro Delgado, winner of the 1985 Vuelta and one of Spain's best riders, had opted to compete in the Giro d'Italia as preparation for the Tour de France. In 1987, he'd lost the Tour to Stephen Roche by 40 seconds only and the loss smarted. At this time, the Vuelta was run in May, more or less simultaneously with the Italian tour. Delgado's desertion was, of course, seen by both the Spanish fans and the organisers as a flagrant betrayal.

Sean Kelly, now nearly 32, had had to abandon the race the year before and, famously, said that it 'left a thorn in my side. I'm ready to pluck it out.' His principal rival, the young Spanish climber Laudelino Cubino, took the Amarillo (yellow) jersey early on, but Kelly was unperturbed.

Stage 13. Cubino had won at Cerler in 1987 so it seemed a good place to make a decisive attack on Kelly but, though he was up with the leaders till the steep section of the final climb, he faltered there and fell away. He later claimed that his gears had jammed. However, Kelly, the soul of nerve and patience, cranked up the pace and, with help from Robert Millar – the Spanish weren't amused – arrived in Cerler as the clear favourite to take the overall. Cubino's lead over his team mate José Manuel Fuerte was reduced to 3 seconds and on Kelly to 33 seconds.

The 14th stage from Benasque to Andorra (191 kilometres) crossed four puertos: Fadas (2nd category); Viu (2nd); Perves (2nd); and Cantó (1st category). There was to have been a fifth puerto near the end, the 2nd category Comella, but it was scrapped because of a religious procession, a 'romería'. Ah, Spain…

Kelly took the lead in the final time trial and the race overall in Madrid. In 20 of the race's 21 stages he had finished in the top ten and, on the podium took the final yellow, the Points competition and came third in the Mountains prize, behind Cubino. It really was a most singular triumph.

Vilas de Turbón 1300m

A glorious ride. With added spiritual uplift

LENGTH: 18 KM

HEIGHT GAIN: 609 M

MAXIMUM GRADIENT: 7%

The hermitages in the stony wilderness of the Macizo (massif) de Turbón east of Campo are as English ex-pats in southern Tenerife: everywhere you look. More ermitas than you can wave a thurible at. Come on, you know what a thurible is; if you don't, it's a censer. Did the recluses – one wonders – regularly send out invitations to the other recluses not to attend their particular saint's-day celebrations? Did they hold silence-keeping and prayerful ESP communication competitions? (Who adjudicated? God presumably, in the form of lightning bolts and electric storms for the gossipy losers and rainbows for the tight-lipped winners.) Did they develop eye-catching techniques for the attention of visiting pilgrims and then, seeing them traipse up the rocky thorn-strewn hill, perversely brandish signs warning them to keep their distance, much like Greta Garbo trumpeting to all and sundry, 'I vont to be ah-lohne'? Whatever the case, scratch a boulder hereabouts and it will wince at being disturbed. The air is full of ancient orisons.

Old Campo (691m), lying off the N260 east from Ainsa, is a shaded warren of flagged streets with an arcaded square, shops, bars, a sizeable square in front of the church and ayuntamiento (town hall). New Campo is an extended building site through which runs the small road east along the bank of the river Rialgo. There is no shade, the narrow road rolls smoothly for 3 kilometres up small summits and over, grabbing metres then dropping a few of them, to a bridge and a fork in the canyon. Right leads to the cul-de-sac called Espluga, left heads up the angled defile of the re-entrant filled by the course of the Las Ziallas River, for Egea. Two kilometres on at Casa el Moline, the road begins the round-hill contours under the plateau, looking down over the wide basin of the Espluga.

At Egea (1018m, 11km – hermitage nearby, overlooked by another hermitage), bear left on a smooth undulating road, open to the mercy of the sun, for another 7 kilometres at a steady pitch of 5% with occasional sneaky steeps and shy reductions. The orange-brown earth is studded with stone and a profusion of dwarf holm oaks – the evergreen scarlet oak, indigenous here and originally a symbol of the dying until usurped by the holly.

There is a barking dog on the leafy outskirts of Vilas de Turbón. In town, a shop and a hotel/bar/restaurant and attached Balneario (spa bath) whose waters are carbonated with calcium – oligometallic and highly hypotonic – which make them jolly good for renal complaints in particular. The spa opened in 1934, was used as a refuge for displaced children during the Spanish Civil War, 1936-39, and later reverted to a spa.

The descent back down the Barranco la Torizda to the left turn for Torre la Ribera is fast and pleasurable, the landscape ahead and below laid out like a rust and almond-green lozenge-patterned carpet.

Collado de Fadas 1470m and Collado de Espina 1407m

North of Bonansa

LENGTH: 32 KM
HEIGHT GAIN: 457 M
MAXIMUM GRADIENT: 7%

These linked cols straddle the N260 to the north of the Bonansa. From Bonansa, therefore, ride about 4km north towards the N260 and Castarnés. From the junction (1060m) the road is of two-car width, smooth and flowing for a short way before falling away in a long downhill into a leafy, flat valley bottom at 3km, 950m. The soil is a dusty maroon red. The climb out is barely perceptible – 5km stands at 1000m – before another long drop into Noales and a bridge over the river Baliera (6.6km).

A sign indicates the Collado de Fadas. The climb proper begins: a gradual winding-up of the altitude at between 6 and 7%. At 12km, 1360m, the terrain opens out into grassland and a side road off to the right leads to the tiny village of Neril. There is a charm in these manifestations of human activity. Pictures of evenings at such places in old Spain typically show men and women sitting outside the houses, chairs planted on the cobbled square of the village, the women spinning, knitting or mending, the men idle, ready to chat, presumably... the rhythm of centuries yet uninterrupted.

Half a kilometre or so further on comes the Collado de Espina (1407m, 12.5km). Painted on the back of the col sign is 'Ribagorça', the old name for this part of the kingdom of Aragón. From here the road traverses a plateau of flat meadowlands, taking in the brief rise up into Laspaules (1436m, 14.5km). The surface is excellent, the countryside bonny, the climbing steady, to the Collado de Fadas, 50 metres or so short of 20km, 1470m. A fine close view of the high, snow-capped ranges lining the border, among them the Pico de la Maladeta, Peak of the Accursed Woman. Wouldn't you show some pique if your name had been scandalised?

Two kilometres on, past a series of quite tight bends, the road goes through a patch of woodland – oak, pinus silvestris, poplar and hawthorn – and on downwards round a big sweep of the valley side to Bisaurri (1150m, 26km) reaching the bottom in Castejón de Sos (960m, 32km), with a number of shops, restaurant/bars and a hotel.

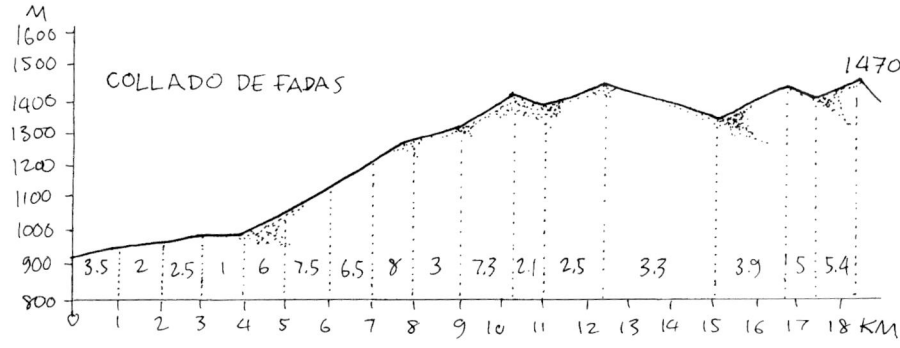

Collado[9] del Plano / Puerto de Bonansa 1380m

An easy loop

LENGTH:	8 KM
HEIGHT GAIN:	430 M
MAXIMUM GRADIENT:	6%

The road sweeps joyously down to the Barranco la Ball as if it were having one – a ball, that is – and then metamorphoses into a broad-lane highway by-pass, cocking a snook at Torre la Ribera, 1040m up on the hill to the left. This is odd. A short step from the wily roads-cum-tracks along which the brooding hermits trudged in fear and trembling of meeting another of their solitary kind, suddenly we're in big EU land, construction subsidies sloshing about like payola. It doesn't last. Normality is restored on a more unkempt passage of 2 kilometres which has not had the tarmac makeover.

Turn left at the junction with the A1605 for Bonansa and thence to the Vielha tunnel. The surface is smooth again, there's a verge cycle lane and quite soon, following the river Isabena, you're in the Obarra gorge. Almost inevitably, a wandering chapter of monks set up close by; 7 kilometres from the road junction (1040m) stands the Monasterio d'Obarra. The gorge becomes very narrow and hemmed in, the water races through its conduit at an impressive depth and a series of tunnels, lit by large window embrasures, fend off rock falls.

The gradient is untroublesome, the road straight, the tunnels shady, the scenery that of a ravine for 6 kilometres to a short tunnel at Tusal de la Font (1280m) at the far end of which the landscape turns to an open-summit approach with extensive woodland to the right. A sign at the start of a track which disappears into the Bosque de la Pegá clarions 'The passionate world of mushrooms', marking a round-trip forest walk of 1hr 40min. Growing in the mulch below the mixed spinneys of Pino silvestris (Latin Pinus silvestris – Scots pine or fir), Haya (Fagus silvatica – Beech), Boj (Box), Ilex, Avelláno (Hazel) are a variety of fungi, edible and inedible, including the hallucinogenic amanita muscaria – the spotted toadstool on which sits the caterpillar with the hookah in Alice in Wonderland – and a great abundance of the very toothsome lengua de vacá (hydnum repandum – cow's tongue) which can be pickled or dried as well as picked, cleaned and plopped straight in the frying pan.

Here is the Collado de Plano (1320m) and, just beyond it, the Puerto de Bonansa (1380m) with an open view of the road falling away to Bonansa, a kilometre below where the bar/restaurant is popular with locals (always a very good sign) and very friendly.

9 *Collado* means 'pass'

Collado de Perves 1350m

Gorges and lost hamlets

LENGTH: 15 KM
HEIGHT GAIN: 509 M
MAXIMUM GRADIENT: 7%

From Pont de Suert (841m) take the N260 direction La Pobla de Segur. The road is wide, well-surfaced, sweet-tempered. A kilometre along there's an unlit tunnel about 140m long and at 2km, 860m, the road narrows into a ravine, the water quite close, and mimics the meander of the river on a gentle gradient. At 5km, 999m, the slope kicks up somewhat to 6%, and at 6.7km, 1100m, comes another tunnel but a titch at no more than 30 metres. The climbing gets marginally more difficult, now – 7% up towards the village of Viu de Llevata (1325m) just before the 9km mark. There's a spacious view west over the long gorge splitting the rock mass underpinning the Spanish share of the frontier massif, the Maladeta to the left.

Apart from the denizens of Viu, there are few people up here, the dry scrubland offers scant hospitality to humans or animals. The slopes ease onto another familiar feature of these transitional Spanish routes, the plateau ridge, open to the wide, atop which, though barely a significant high point, is the col itself, Perves, at a little beyond 13km.

The hairpins tumbling away from the col are very tight, and 2km down at 1240m sits the tiny village which names the pass – about ten houses and a church. Once the inhabitants would have subsisted on smallholding and sheep-herding; now perhaps they drive distances to office and workplace. Nevertheless, there is something timeless even in the continued existence of these mini pueblos, clinging to the dust of their patrimony, their days punctuated by the clangour of the church bell, the electricity in the old houses supplying computers, CD players and televisions on which they can watch the bullfighting from Madrid... Sevilla... Palma de Mallorca... This village, like most of them, has no bar, so, stranger, cast a cold eye on life, on death, and ride on.

Puerto de Beret 1860m

Eastern approach

LENGTH: 7 KM
HEIGHT GAIN: 431M
MAXIMUM GRADIENT: 8%

The turn off to the Beret comes just over halfway on the western approach to the Bonaigua. From Vielha (960m) – a characterless retail-outlet border town, albeit the actual frontier is some way north – the C28 heads east for Arties and the Puerto de Bonaigua, linking the Vall d'Aran with the Vall d'Aneu. This begins as a highway, broad, newly-surfaced (for the Tour de France, maybe) with a verge cycle lane, the villages en route passingly attractive, the land beyond the road green and manicured. After Arties (1180m, 6km) the road used to narrow but it has been widened, presumably to accommodate the influx of traffic for the winter frolics. Salardu (1240m 8km) is a big ski town, high-rise apartment blocks and the usual appurtenances, the road surface rather hacked, cracked and crazed from the amalgamated hostilities of ice, sun and snowplough. Here the climbing starts and there is no verge lane. At Baqueira (1429m, 14.5km), another large ski resort, there is a satisfying long view back down the road, and the C142b swings left for the extremely well-heeled, pricey and fashionable snow Shangri-la which is the Beret. King Juan Carlos of Spain skis there. The ski-lifts are the costliest in Spain. The ride in summer is a beauty.

Up past the five-star plush of the lodges, the road switchbacks on a gradient tailored not to overstress the limousines and de luxe coaches, nor yet (by coincidence) the cyclist. The views which unspool on each succeeding ramp are fine, the zigzags of the way ahead clearly visible, the gradient steady at around 6%. On the far side of the valley, the mountainside is folded in huge Roman nose spurs and clefts down which tumble the tributaries into the main flow of the Vall d'Aran.

At 5km, 1790m, two snow tunnels with open sides put a brace on the road but, thereafter, it flows again with energy and pace. It feels high up here, exposed, rugged. The Puerto comes through a natural gateway of rock and the final 2 kilometres to the ski station on the Pla de Beret (1840m) are pretty well flat. The plateau is broad and the road continues, unmetalled, in a long loop to the Vall d'Aneu, under the Port de Salau.

I made my first cycle crossing from Spain to France via the Port de Salau on grass hairpins, dirt track, sheep track and no track at all.

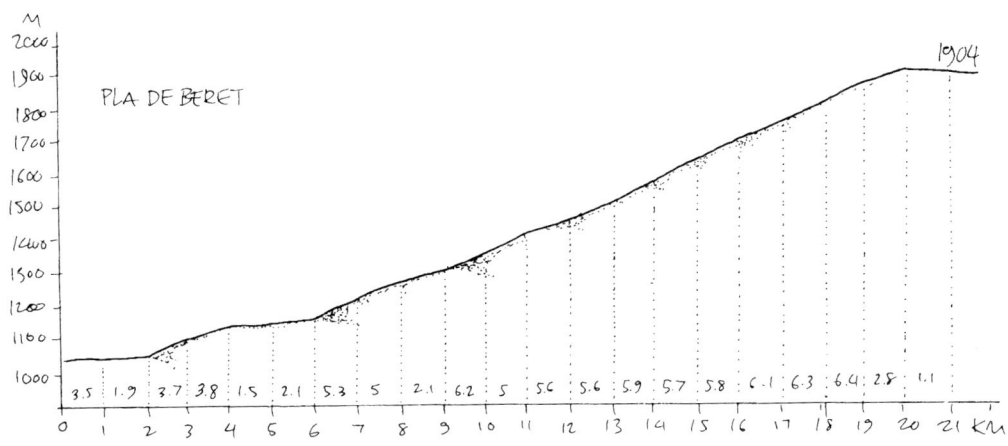

VUELTA A ESPAÑA 1995 STAGE 16
Zülle resurgent

Earlier in the race, Zülle had lost 18 minutes on the Sierra Nevada and, worn out and demoralised, crashed on the way back down the final climb to his hotel. He had come close to quitting but, showing remarkable pluck and resilience, stayed in the race and, this big stage into the Pyrenees, showed the kind of class that would bring him two overall victories in the Spanish Tour – 1996 and '97.

The day was wet and chilly, with snow on the mountain top finish at the ski station. A break of eight men, including Zülle, went clear 107 kilometres from the end and the bunch showed little interest in chasing. Within 30 kilometres, their lead was over 8 minutes.

However, at the foot of the 20 kilometre climb of the Puerto de Bonaigua, Zülle suddenly upped the ante and attacked. Only three riders stirred themselves to attempt to stay with him but he rode them off his wheel and settled in for a lashing lone attack, like that which had brought him a stage win, to La Plagne, in that year's Tour de France. Riding with imperious ease, he had almost 4 minutes lead on the bunch where the tussle for second place began to rev up. Axel Merckx jumped clear on the descent towards the turn off for the Pla de Beret and got a lead of 30 seconds which the chasers gradually whittled away on the final climb. Then David Garcia of Banesto rode clear with Michele Bartoli of Mercatone Uno and, almost inevitably, Laurent Jalabert, Zülle's team mate at ONCE. He it was who took the sprint for second (and thereafter final victory in Madrid) but Zülle had already taken a superb victory by 3 minutes 20 seconds. One of those riders of whom it might justifiably be said that he never quite seemed to fulfil his promise, Zülle was nonetheless always a rider of great courage and flair. His honesty during the tawdry Festina affair, when so many others were keeping shtum, was impressive.

TOUR DE FRANCE 2006 STAGE 11

Climbing as teamwork

At the foot of the Portillon in Bossost, with the early break still away, an elite group set off in pursuit of an early break, among them Landis, Leipheimer and three Rabobank riders Menchov, Boogerd and Rasmussen, known climbers all. There followed one of the most impressive examples of team support and sacrifice witnessed in a long time. Rasmussen, King of the Mountains in 2005, having ascertained that Menchov was feeling good, went to the front of the bunch and worked… and worked… all the way to Baqueira (28km), Boogerd on his wheel. It was uncompromisingly selfless. Rasmussen, with ambitions, surely, for the polka dots of the Mountains prize, was simply driving himself into the ground for his team leader, winner of the 2005 Vuelta after the disqualification of Heras for doping.

As they swung onto the final climb, Rasmussen quite simply fell away to the side, utterly spent, and Boogerd took over the relay. The image of the ex-mountain bike champion slumping as his team mate upped the pace once more was poignant. Boogerd did not spare himself, either: he knew he wouldn't last long but for 2 kilometres of the long hairpins up to the Beret, he drove the pace as high as he could and then, in his turn, peeled off, his work done. His face was puce with effort. And so it was left to Menchov and he repaid them with the stage victory. Inspiring.

Puerto de la Bonaigua 2072m

Western approach from Baqueira

LENGTH: 9.3 KM
HEIGHT GAIN: 645 M
MAXIMUM GRADIENT: 7%

Continuing the western approach of the Bonaigua from Vielha and the turn off to the Beret, the broad road chews at the tyres for a kilometre or so but at 2km becomes a smooth-surface corniche road snaking round the rock wall, the valley way below. At 5km, the road narrows, trees appear like spectators, the surface gets bumpy but the feel of the climb is more intimate, the hairpin an indicator that the col is getting closer. A long stretch of straight with an ashlar side wall seems to head for oblivion and the final 3 kilometres are a bit rough underwheel, but this is a very satisfying col, lofty, long and somehow generous in its dispensing of praise at the achievement of riding it. The top, clearly visible round the last corners, levels out onto a spacious car pull-off and reaching it is a real 'hats off' moment.

However, the Cafetería Bonaigua to the right is unreliable, as is the Gothic, octagon-towered Cap de Port hostelry, a dead ringer for Frankenfurter's Rocky Horror Schloss on the east side. Just before it, proudly displayed, is an early earth-moving tractor, Le Peeter, which helped open the Bonaigua to automobiles, 1944-62. 'Men and machines' reads the inscription in Catalan 'played an important role in the development of the Pyrenees'. This area was part of that vast territory ceded to the French crown by the treaty of 1659. The view down into the eastern side of the valley is heart-warming: hairpins and a long, long drop. This is the Bonaigua saying 'bonne route'.

Eastern approach

LENGTH: 22.9 KM
HEIGHT GAIN: 1122 M
MAXIMUM GRADIENT: 7%

If you are keen to repeat my eccentric approach to the border and proceed over the Port Salau into France by grassy sheep track (it wasn't my idea), then head north from Esterri and keep going through various hamlets until the road runs out. Otherwise, check in at the Fonda Augustí, set back from the road beside the church, and treat yourself to a Lucullan menu del dia rounded off with a siesta by the lake a few kilometres south.

The C1412 leaves town up the valley of the Bonaigua at a leisurely 4–5% and gets playful round the bends within a kilometre as the roofs of Esterri appear like a jumble of Scrabble tiles below. There are trees, an avenue of poplars, but not much shade, the hairpins flicking you on into the village of València d'Aneu (1080m, 2.7km). Beyond the village the road shakes away its tease and gets sombre – straights and bends with the way ahead looking ominously long. A sign reads 'Port de la Bonaigua 14'.

Dense thickets of birch line the river banks and at a little over 4km, a bridge over the river ushers in the hairpins. The gradient slackens marginally, the craggy cliffs of the ravine walls close in, and a few intrepid birch trees with hermitage on their mind have made it up away from the crowds at the bottom, seeking sun and the better company of solitude.

The camber is awkward – descenders, please note – and around 12km the road suddenly loses all sense of humour and turns into a cheerless straight broad highway, a pig to ride: long wide and occasionally feeling quite disproportionately steep, although the statistics argue against that.

At around 17km, 1730m, stands a squat, rhomboid, stone-built tower with a peep-bo belfry, an ermita dedicated to Mare de Deú ('mother of God') de les Ares, and, across the road, a restaurant/bar with the same name.

From here the hairpins, varying in size, crank up the altitude at a steady 6–7%, the confines of the ravine falling away, the bare rock of the mountainside (and the ski runs into which they transmogrify in winter) bleaker and harder of question. But there is grim confidence, too, in the rounding of the bends, the settling into the straights between, the twists and turns that coax rhythm.[10]

---

10 The Tour de France has crossed the Bonaigua twice, both times from the east, both times destination Saint-Lary Soulan: in 1974, when the stage was won by the perennial Raymond Poulidor, and in 1993, topped first by Tony Rominger, that year's King of the Mountains.

Collado del Canto 1725m

Western approach

LENGTH: 20KM
HEIGHT GAIN: 1005M
MAXIMUM GRADIENT: 8%

Both this route and the crossing of the Faidella and Boixols lead east into Judgement Mountains.

The climb out of Sort, at the junction of the C147 south from Esterri d'Aneu and the C260, is tough, 6 kilometres of around 7% on a good surface, a winding, quiet road, unblessed with shade, before relaxing a touch and levelling out into Vilamur (1280m, 9.8km) and for a couple of kilometres beyond. Two side roads trickle off to the right, one at 11.1km, 1310m, to Soriguera, another at 11.8km, 1340m, to Llagunes. There is no evidence to suggest that the Lily of Laguna celebrated in popular song of yesteryear did hail from this remote pueblo (village) in the remote Spanish Pyrenees, but nor is there evidence to suggest that she did not. 'She is my Lily of Laguna, she is my lily and my rose,' and roses grow in abundance not so far away on the valley floor.

The gradient stiffens for 5 kilometres and I passed a French guy riding a recumbent on this stretch. He seemed to be going quite well, making the complete traverse of the chain, all his gear packed into a capacious pannier behind the saddle. He smiled, we took a picture, but there was a sadness in him, as if he were grappling with some form of demon, a cycling hermit, for sure.

Past Rubio on the left (1645m, 18km), the road dips and crosses the river Rubio, (1620m, 18.5km) before gathering itself for the final steep assault on the mighty Canto. Just before it reaches the sign and the col, with a grand perspective into the hazy distance of Judgement Mountains, it passes an excellent restaurant run by (and named for) Elisabet i Francisco, menu in Catalan and inscribed with lines by the 17th-century Catalan poet Francesc Vicenç Garcia:

*"De tots los pans que ha posat en la sua taula
Amor sens dubte que es lo millor."*

'Of all the food that is put on your table
Love is without doubt the best.'

The road rolls across another ridge plateau for 6 kilometres, passes a side road to Guils de Canto (1575m) and then plunges quite steeply (up to 8%) for 3 kilometres to a bridge over the riu (river) de Pallerols, 1315m, on a hairpin. A short flattish section leads to a sharper drop into Pallerols itself (1248m, 13.2km) and another plateau of sorts to the start of the final long and quite steep drop into Adrall, the road plunging down across open country, a plaid of small fields, studded with buildings, like brooches, into the twistier, leafier, closer way leading into La Parròquia de Hortó (810m, 23.1km) and a final kilometre of decelerating gradient to Adrall.[11]

---

11 The main C1313 south 20km to the turn at L401 is busy, but has a verge cycle lane.

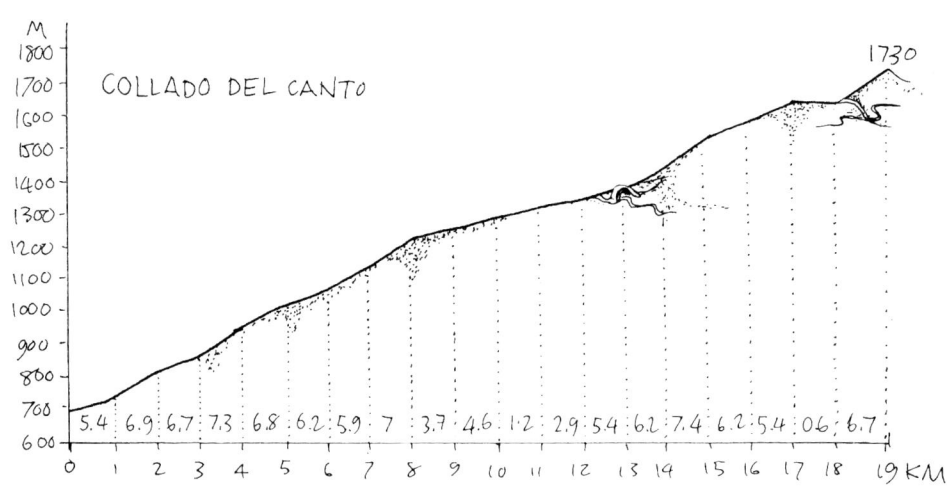

Collado de Faidella 1250m and Collado de Bóixols 1380m

Towards the Sierra

LENGTH: 9.3 KM
HEIGHT GAIN: OVER 800M IN TOTAL
MAXIMUM GRADIENT: 7%

Poppies stain the oats and barley fields to either side of the L511 which leaves the C1412 east of Tremp at Figuerola d'Orcau. There is a beautiful view of the sierra ahead, the rock cradle of your back and leg pain to come, as the long, straight, surely Roman, road passes between extensive cherry orchards at scarcely a murmur of gradient. At 3km, 790m, the road begins to swing on a smooth ground as if it hears sweet music, a local cantilena not a Roman marching song, which would be hobnailed, militaristic and almost certainly lewd.

A tree-clad ravine appears to the right and the climb gets under way, spindly-trunked pinus silvestris aplenty, the slopes at around 6%. At 7km, 1020m, a speed limit imposes 40kph then cancels it for 50 metres, leading into a sharp bend. Some homicidal sign-poster has been this way, it seems. Cast a complacent eye back over the wide acres of the valley, its fields and orchards mottling the sandy yellow and stripes of green.

Up to the right stands a long ridge like a castle mound, its slopes spread with stunted trees, its bare rock crown, ribbed and fissured, looking like a crew cut, a long frill, the curtain wall of a natural fort.

This may be a transition road but it is a stunner as it finds the last hidden beauties of Lost Mountain. There is no shade, but plenty to see and enjoy. The Faidella arrives at around 12.3km and the road instantly drops away left past a house built up on a rocky projection, a domestic castle. [This is not the place for speculation about the origin of 'castles in Spain'. I have done that in my book about the Arthurian legend].[12] The tarmac below it is stencilled with a family of zebras but they do not constitute a crossing, they move along the line of the road.

Dropping at 6% round easy bends reveals a curious natural bridge – a curtain wall of rock joining the two sides of the ravine, with a deep breach in it.

The tiny village of Bóixols (1180m, 16km) – church, houses, school – sits either side of the road overlooking deep gullies, while to the right a sort of collapsed watchtower, an enormous prominence of rock whorled like a snail-shell, squats athwart its grassy floor.

The road to ride appears, carving up through the trees, a long way off. Whether this is encouraging probably depends on the mood at the time. At around 20.5km, 1300m, a green sign announces passage between Pallars Jussa and Alt Urgell and 1.5 kilometres further on comes the Collado de Bóixols, spangled with flowers; it's a quiet stretch of road, with a fast descent in prospect – long straights, fewer bends, more open country, a short stretch of gorge near the bottom and the imposing presence of the Sierra de Moumort in the background.

---

12 *Arthur the King: a study of mediaeval romance in its historical, literary and social context*, London, BBC Books, 1990.

4. Circle of Death

One of the defining Pyrenean landscapes: a line of huge mountains like watchtowers looking in both directions over the long roads weaving up the deep glacial valleys towards the passes.

The mountains which make up the Circle of Death ring the northern part of the ancient French viscountcy of the Béarn and the mountains of the Bigorre. Gaston Fébus (1343-91), Viscount of Béarn and Count of Foix, declared the Béarn 'a country apart, of itself and separate from the crown of France'. He held power, he said, 'through God and my sword'. The tradition was preserved by Henri IV, born in Fébus's chateau in Pau in 1553 (assassinated 1610), and the Béarn remained autonomous until 1620 when Louis XIII put aside ancient custom and law to incorporate it into the kingdom.

The old region known as Bigorre became the department of Hautes-Pyrénées and is popularly known as 'the Gateway to the Pyrenees'. The Bigorre Mountains are home to the isard, the mountain goat closely related to the Alpine chamois; the marmot – a large rodent of the squirrel family, given to announcing its presence by a warning whistle; and the mouflon – ancestor of the domestic sheep, now reintroduced to its mountain habitat and notable for large, curved horns. Griffon and lammergeier vultures are common, cruising the thermals of the airy chasms, so too Golden and Bonelli's eagles and buzzards. The Donjon des Aigles, near Argelès-Gazost affords the chance to view these magnificent raptors in flight. On the Pic de Pibeste 7 kilometres south of Lourdes, the Mediterranean microclimate of the so-called 'Enchanted Mountain' attracts a profusion of butterflies, and through spring and summer the upland meadows and forests are spangled with a variety

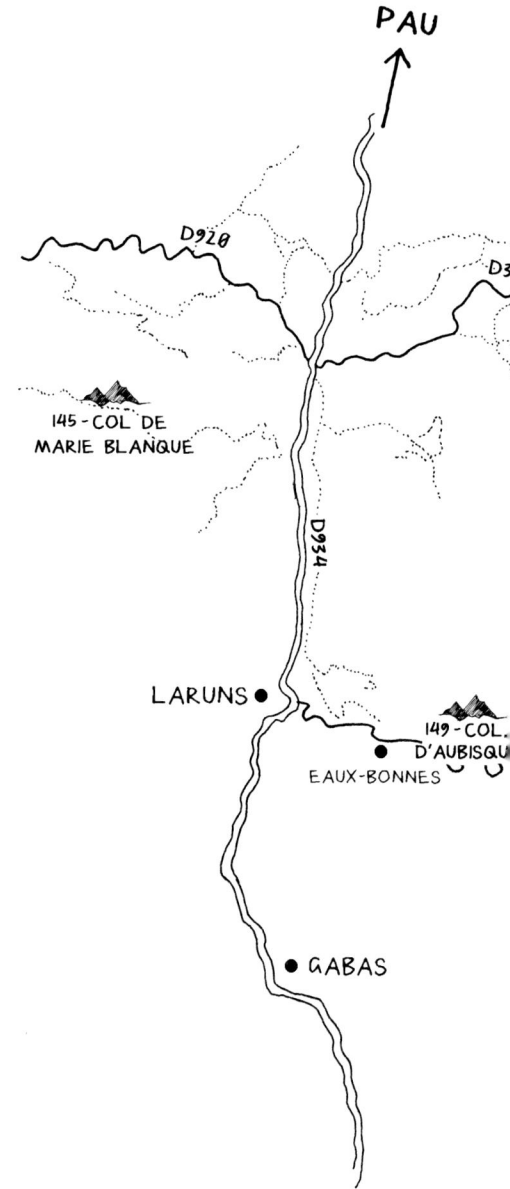

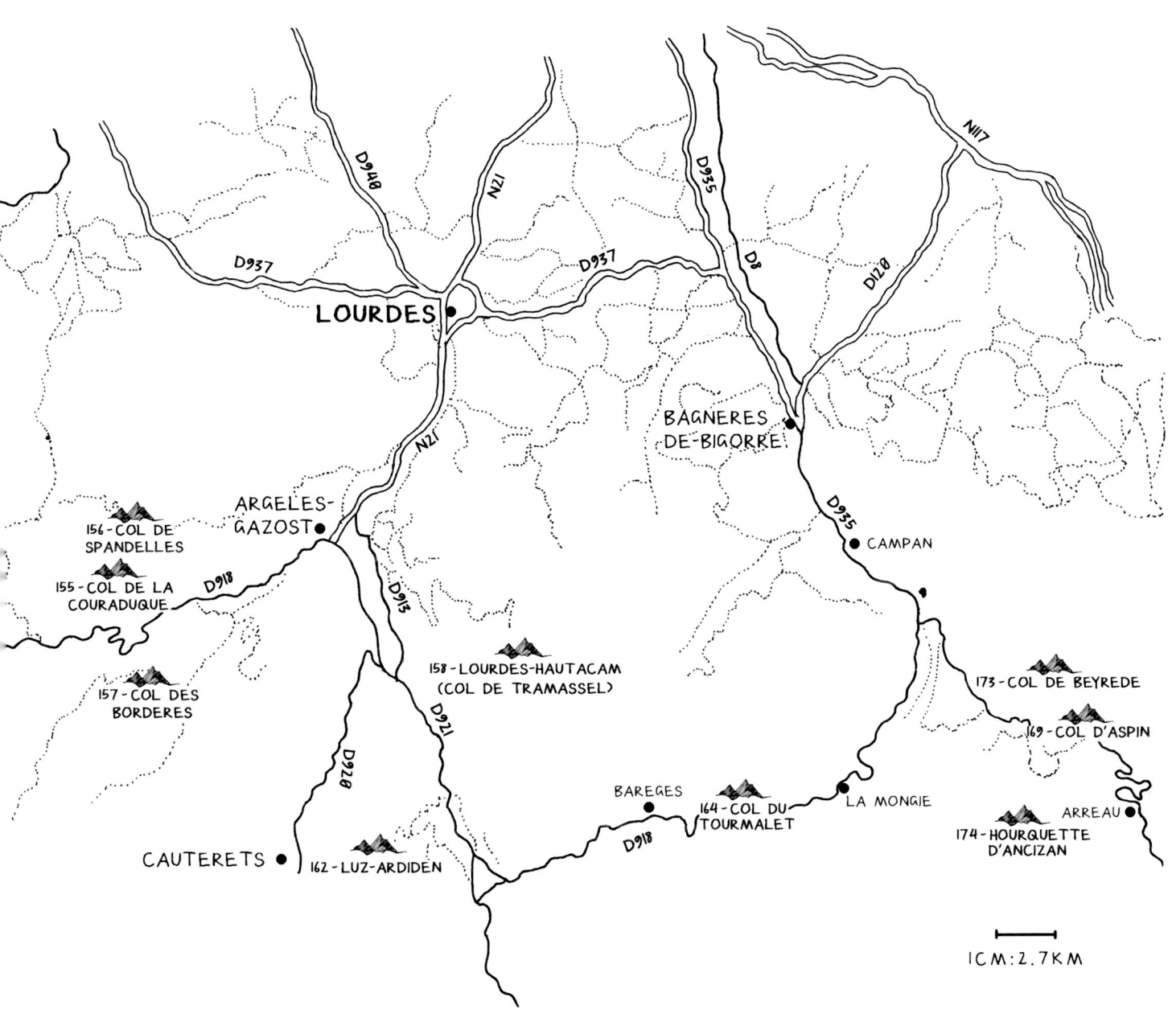

of wild flowers. The rocks of the Bigorre are also richly varied – granite, gneiss, schist, limestone and marble. White marble from the quarries of Saint Béat in the east of the region were used in the fountains of Versailles and, possibly, for Trajan's Column erected in 113AD in his new forum in Rome.

Béarn and Bigorre straddle the north-south Aspe and Ossau valleys: the Aspe is characterised by woods and upland pastures, the Ossau giving onto the barer, more barren rock landscape of the Pic du Midi south of the Aubisque and the Massif de Néouville just beyond the Tourmalet, whose name means 'bad detour'.

Allied airmen on the run and Frenchmen evading forced labour crossed these mountain passes into neutral Spain, helped by border escorts such as shepherds who were known as 'passeurs' – literally 'pass-men' – who risked death (in the words of one commemorative roadside plaque) 'for the honour of serving the cause of Liberation, 1940-5'.

CUISINE SPECIALITIES

Filling garbure – a hearty vegetable soup often resembling a crude cassoulet when fortified with added pork, sausage or goose, four varieties of cheese from mountain farms – Ossau, Iraty, Brébis, Pyrénées, egg-batter, spit-cooked gâteau à la broche (a rum and orange sponge) local Madiran wine – red in the middle of a region which otherwise produces only white wine (St Mont, Pacherenc, Jurançon).

P121 Departmental sign at the *Cirque du Litor*

P122 The *Cirque du Litor* below the *col d'Aubisque*

P124 Archway on the climb to the *Aubisque* from the *Soulor*

P126 The *Hôtel des Crêtes* about to be smothered in mist, west of the *Aubisque*

P128 *Marie Blanque*… Some encouragement for riders from Sainte Suzanne

P130 Approaching the final corner of the *Marie Blanque*

P132 The westerly swish and bend of the *Tourmalet* ascent

P134 Nearing the *col du Tourmalet*, glance back at the road just travelled from the west

P136 Inside the café at the top of the *Tourmalet*

P138 The road up to *Lourdes-Hautacam*

P140 Stunning scenery in the Circle of Death

P142 The quiet twisting road dropping north off the *Hourquette d'Ancizan* towards *Sainte-Marie-de-Campan*

P144 The central Pyrenees from the *Boulevard des Pyrénées* in *Pau*, the *Pic du Midi* prominent

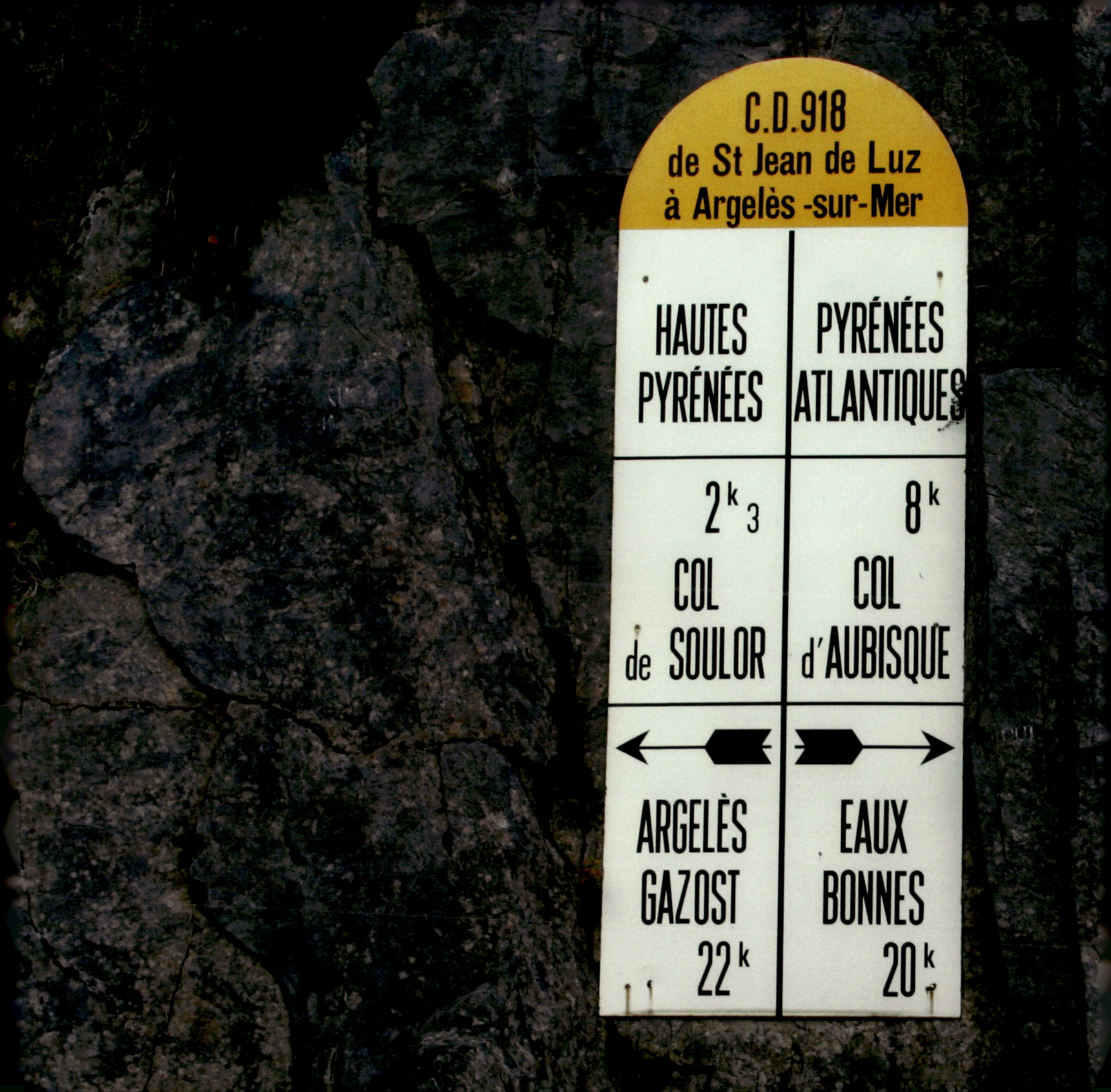

Col de Marie Blanque 1035m

Western approach

LENGTH: 9.5 KM
HEIGHT GAIN: 700 M
MAXIMUM GRADIENT: 11%

The Col de Marie Blanque lying on the D294 (Michelin 342, Local I 4) straddles the ridge between the Gave (gorge) d'Aspave to the west and the Gave d'Ossau. Not included in the Tour de France until 1978, it has been visited nine times since, including 2005. A classic Pyrenean ascent, twisting through mixed woodland with fluctuations in gradient, some very sharp, along a narrow road not much used by cars. A tranquil location but a killer of a climb from the west. Allow 1½–2 hours, both directions.

The pass is open all year round, there's room to park a car at each end and on both sides the road surface is generally good. However neither side offers a café or buvette (refreshment bar/kiosk) nor any source of water. So be prepared.

"As far as these Pyrenean climbs go, I think the Marie-Blanque is one of the hardest there is. It's only 10km long but there are 4 or 5kms that really make you suffer. You will need a 19 to 23 to get up this one. A 21 is no good." Fernando Escartín

"Hitherto unknown and underrated in the hierarchy of climbs by the Tour organisers who have, since its first inclusion, put that act of treason right." Henri Quiquéré

The western approach begins at Escot, off the N134-E7, a green-line route following the deep Défile d'Escot. 9.4 kilometres to the col, height gained 705m, average gradient 7.5%. If the introduction is gentle enough – 5 kilometres varying from 2 to 6% – the remainder is severe: 8, 11.5, 11.5, 11.5, 11. The lower slopes are very exposed to the sun, the final section shaded by flanking woods, the summit recently shorn of trees.

From the N134-E7, the road drops down into the tiny village of Escot and turns right onto the approach to the climb. Don't miss the octagonal church tower and unusual conventual cloisters in the quiet open square of Sarrance, 4 kilometres south of Escot. At the side of the road just to the north of Sarrance stands a plaque in memory of the brave passeurs.

The road to the col through the Défile d'Escot follows the fast-flowing stream of the Barescou – a friendly presence, babbling brook, cool chatter – and the first 3 kilometres are easy enough. Steep, grassy hillside to the right beyond the cordon of trees, while tall oblong signs indicate kilometre, altitude, height gained.

At around 3km the gradient goes up a notch, from 4 to 5% and a large overhang to the left suggests that this road has been blasted through the living rock along the path opened up by the torrent. The gradient changes gear, 6% into 8%; an access road to your left leads to a few farmhouses with a swathe of mountain pasture beyond.

Long curves, both a characteristic of this climb and part of its difficulty, bully the road as it crosses the stream to continue up, by steeper lifts, as a winding shelf cut into the southern flank of the gorge. Across to the left the land falls away to the valley bottom.

At 6.5km a large signpost in the domed, rectangular shape of a kilometre stone (borne), white capped with blue, indicates 'Camping Mont Bleu' to the left. (A graffito on the road, surely to an Etape du Tour [the 'have-a-go-at-the Tour one-day ride'] participant: 'Keep Going Dad', plus the outline of a heart. Also 'Go Lance, go home'.) Now the going gets tougher: be prepared for 8%, then up to 11.5. A long spur of the mountain jutting out from the valley head appears, its long spine

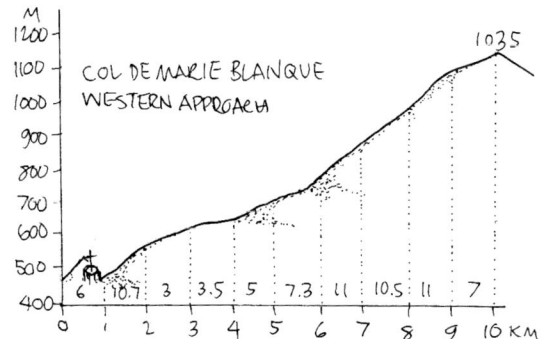

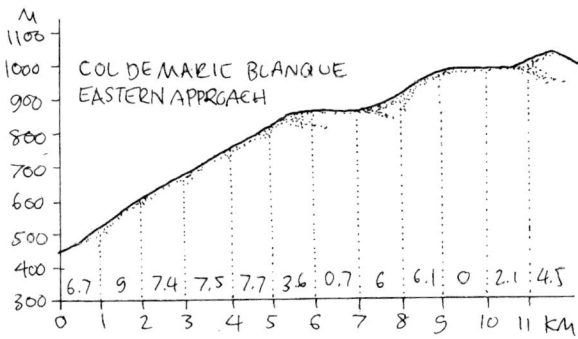

CIRCLE OF DEATH

sprouting trees like the stubble of a Mohican.

There are several elements which make the Marie-Blanque from the west particularly testing. The lower slopes are very exposed to the sun, and the long straights of the road are like lengths of tough wire being stretched to remove the kinks. Seeing what lies so far ahead along the unforgiving tarmac is always added misery. And this surly lack of movement in the road itself, coupled with the crowding attendance of trees to the left and the damp rock wall at the foot of a sheer, tree-flanked slope to the right, hems you in, cramps you. The shade offered here is only small comfort on a road leadenly tracing the path of an old mule track, getting to the top by as direct a route as possible, just to get the rotten job done. You can feel such grimness of purpose. It's oppressive. The view, even across the valley, is pinched. This is a tense, cheerless climb and, for the final 3.5 kilometres, horribly steep – an unrelenting 11.5%. What if it does dip to 11 at the top? You think by this stage you can tell the difference?

Suddenly, as if to emphasise its harsh, bucolic origins, the road narrows to not much more than a car's width and, at last, gets some life: a jink of hairpins before the slight hummock of the col hoves into view. On the road, another plea for the Etape riders: 'Sainte Suzanne, priez pour eux' (Saint Susan [a martyr known for her long sufferings], pray for them). The summit clearing is no more than a swatch of tarmac tossed onto the bare earth. To the right, the encroaching trees have been cut back; to the left, the summit drifts away downwards. The views are meagre, blocked by surrounding heights to the north, the long tree-crested spur west, woods east and south. Your sole reward is the relief of getting to the graceless marker and launching happily onto the descent.

Eastern approach

LENGTH: 11.5 KM
HEIGHT GAIN: 586 M
MAXIMUM GRADIENT: 9%

The eastern approach begins at Bielle, off the D934, a trunk road running south from Pau to the Col du Pourtalet on the border with Spain. It's 11.2 kilometres to the col, height gained 600m, average gradient 4.2%. The first 4 kilometres hit hard, 8.5, 8, 8, 8.5, easing to 6.5. A wooded, near-flat 2 kilometre stretch of hairpins leads to a comfortable open plateau 2 kilometres long, then a kilometre of 7.5 and a steady untesting swing up to the col.

The view southwards up the valley past Bielle is magnificent: caught dramatically in the V between the opposing flanks, a series of lofty peaks overtopped by the great massif of the Pic du Midi d'Ossau, below whose collar-blades lies the Col du Pourtalet on the border with Spain.

From a roundabout on the D934, the D294 leads (right) past Bielle (left) and onto the beautiful, smooth meandering approach to the 11.5 kilometre climb, the flat meadows of the wide river valley away to the left and the cluster of houses and prominent church of Bilhères, close neighbour to Bielle. (Bielle, the old capital of this valley of the Ossau, has some 15th and 16th century houses and a church worth a visit.)

The gradients aren't especially kind – 4.5 kilometres of between 8 and 8.5% – but the expansive nature of the ride – trim pastures, houses dotted about, the grandeur of the view south, the tapering perspective north – lull any futile brooding at how steep and how long this initial work-out is. The summit is far away, the upper reaches of these first slopes masked by trees and the fugitive configuration of the mountain. Quite quickly the road develops hairpins, in succession very steep and fairly mild, as is so often the pattern. This is a right-handed climb: acute right-hander hairpins, a real jolt of metres gained, the left-handers far more lenient. This marked variation in gradient is ironed out by averaging. Kilometre signs count down the total distance covered.

At 5km, in a flat grassy glade in the shade of sparse trees to the right of the road, the small Chapelle de Notre-Dame de Houndas commemorates three local men who died while being deported for the crime of 'rebellious aid given to allied parachutists' 1942-44. 'Rebellious' means that their activities were not only against the law enforced by the hated milice (militia) working for the occupying Germans, but were also frowned on by German sympathisers fearing reprisal. As if in subdued reflection upon the heroism of such men, the road suddenly narrows introspectively, eases to a gentler 6.5%, throws off its veils of trees and goes bare-headed onto the Plateau de Bénou, a 2 kilometre stretch of flat moorland. The route winds through furze and outcrops of boulder, past a farmhouse and grazing horses towards the next lump of the ascent, cloaked in trees, the surface pitted and scored from the passage of farm vehicles.

Into the trees where a sign welcomes us to the communal forest, and from here the ascent, a kilometre of leafy 7.5%, is as pleasant as any you'll find: sunlight dappled through the pines, a curvaceous swing of road and the gradient suddenly topping out onto the final 3 kilometres of easy climb, an undulating rather than a steady and flat 2.5%, but no great trial. On the penultimate hairpin worth the name, a torrent crashes down the mountainside to the left and under the road. Then a last turn to the col, marked by a line drawn across the metal.

TOUR DE FRANCE 1978 STAGE 10

The misery of abandoning…

The 1978 Tour saw the first inclusion of the Col de Marie Blanque towards the end of stage 10 as the only significant climb of the day. The build-up to it comprised the Col de Pagolle (211m) and Col d'Ichère (681m), then a final slap from the Côte des Indats (519m).

Thévenet had won overall twice: in 1975, when he defeated the hitherto unbeaten Merckx, and in 1977, after an amazing scrap on Alpe d'Huez to save the yellow jersey from Kuiper by 28 seconds.[13]

Stage 10 of the Tour, to Pau was dominated by an attacking group containing several contenders for the overall win, among them the 23-year-old Bernard Hinault, winner that May of the Vuelta. On the slopes of the lowly Pagolle, Thévenet was in awful trouble, clamped to the bars like an asthmatic and desperately gasping for breath. Such distress is always pitiable; for a noted climber, double-winner of the Tour, it carries the undeserved stigma of shame. Nonetheless, pride overrode the physical misery and Thévenet fought his way back, as he had done that famous day on the Alpe d'Huez.

The lead group, Aghostino, Hinault, Kuiper, Martinez, Pollentier, Zoetemelk, hit the decisive climb of the Marie-Blanque hard and Thévenet, shelled out straight away, was left to struggle on his own. The weather at the foot of the 11.5 kilometres was scorching hot and Thévenet, his face 'white as saliva' and coated in a slick of chilly sweat, stopped a long while to recover. He remounted. A short way on: a problem with the rear wheel. He stopped once more. The team car drew up. While the mechanic changed the wheel, the team driver tried to persuade Thévenet to abandon. He refused.

As the road wound up through the trees onto the long curves of the higher plane in thinning air, the mist closed in, cold and damp, soaking into Thévenet's enfeebled legs and tortured lungs. He recalled the misery of the ascent: 'At the

---

[13] That Tour finished, for the first time, on the Champs Elysées. In a deluge of rain, Thévenet, Merckx and others fell heavily. Thévenet told Jacques Chirac, then Mayor of Paris, that they'd been riding in constant fear of crashing. Chirac laughed and said that the rain was good for drama. Thévenet remarked, drily: 'He can't have cycled much in the rain.'

start [in Leyden, Holland] I was in fair shape – I thought I would ride into form after a few stages. It didn't happen. I feared this col because I didn't know it, though friends had told me how hard it was. From the first slopes, I felt bad, no strength, incapable of rising to this hellish gradient. At the summit, in that rain which I hated, I must already have lost ten minutes. I couldn't believe I was so shattered. On that climb, I went through one of the worst experiences in my life.'

The dense crowd lining the road either side of the col, many of them visibly shocked at the sight of his torment, cheered and applauded him through, knowing that the expense of effort just to survive in a man of Thévenet's class is far more excruciating than when he dominates the race. His team mates Guy Sibille and Régis Delépine, sprinter-domestiques (sprinter team-mates), were waiting to nurse him home. He slipped gratefully onto the long descent but what agony to finish.

The two hills which lay ahead were paltry – a 50 metre rise to Sévignac-Meyracq and a withering slog up the Côte des Pindats, at 519m – but the punishment they meted out was gruesome, final. Thévenet arrived in Pau spent, over 13 minutes down on the winner, Henk Lubberding, that year's Best Young Rider. The following day, he toiled up to Barèges at the start of the Tourmalet, stuttered to a halt and climbed off.

Abandoning the Tour de France is one of the most traumatic experiences for any pro rider: they will endure almost any level of agony rather than quit. For the man who had crucified Merckx in the Alps in 1975 and taken the 1977 Tour against specialist climbers like Van Impe, Zoetemelk and Kuiper, leaving the race on his preferred terrain was doubly bitter. Yet knowing when to quit is a mark of a champion, for it is to acknowledge a truth central to the understanding of suffering on a bike: no rider ever beats the Tour; the best he can say is that, for the moment, the Tour has not beaten him. As that magisterial writer on the Tour, Antoine Blondin, said, the essential is knowing what it means to exceed one's limits.

Col d'Aubisque 1709m

Western approach

LENGTH: 18.4 KM
HEIGHT GAIN: 1200 M
MAXIMUM GRADIENT: 10%

The Col d'Aubisque, 'queen of the Pyrenees', sits atop the main passage over the high buttress dividing the old frontier province of Béarn from the Bigorre region and two river gorges, Ossau to the east, Pau to the west. First climbed in the 1910 Tour de France and included in every race thereafter until 1958; since then, excluded only 16 times.

The road surface is variable on the western approach, generally good on the east side, with the pass open between June and October/November. The col (but no further) is rideable from the west most of the year, kept open for cross-country skiing.

Allow between 2 and 3 hours, whichever way you ride up to the Aubisque. No problem with refreshments, cafés on Aubisque and Soulor (these linked by the Route des Corniches). The northern and eastern approaches afford a splendid panorama as you ride on to the final stretch to the col. One of the great, historic Pyrenean climbs.

"There is nothing in the world more hypocritical than the 1709 metres of the Aubisque. Because one rolls out of Pau on deliciously flat country. Because, from the beginning of the climb, all the way to Eaux-Bonnes, there are 5km of a very beautiful road, mounting 'prettily'. It isn't till after Eaux-Bonnes that the treachery of this Aubisque declares itself. It is cruel, tortuous, frequently thick with shit when it isn't choked with dust and littered with stones." Henri Desgrange.

He was perhaps referring specifically to the 1926 Tour de France, at 5745 kilometres the longest ever. Bayonne-Luchon in heavy rain, by midnight only 47 of the 67 starters have arrived. 12 riders finish the stage by bus. Lucien Buysse wins by 25 minutes, takes the Tour and, in souvenir of the hell they all endured over the Pyrenees, names the hotel he buys 'L'Aubisque'.

Start at Laruns. Out of Laruns, (from a Basque word 'lar-un' for pasturage) across the river Arriuse (0.5km) and the bridge over the Ossau gorge (1.5km). Junction at 1.9km: the D934 heads on south towards Col du Pourtalet. Two sizeable parking spaces either side the D918 (the old coaching road across the Pyrenees) which swings east.

The climbing begins quite easily, between 4 and 6%, all the way to Eaux-Bonnes, (720m, 5.9km). Some bad gouging and pitting in the road (snowplough damage), ancient pines standing sentinel along both verges, a fine aerial view of Laruns below. A sign trumpets the virtues of the Eaux-Bonnes thermal

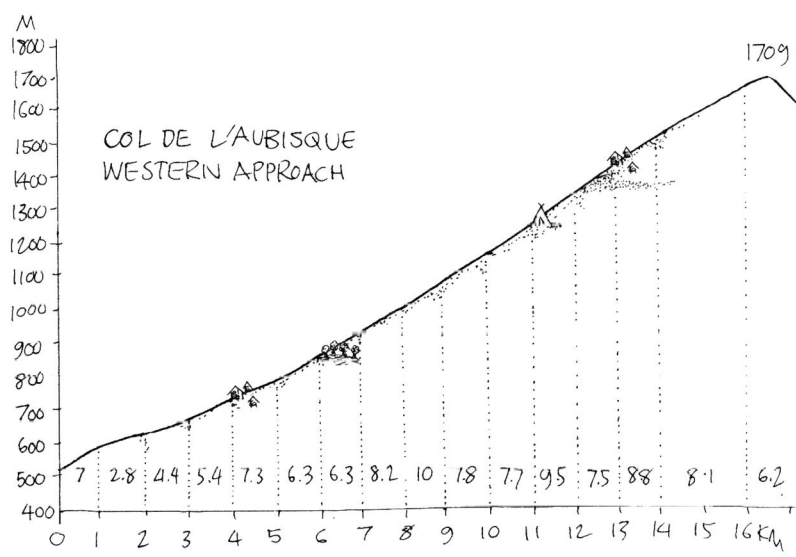

Col d'Aubisque *continued from previous page*

baths – a cure for 'aching joints, breathlessness, stress'. Be encouraged. Into town, a rather decayed spa, elderly five-storey terraces parading a faded grandeur, a Casino, a rectangular central reservation you will have to ride round, and back to the turn.

Certainly used by the Romans, the spa first came to later notice when its sulphurous waters aided the convalescence of Béarnais soldiers, returning wounded from the Battle of Pavia in February 1525, in which the Hapsburg emperor, Charles V, trounced the French army of Francis I, who was taken prisoner. Some fine cascades a short walk up the neighbouring southern slopes.

Out of Eaux-Bonnes, the road snaps up sharply then swings into 3 kilometres of long bends, 7, 4.5 and 7%, a sudden slap of 13% and on across two bridges over deep-set rivers. This marks the real start of the climb. You ride a kilometre of 10% and the rest of the way varies between 8 and 9%. The screen of trees crowds you, allowing not much in the way of a view down or up, just the sour-faced wide road ahead. Wide roads are harder, somehow. The gradient slackens fractionally into the snow tunnels, then a flat left-hand bend at a car park ('Gourette Welcomes You') before swinging left up a wide ramp into the winter resort (variously named Gourette or Gouretta – 1346m, 8km) and a sudden twinge of discomfort. The big wide unyielding slab of concrete hauls you coyly into ski-town – the routine gaudy chorus line of bars, restaurants, hotels and resort tat – as if to say 'well done, you made it, take the weight off' only to spit you straight out the other side (steep) onto the final run-in with the Aubisque.

The 4.3 kilometre approach to the col is hard but scenically more engaging. The road – a much better surface – narrows and has more movement in it, giving you a better sense of your own progress. It hugs steep buttresses to the right and intermittently sneaks a glance through the trees over the deep valley way below to the left and to the large cream-coloured Hôtel des Crêtes (Rock Ridge Hotel), perched on a bluff way ahead. As the trees thin out, the road emerges at 9% onto a bare mountainside – sheep grazing lazily on cropped furze – and the hotel at 1571m, 16.6km. You're on the bare mountain for sure now, travelling a high-rise, pinched track, exposed, unprotected – the Aubisque is one of the bleakest of summits. You begin to get tantalising glimpses of the great wind-scraped massif lurking round the last bends, testing your patience, your nerve. The stonewall parapet gives way to wooden post barriers. Suddenly round a big right-hand hairpin, it arrives, the bald dome of the Aubisque in full view. A final 0.5 kilometre kick of 8% and you're onto the pate of the summit.

There's a good café to your left by the broad car park of the col: souvenirs and postcards, food and drink, a friendly owner. (It also serves as a Raid Pyrénéen control.) A summit sign for photographs. A truly magnificent vista eastwards over the deep valley to your left and the yoke of the Soulor ahead. One look down there and you can begin to gauge how Lapize and the others felt in 1910 when they first rode up here.

Eastern approach

ARGELÈS-GAZOST TO COL DU SOULOR: 19.4 KM

HEIGHT GAIN: 1050 M

MAXIMUM GRADIENT: 9%

SOULOR TO THE AUBISQUE: 10 KM

HEIGHT GAINED: 1264 M

MAXIMUM GRADIENT: 7%

Both eastern and northern approaches offer a mildly intimidating conclusion to the climb because of the imposing presence of the Aubisque itself, squatting on the high chine of rock way ahead as you crest the intervening Col du Soulor.

From the start: 4 kilometres of 6…7.5…7…5.5 to Arras-en-Lavedan (680m) by the Lac d'Estaing. 8 kilometres of breathing space, more or less flat, over the nominal Col de Couraque (855m) to Arrens (870m) at 12km. Turn right up the D918, 7.5 kilometres of dogged 8 or 8.5% to the Col du Soulor at 1474m. (A good café here.) The road drops to 1390m over the next 2.5 kilometres onto the corniche of the Cirque du Litor, along which it rises gently for 4 kilometres, 2.5…4.5…3.5, to the final 3 kilometres of 7% to the Aubisque.

Via Col du Soulor 1474m

LENGTH: 10 KM

HEIGHT GAIN: 235 M

MAXIMUM GRADIENT: 8%

From the Soulor, a majestic view across the great chasm that yawns below the peak of the Aubisque. The road curves right onto a 2 kilometre drop which robs you of 116m. Beware cattle straying across the road: they have unfettered grazing on the grass outcrops on either side. The start of the climb follows the spectacular Cirque du Litor, a narrow ledge cut into the side of the sheer mountain wall – a vertiginous drop to the right. This road goes through two unlit snow tunnels, the second (3.5 kilometres from the col) particularly uneven in surface and slick with water seeping out of the rock – a notable hazard if descending from the Aubisque to the Cirque, so be careful to remove shades before entering.

A little further on, a plaque fastened to the rock wall on the left commemorates the spectacular fall into a ravine of the yellow jersey Wim Van Est (the first Dutchman to lead the Tour). He punctured on the descent in 1951, wobbled into the parapet, toppled some 50m over the side and, miraculously, was unhurt. Hauled up by a rope of tubulars tied together he was too shocked to continue the race.

There are four relatively easy kilometres – 2.5, 4.5, 3.5 and 3.5 – before the final moderately steep climb at 7% to the summit. The tarmac is rather old and pitted here, another peril on the descent.

From the crest of the climb, the panorama of the long sweep of the Cirque du Litor's road hugging the beetling cliffs is one of the grandest panoramas of the Pyrenean chain.

To the Soulor from Arrens 870m

LENGTH: 7.4 KM

HEIGHT GAIN: 604 M

MAXIMUM GRADIENT: 8.5%

The approach to the Col du Soulor along the Gave d'Azun to its base at Arrens Marsous, affords one of the finest valley perspectives in the Pyrenees, a deep V narrowing focus on the big ranges – Grand Gabizos in the foreground, beyond it, the Pic de Ger, overlooking the Aubisque.

The D918, much used by the Tour, is clean-surfaced and well maintained but the 12 kilometre approach from Argelès-Gazost (a good bike shop) to Arrens at the start of the climb is by no means a doddle. It begins fairly steep, 5–7%, before dropping to 4 then 2.5%, and finally running tea-tray flat into the souvenir and ski-stop town of Arrens. A sign announces the col at the foot of the climb proper and cherry-red-capped cream kilometre stones tell off the distance. This is a genial climb, as they go – long bends, a smooth passage, trim countryside, pleasant views, 7 kilometres of a good steady 8–8.5%. This allows you to develop a rhythm, with reassurance in the state of the highway, its gracious sweeping movement and the greenery to either side. At about 5km from the top (1258m) the treeline slips away – always a sign of getting close – and the hairpins arrive. They get quite tight as the road hugs the wall of the mountain to the right, but they flow and draw you on up to what you know must be a fine belvedere of a col, showing off the sunken ground from which you have just ridden. And it is so. A vast panorama where eagles fly.

Col d'Aubisque *continued from previous page*

Northern approach

LENGTH: 22.6 KM

HEIGHT GAIN: 954 M

MAXIMUM GRADIENT: 9%

From the D35 between Lestelle-Bétharram and Louvie-Juzon take the D126 which follows the course of the river Ouzon. For 15 kilometres, via Arthez-d'Asson (6km) to Etchartes (9.4km) the gradient goes no higher than 3% in one short stretch with 1-2% for most of the rest. The tranquil, narrow road crosses and recrosses the river, pasture to right and left. A forbidding or, depending on your mood, grand view up the valley: mighty spurs of mountain rock project at about 45° on both sides, framing a long view of the massive peaks on the distant skyline. The first experience of riding mountains is always spiced with the amazement that any road could possibly reach up into the giddy heights you can actually see. That amazement can easily translate as disbelief and apprehension.

The stream plunges happily alongside you down the gravity chute, the road twisting through ever closer crowding trees. Wayside statues in rock niches, a mill house, a cascade, a restaurant/bar Le Moulin (recommended) just short of Ferrières, where the slope stiffens to 5%. A sense of foreboding, perhaps: this drawn-out, quiet approach must lead to something unpleasant, but when is it going to start?

A road left goes up to the Col de Spandelles, a 'route pastorale', a shepherd's track by origin. Into Ferrières, a shabby, nondescript village: restaurant/hotel, school, church, post office, small information booth, the road very broken up, gouged, pitted with potholes, what the French call 'hen's nests'. The road swings abruptly right on a steep bend into 6.5%, as if sprinting to gain momentum for the next 11 kilometres. Strings of poplars obscure the view right, the road surface very poor. Such byways crave a regal visit from the Tour de France and mandatory repairs. To date, this is like the backstairs approach to the Soulor, for lowly postmen and tweenies: the royal highway for the grandees of the peloton comes up from Arrens.

At kilometre 1, an outcrop of rock to the left, dimpled and mottled black grey ochre, like some confection by Gaudi. For 3 kilometres the road winds along a corniche, a relatively steady gradient of around 7%. Into the tiny central square of Arbéost (14km) – a Gîte d'Etape (lodging for walkers/cyclist, originally a military staging post) – the road tilts sharply down then, with a burst of glee, jinks left and up a steep pull into a stretch of 9% and 8.5%, the next upper storey of the climb. At just under 5 kilometres short of the col, the flanking trees thin and disappear and the road is at once very exposed to the right, offering a majestic view down into the valley and across to the range topped by the Pic du Moulle de Jaout (2080m). This stretch is bleak, rough, daunting but beautiful. At around 3.5 kilometres from the top, a lay-by overlooks the Piste du Litor, a long, serpentine track for walkers down into the basin of the valley head. A sign warns against dropping litter and approaching animals closer than 10m. The café on the Soulor appears on the rim of the col and 7.5-8% brings you home.

TOUR DE FRANCE 1910
Murderers!

After the first Pyrenean stage – Perpignan–Luchon, 289km over cols de Puymorens, Port, Portet d'Aspet, Ares – Henri Desgrange, the organiser, returns to Paris having summoned his deputy, Victor Breyer by phone. Rest day in Luchon.

21 July, 3.30am: The riders set out for Bayonne on the Atlantic coast, 326km across the cols de Peyresourde, Aspin, Tourmalet, Aubisque.

Breyer reports: 'Having crossed the Tourmalet, we parked three quarters of the way up the Aubisque which, according to [Alphonse] Steinès (the man who had reconnoitred the Pyrenees the summer before and declared them rideable), was the major obstacle on which the decisive duel would be fought. From our vantage point we would be able to see the riders coming. I calculated that the first would arrive in about fifteen minutes. A quarter of an hour passed, then another, then a third, me consulting my watch the whole time. The sun, almost at its height, blazed out of a clear blue sky, its implacable rays unleashing a suffocating heat. An absolute silence reigned in that desert of nature. And still nothing. I had the feeling that the enterprise entrusted to my care was in the process of coming to grief. I was now persuaded that the Tour de France was about to disappear into oblivion.

'Suddenly, round a corner of the road, appeared a rider whom I didn't recognise, a heavy lump of a man, squeezed onto the machine which he rough-handled, panting with every stroke of the pedals. He moved forward very slowly, but he was moving forward. I ran over to him: "Who are you? What's happening? Where are the others?" Bowed over the handlebars, eyes fixed on the road, the man didn't even turn his head, he didn't say a word. He went on and disappeared beyond a bend. Steinès had lifted the number on the man's jersey and consulted his list: this was the independent (i.e. not riding for a team) François Lafourcade. He'd rejoined and then dropped all the 'cracks', the top men. Once again, minutes ticked by. Another fifteen passed after the arrival of the man from Bayonne, before a second rider, identifiable by his blue jersey with the red collar: [Octave] Lapize. He was walking, leaning on the bike which he had no longer the strength to ride. His eyes bulged, mark of his intense distress. But unlike Lafourcade, he spoke, and volubly. "You are murderers. Yes, murderers."

'In such a place, to engage in conversation with a man in such a state, would have been stupid and cruel. I walked along beside him, holding my peace while he continued to curse us before rounding on me and saying to my face: "Don't worry, when I get to Eaux-Bonnes, I'm packing it in."

'It took me some minutes to recover my composure. There were still 150km to the finish.'

Lapize didn't pack it in. He won the Tour and Lafourcade came 14th. Of 110 riders who started, 41 reached Paris.

Col de la Couraduque 1367m

From Aucun

LENGTH: 6.2 KM

HEIGHT GAIN: 507 M

MAXIMUM GRADIENT: 9.5%

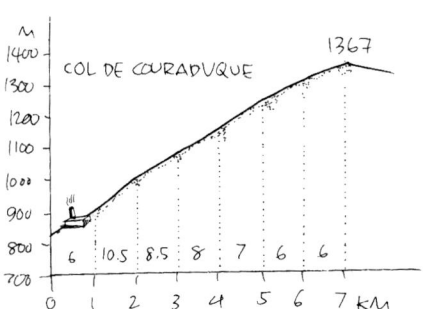

At Aucun, 10 kilometres from Argelès, turn sharp right towards the col onto a steep climb past the Place 19 mars 1962 (commemorating the ceasefire in Algeria). A pleasant little village gathered round the main road with quite a few new buildings – the community has expanded. The ascent winds up past slopes of meadows and a long view back across the valley to the ridge and the Col de Bordères, a large copse of cypresses on its flank. Two-lane road, excellent surface, tree-lined lower down, clearly following an old track cut into the hillside with one or two quite steep hairpins at the lower end. Overall, an easy enough gradient despite the fact that the first kilometre shows 9%. (Averages are so often deceptive and the nature of the road makes a big difference: the attractiveness of the passage, through woods and avenues of trees or along ledges with grand views – such as this climb – will often substantially dull the ache of hammering the pedals.) Another kilometre of 8.5% onto a stretch of exposed road with a massive view of the Gave d'Azun followed by a patch of cover, a gentle sweep downhill, a sharp hairpin right and 7.5% with a view up to the heights from where the parapentes (hang gliders) launch. Hairpins and bends dictate the swing of the road up the final kilometres of open road on the bare hillside to the Col de la Couraduque from where the views are stupendous. A bar/restaurant with a wonderful belvedere of a balcony, and a very friendly guy in the adjacent ski and mountain bike hire shop.

(This makes a very pleasant descent but be careful on the steep final hundred metres or so which hit an abrupt junction with the main road.)

Col de Spandelles 1378m

From the west

LENGTH: 10.6 KM
HEIGHT GAIN: 853 M
MAXIMUM GRADIENT: 9%

From the Couraduque, 3.8 kilometres of downhill forest piste, very rough, badly gouged and strewn with stones, to the junction with the metalled road linking Argelès-Gazost (via Gez, 13 kilometres) and the foot of the Soulor on D126. Just before the junction a welcoming chalet, the Refuge Haugarou – auberge, rooms, meals.

There are no kilometre signs either side of the Spandelles. From the junction, the road climbs steeply up 2.4 kilometres and exacts a fierce maximum of 10% up to the rim of a deep gorge under the gaunt Soum (summit) de Granguet, its sheer grass-covered flanks split by long, protruding scars of jagged rock. The view from the col is even larger, more breathtaking than from the Couraduque, a magnificent vista as well as a satisfying look down at the switchback of hairpins of the upper part of the northern ascent.

The approach begins on a route pastorale (shepherd's track) between Etchartes and Ferrières (525m) some 300m up the D126 from Le Moulin restaurant – excellent food, a terrace by the old mill, greylag geese in a coop, the river chuckling along under a canopy of trees.

This must be the old route over the ridge. What has become the main route goes to the head over the Col du Soulor of the valley and will offer a gentler climb, but when time was against the drover or the shepherd, steeper meant quicker, and man and donkey loaded with wood or wares can go where no wheeled transport can venture. In this case they were going from the sheltered northern side to the open, sunnier slopes, in Latin apricus, hence 'apricot'. Such reflection on why these roads exist at all is surely integral to the challenge, pleasure and allure of the Pyrenees. Cycling them is quite the best way of getting to know large chunks of the region: its people, towns, villages, local cuisine and varied terrain.

Two kilometres up there is a beautiful view to the left of a precipitous (75-80°) hillside, its smooth, grassy flanks reaching up to a considerable height, sprouting clumps of dark pines, cut across by scars of old terracing and scattered farmhouses.

This col is steep, never less than 7% and most of the way 8 or 8.5, though it feels worse. Not for the fainthearted. A good surface, very tight hairpins, unremitting gradient, this is serious climbing, no signs, no indication at all of where you are. You are absolutely on your own, and the frisson of such climbs as this is that you simply have no gauge of how you are doing – the way ahead is hidden, the sudden shots of the way up which you have come so faraway, remote and testing that you are caught between surprise at what you have done and dismay at what you still have to do.

There are variations in steepness, which averaging irons out, and after the first real hit of the climb there is a brief levelling, but no great change.

Some dwellings. A farm selling sheep's cheese. These signs of habitation do help the morale a bit, if not the legs or lungs.

The road – good surface – tucks into the flank of the mountain, half the way through trees, and there are occasional glimpses ahead of the next section in gaps of the cover – what looks like an impossibly abrupt track knifing upwards, enough to make you say 'how am I going to ride that?' But in the mountains, seeing is not believing: trust rather your instinct for persevering and the fact that you have got this far, so why not further? And if not, not, so get stuck in.

Wonderful perspectives of the valley behind open out and up ahead looms the huge Granguet summit, part craggy, part cloaked with trees. The road has a lot of movement in it and at around halfway, as the tree cover thins, it opens out a bit with wider verges. However this isn't the treeline, only an intervening baldness. A deep recess to the left, a small hollow of earth as if scooped out for a sort of corrie in the hillside as shelter for sheep, a floor of cropped grass.

This is a climb full of interest – every now and then, to begin with at least, you turn a corner and there is a house. The slopes do ease intermittently, a slight respite, but you are always conscious of being drawn directly into the mean business of the mountain, a very strait and narrow twisting buckling road.[14] So, both exciting – the challenge of the new – and if you are not used to such bran tub climbs, quite daunting.

Nearing the treeline, around 3 kilometres from the top, the road becomes a ledge not much wider than a car with a vertiginous drop straight off the tarmac to the right and a stunning view out into the emptiness. On into a wooded stretch with broader verges. Above the treeline, the bends tighten all the way up to the col. (The descent will be nervy but exhilarating as you plunge towards the zigzags of the snapcomb bends as they flick back and forth.)

---

14 'Strait' and 'narrow' are synonymous. Think strait jacket, dire straits, the Straits of Messina. As Scott says of an obese individual in *Ivanhoe* 'If the stairs be too strait to admit his fat carcase, I will have him craned up from without.' So, it is the strait and narrow path, often twisting and winding and full of arduous difficulty and hairpins and bends and taxing gradient, which leads up to Paradise, and the broad, smooth highway – the Nationale – that leads on a gentle easy-peasy slope straight, unbendingly, to Hell. Misspell your 'strait and narrow' hereafter at your dire and straitened peril.

Col des Bordères 1156m

From the east

LENGTH: 15.3 KM
HEIGHT GAIN: 950 M
MAXIMUM GRADIENT: 10%

Head out of town towards the Soulor and take a small turning right to Gez, direction Sère-en-Lavedan. In Gez turn left onto the narrow, well-surfaced road which follows the re-entrant of the Bergons valley. There is tree cover most of the way and the first 6 kilometres are quite demanding, between 7 and 8%, with a short stretch, halfway, at a more moderate 5%, but this is beautiful, quiet country. At around 6km, the gradient eases into a long stretch of fairly undemanding work: five or so kilometres with no nasty surprises and a gentle average, even near flat for some distance. The final 2 kilometres to the junction with the track from the Couraduque, where the road crosses a bridge over the Bergons, get markedly steeper to tax your legs before the final 2.4 kilometres to the col.[15]

From Arrens

LENGTH: 4.5 KM
HEIGHT GAIN: 286 M
MAXIMUM GRADIENT: 9%

This is a gem of a col, a great alternative to the main road from the foot of the Soulor to Argelès-Gazost and vice versa. It's been included on the Tour route only twice, in 1987 and 1989 on the stage Pau-Cauterets. That day saw the emergence of Induraín, loyal domestique (support rider) of Pedro Delgado, the 1988 winner, as a rider of exceptional class. He attacked on his own a long way from the finish, continued over the Aubisque and the Bordères to the ski station which, like Hautacam, has welcomed the Tour but three times since 1953. Behind him, several big names lost hatfuls of time, including the 1987 winner Stephen Roche who ceded more than a quarter of an hour.

A short burst of climbing on a jolly little road lined with silver birch and ash. The restaurant above the col (Auberge du Pic de Pan) is a bit of a cheat: reservation required, noon and evening.

From Argelès-Gazost

LENGTH: 13.2 KM
HEIGHT GAIN: 750 M
MAXIMUM GRADIENT: 10%

A back route follows the D101 south to Saint-Savin – a pleasant, well-groomed little town with a fine view across the valley – through to Arcizans on the D13. A windy, hilly ride but quiet and bucolic. Up past Sireix and onto the D103, a steep drop into the valley, the Gave de Labat de Bun, and a beautiful ride along the banks of the stream to Estaing (14km) where the narrow road to the col swings off to the right and asks of you 2 kilometres at 10%.[16]

A quite exceptionally joyous detour, this.

---

15 There are superb views of the Pic du Midi Bigorre on the way up to the village of Peyras from an appealing, newly-gravelled road that leads south from Rimoula, just north of Sainte-Marie-de-Campan, and loops back to near Campan. However it's very steep and peters out into rough piste higher up. Not recommended.

16 Savinus, a Spanish hermit-monk, lived here and the partially restored abbey church dedicated to his memory is one of the finest in the Pyrenees, more fortress than church, reputedly founded by Charlemagne on the ruins of a Roman palace and rebuilt and enlarged over several centuries.

Lourdes-Hautacam 1535m (Col de Tramassel 1615m)

Fron Lourdes

LENGTH:	15.6 KM
HEIGHT GAIN:	1052 M
MAXIMUM GRADIENT:	10%

In 1858, an illiterate 14-year-old peasant girl, Bernadette Soubirous, claimed to have seen 18 visions of the Virgin Mary in the Grotte de Massabielle near the Gave de Pau. The ecclesiastical hierarchy cheered and established a feast day on the anniversary of the first apparition – 11 February – when the pallid spectre had proclaimed: 'I am the Immaculate Conception'. The epiphany of Lourdes as a 'Cité religieuse' and the attendant commercial bonanza ensued.

Unless you have a perverse taste for the grotesque, the maudlin, the lurid, for pietistic excess and the kind of canonical trinketry and consecrated kitsch for which the Roman Catholic church has a particular fondness; unless you exhibit an irrational craving for holy water dispensed promiscuously from rows of taps in stand pipes into opaque plastic demijohns (on sale everywhere) the colour of glaucoma; if you suffer, even intermittently, from pangs of a dark sanctimonious brooding introspection or morbid intimations of mortality ('being immortal is to be half dead,' said Antoine Blondin, that peerless chronicler of the Tour de France) then, for your own sake and peace of mind, avoid Lourdes. Alabaster-visaged identical nuns scurry like scary troops of cloned triplets. Soutaned priests loiter like traffic wardens with halitosis. Creeping Jesuses shuffle more holily than thou along every pavement and there are vastly more churches, chapels, shrines, seminaries, pilgrim hotels (and pilgrims) than good bars and restaurants. Not an attractive imbalance. The 3-D eyes of numberless crucified Christs blink open and stare with the blank intensity of zombies from holograms crucified on card racks as you hurry by looking for a way out. The forecourt of the basilica is miraculously smooth and perfect for cycling, but beware: the odour of sanctity can be quite as noxious as the sulphurs of Old Nick and the forecourt of the basilica is perilously close to the source and the grotto of Saint Bernadette. She was, like most of the saints, a remote stranger to personal hygiene and mens sana in corpore sano.

One visitor to Lourdes who came with the firm intention of penning a scabrous exposé and denunciation of its false promise, its vanity and the pernicious delusion it spawns was the novelist Emile Zola.[17] However having spent some time there, he concluded that human beings somehow need and depend on the kind of fatuous hopes that Lourdes purveys so prodigally in order to meter and dull their abiding despair. Battered, bowed and sometimes embittered by reality, human kind, as T.S. Eliot puts it, cannot bear too much reality. Belief, and hope, makes life tolerable.

Lourdes has a bike shop where ailing machines can get repair and prosthetics in exchange for hard cash. No genuflection. No Ave Marias.

Draw your own conclusion about the place once called 'the key to the Lavedan valley', but there is a fast, flat, even-surfaced, two-lane cycle track along the old railway line that shoots straight out of Lourdes south all the way to the resolutely secular spa town of Argelèles-Gazost and beyond to Pierrefite-Nestalas. Alongside it, the D13 winds along the river towards the Gorge de Luz and is liable to flooding, though not in summer, past a town called Boo. (The French say 'coucou' for 'boo' by the way.) Turn left onto the D100 towards Ayros (480m) and the beginning of the climb to the ski station at Hautacam.

---

17 His unwitting rôle in the institution of the Tour de France merits a fuller account. See *Tour de France: The History, the Legend, the Riders* by Graeme Fife, Edinburgh, Mainstream Publishing, 2006, fully revised edition, includes a report on the 2006 race.

The road is quite narrow, two car widths only, intermittently shaded in and out of tree cover and the surface is good. The Tour has been here three times, most recently in 2000. The first 3 kilometres take an immediate toll, 9, 8.5 and 10%, then ease into a couple at 6% average, although here is another example of how mean figures distort the picture: some of these notionally mild stretches deliver sudden tight squeezes. Excellent views down to the right across the valley and to Argelès-Gazost (which also offers an approach to the climb on the D100 north).

There is a bar/restaurant/hotel in Artalens and, juxtaposed at the end of the tiny square, a small Mairie gaily decked out with miniature tricolour standards. Also a wayside shrine – niche and statuette – to the ubiquitous Notre Dame de Lourdes… just keeping an eye, of course…

The lawns, verges, meadows, hedges and shrubs which adorn the tiny village of Saint-André a bit further on (more 9%) are as neatly manicured as trimmers, clippers, mowers (and nail scissors, possibly) can make them. At 6 kilometres from the col and another slug of 10%, the trees thin out and look stunted as if huddling from inclement weather of which the mountain gets plenty. Next there's open ground, bracken and rocky outcrops, the climb taking on a more rugged aspect, getting down to hard cases and a steady rack of 8 and 9%.

When I rode this climb, the tarmac on the upper reaches was awash with white paint. Now the blackboard is pristine again, clean slate. Past the Auberge d'Arriotou a belvedere intervenes on the long straights driving on and on towards the twists and turns of the final risers; beware a cattle grid. A graffito on the low parapet wall advises: 'Attention à vos fesses' (watch your arse). Is this more helpful, even friendlier, than a wayside plaster-of-Paris statuette of a virgin in a niche? Certainly more relevant. In July 2005, a one-armed cyclist made the climb. Hats off.

The road to the Col de Tramassel (another 2.6 kilometres) continues beyond the turn-off to the huge open space of the Hautacam, but the metalling runs out after 600 metres. In summer the ski lifts do duty dragging small, low-level carts up the grass of the piste for the drivers to slalom back down under their own momentum. This is the main activity on offer courtesy of the Parc des Loisirs Espace Rollerbe: the café was shut. The car park is unmetalled, stony and unlovely but the views are fine indeed and the descent is a cracker. There is, after all, something particularly satisfying about going back down what you have just ridden up, inexplicable to those who do not cycle the cols but an idiosyncratic treat for those who do.

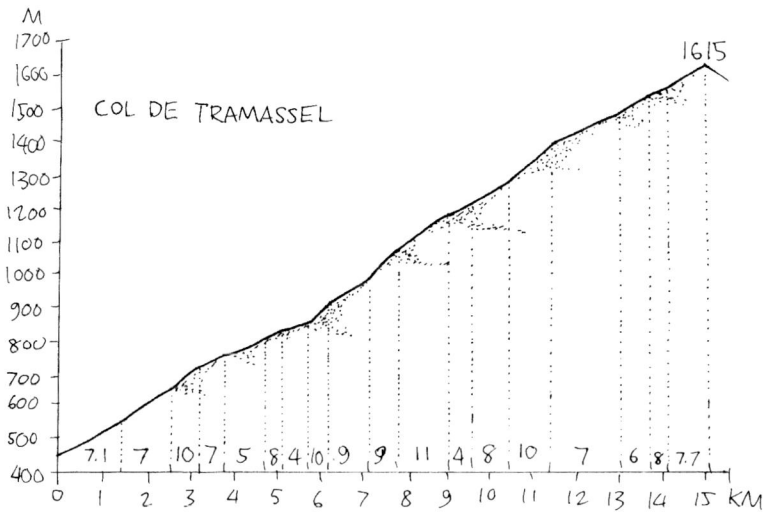

TOUR DE FRANCE 1994-2000
Rare but decisive

Lourdes-Hautacam (Hautacam means 'highland') has appeared on only three Tour itineraries. In 1994, it shelled out Tony Rominger, who lost 2 minutes, and Claudio Chiappucci, who lost over 20. They were both suffering from the onset of gastro-enteritis, a common affliction in stage races. The Italian endured a debilitating attack of vomiting on the lower slopes; both riders abandoned. The winner that day was Luc Leblanc – with 2 seconds on Miguel Induraín riding to his fourth consecutive overall victory and 18 on Marco Pantani. He also took that year's rainbow jersey on the road, ahead of Chiappucci.

Shortly afterwards in October, Rominger extended the mile record to 53.832 kilometres and a month later increased it by an astonishing margin to 55.291 kilometres, each time on the Bordeaux track.

In 1996, Bjarne Rijs raised eyebrows with his extraordinary chase-me-Charley tactics on the Hautacam. Sprinting ahead of his immediate rivals, he then waited for them to catch up before flirtatiously sprinting away again. He eventually left them for dead and arrived at the summit alone, 49 seconds clear of Virenque, that year's winner of the Mountains Prize.

In 2000, the stage was taken by Javier Otxoa but the misty-moisty freezing day of rain and wind went to Lance Armstrong. He rode onto the final 13 kilometre climb with Pantani, Jan Ullrich and Alex Zülle, 10min 30sec behind a breakaway group containing Virenque, Fernando Escartín and Jose Maria Jiménez. Out ahead of them, Javier Otxoa, lone survivor of an early escape.

One kilometre in, Pantani attacked and was instantly checked by Armstrong and Zülle. Ullrich couldn't answer. The pace was ferocious; Zülle fell away, Pantani held on for a while but Armstrong, who had come to the Pyrenees and ridden this particularly taxing ascent several times, was pedalling with impressive fluency and power. His acceleration took him up to and past Virenque and Escartín. Only Jiménez could hold his wheel. Five kilometres from the summit, Otxoa's lead had shrunk to 4 minutes 58 seconds. In 8 kilometres, the American had gained over 5 minutes on him. They were riding through glacial clammy fogs.

On top of the grim inhospitable mountain, journos in the press hall were shivering with the bitter cold of winter in summer.

At 3km Jiménez was done for and Armstrong, still out of the saddle, was hunting down Otxoa. The Basque rider clung on and made it by a mere 42 seconds. Armstrong took yellow and, effectively, his second Tour victory. He had distanced Ullrich by 4min 1sec and Pantani, probably the most talented climber in the peloton, by almost 6 minutes.

Luz-Ardiden 1720m

From Luz-Saint-Sauveur

LENGTH: 5.3KM
HEIGHT GAIN: 1050M
MAXIMUM GRADIENT: 10%

The small town of Luz-Saint-Sauveur ('Radiance of the Holy Saviour') was used as a base by the Knights Templar and then by the Knights of Saint John of Jerusalem who took over the fortified church in the 14th century. It stands near the confluence of the Gave de Bastan (down from the Tourmalet) and the Gave de Gavarnie. The Emperor Napoléon III spent two months here in 1859 with his wife Eugénie, taking the waters at the thermal spa (lavishly modernised in 2000) in Saint-Sauveur, the western half of the main town. It is said that to make the crossing into the town across the gorge easier for fashionable visitors (whom George Sand derided as preening idiots), he ordered the building of a grandiose ironwork bridge, opened in 1861.

Cross from the D921 onto the main central drag of upper Saint Sauveur either by the imperial bridge or lower down the valley to find the start of the Luz-Ardiden climb on the D12.

The road is smooth, views of the valley bottom away to the right open up quite soon and the first few kilometres are relatively gentle, between 5.5 and 8%. It's as gracious an approach to a ski station as any. Indeed, the Pyrenean culs-de-sac rarely exhibit the ugly utilitarian bulldozered hackwork of some of the alpine resort roads.

A tougher belt of tarmac makes kilometre 6 a bit of a pain but, as the D12 tacks round the side of the mountain, the scenery will distract and, when the final zigzags of the climb appear on the far side of the broad east-facing amphitheatre on top of which sits Ardiden (the word is Gascon for 'western peak' thus Luz-Western Peak), a magnificence of geology dominates the way ahead.

The climb is challenging and the intermittent steepness takes its toll. However, the conquest of Luz-Ardiden has more than its fair share of satisfaction if you are prepared to exchange a hard slog for anything so apparently worthless and insubstantial as mere satisfaction. On the other hand, why else are you here at all? After that early warning of 10%, the gradients ease to a varied and more manageable 8.5 to 5. Just after kilometre 11, the high rim of the mountain bowl – a characteristic of the cirque-formed mountains hereabouts – the road crosses a bridge (right turn to Viscos) and the long ramps begin. 9% for starters. That's Nature's way of saying 'last chance'. The gradient does not comply for long and the final 3.3 kilometres are relatively mild. The view is stupendous.

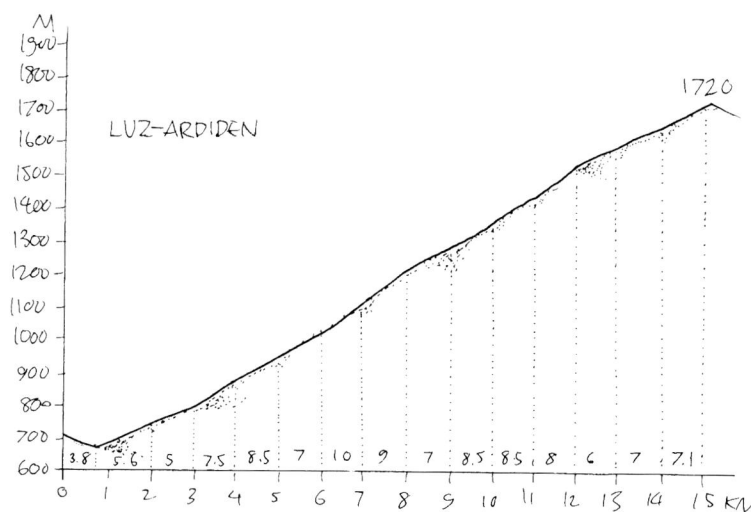

TOUR DE FRANCE 1985 AND 2003

New World v Old

Luz-Ardiden greeted its first stage winner, Pedro Delgado, in 1985. Behind him, a fierce duel was being fought by Hinault, riding for a fifth victory and his dauphin, Greg Lemond.

Hinault, nicknamed 'Badger', had crashed heavily on the road into Saint-Etienne on stage 14 and broken his nose. This made breathing very difficult and on stage 17, into the Pyrenees, Toulouse to Ardiden, he was particularly vulnerable, not only to the specialist climbers Delgado and the mountains' leader Luis Herrera, but also to Lemond, chafing with impatience to take the Badger on. The slopes of Luz-Ardiden were wreathed in thick, clinging mist. Hinault was suffering, gulping air only through his mouth, and the severity of the climb was hurting him.

Lemond up ahead, in company with Stephen Roche and Eduardo Chozas, had already taken a minute out of his boss. He sensed that Roche and Chozas were flagging. He gestured to Paul Koechli, his La Vie Claire directeur sportif in the team car: 'Can I go?' Koechli shook his head. Was this a defining moment? Lemond believed so then and reiterated it many times: by having to rein himself in, he was denied a first victory and Hinault was handed a fifth. But didn't the American know that no man has ever won only four Tours? There are some calls of history which have to be given rather more than a tacit nod.

In 2003 another American, Armstrong, was, some still believe, handed his own fifth victory on Luz-Ardiden. Grazing the lines of spectators too closely as he led on the final climb, Armstrong's right brake hood caught in the strap of a young lad's musette, the bike twisted and down he went, taking Iban Mayo with him. Ullrich swerved past and had a clear road. He did not attack. Armstrong and Mayo remounted. A second time Armstrong unhooked: his gears slipped, his foot came out of the pedal and he went down crotch-first onto the crossbar. Up the road, Tyler Hamilton called for a further truce and Ullrich, at that time only 15 seconds behind Armstrong, once again held fire. Who knows? Back in the saddle Armstrong rejoined, and when, 9 kilometres from the top Mayo attacked, he followed, went past and continued up through the sinking fog to overtake the lone escapee, Sylvain Chavanel, at 4.5km. Going past, he gave the Frenchman a friendly tap on the shoulder.

Col du Tourmalet 2114m

Western approach

LENGTH: 18.3 KM
HEIGHT GAIN: 1450 M
MAXIMUM GRADIENT: 9.5%

Of the first great Italian climber, Luigi Lucotti, in 1919, Desgrange wrote: 'I saw Lucotti cross the Aubisque caked in white dust which made him look like the classic flour-faced Pierrot. But the Aubisque and the Tourmalet so etched into his face the lines of pain and suffering that he evoked, with that cadaverous visage, the criminal clown in Ol' Clothes (a celebrated Folies Bergères vaudeville show). Yet, how, and by what prodigious effort, was he able to finish? "I don't want to race any more," he said, at the top of the Tourmalet.'

From Argelès-Gazost, follow the D921 up the Gorge de Luz to Saint-Sauveur: a steady climb with a fair bit of traffic along the course of the river surging through the deeper cut of the ravine, green with trees and grassy slopes.

Luz is a good place in which to stock up with provisions. A steep climb out of town and a sign warns '18km average 6%' to the col. This is grossly misleading: the first kilometre to Esterre is 5%, the rest of the way never falls below 7% and it mostly hovers round 7-9%.

Quite a few chambres d'hôtes (B and B's) and gîtes dot this road out of Luz, while a campsite to the left on the riverbank just outside town and various other appurtenances of the community are no more than minor distractions. However, the thing about a mountain as high and hard as this is that the foreboding begins early. After the long approach - 31 kilometres from the foot of the Soulor - you're impatient to get on with the climb but once you do start, you quickly realise - or remember - that the toil is unremitting and, though the road doesn't look that steep, it's hanging heavily on your legs from the start. There is a whole weight of history in this road which simply cannot be shaken off by mental juggling of statistics.

Clear of Esterre into the valley which leads to the head of the re-entrant and the beginning of the main climb. Signs show walks leading off to the right up into the higher forest, the river Bastan chumbling past to the left. The road surface is pretty good, the course winding, without much bend in it. Between 17 and 15km, long straights add to the hard work; at 15km a big bend, almost a hairpin but fairly shallow, takes the pressure out of the riding for a short way but then it is back onto the long straight ahead.

Around 14km the road gets into a bit of a swing, and this is cheering as movement always helps; however, after a couple of lengthy bends it tires of benevolence and tightens its grip once more, losing all sway and rhythm. The surface is excellent - clearly it hasn't been repaired for a while, but it's smooth.

The extended view of the tarmac ahead makes the gradient seem worse than it is, though from 14km we're on 7.5, 7, 8, 7 to Barèges, (10.9 kilometres from the col). At 13.5km the road recovers its humour in a sudden burst of curve - these twists do help - before two hefty bends dump you into the unattractive camping/chalet/ski and summer resort that is Barèges, thermal springs to the left.

In 1675 Madame de Maintenon, Louis XIV's mistress, governess to his 7-year-old son, the Duc de Maine, and, later, his wife, came to Barèges (1219m) via the Tourmalet in a chair borne by porters to take the waters. Her visit brought the thermal springs to the notice of the fashionable set, although the community dates back to the 14th century and the springs were

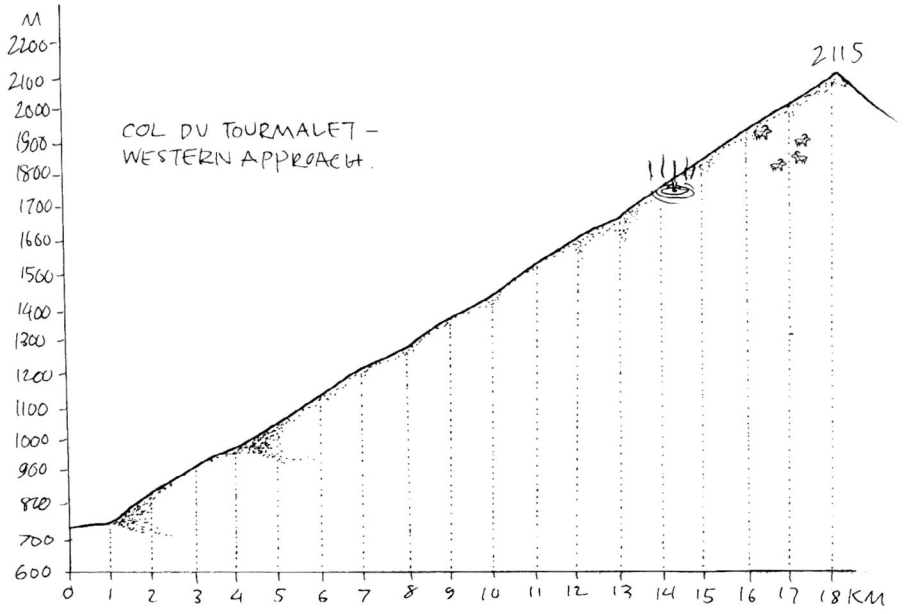

well-known long before the Parisians arrived.

Following the publication in 1742 of a treatise by a Dr Meigham detailing the curative effects of the sulphurated Barèges thermal waters from sources deep in the granite massif on various diseases and disorders, particularly 'Their superior effects in the cure of gun-shot wounds', a military hospital (still preserved) was built here in 1744. The springs offer various massage regimes and hydrotherapeutic treatments for respiratory illness, rheumatism and physical trauma.

The idea of taking the infant Tour de France to the Pyrenees came from Alphonse Steinès, Henri Desgrange's assistant. Desgrange told him he'd gone crazy. Steinès was unabashed. In 1909, he reconnoitred by car, got stuck in a snowdrift at 6pm on the Tourmalet 4 kilometres below the eastern crest, told the driver to head back through the valleys via Lourdes and meet him in Barèges, then proceeded on foot, following the line of poles marking the road. Night fell. In civilian shoes he struggled on to the gendarmerie in Barèges and, when he had recovered, telegraphed Desgrange in Paris: 'Tourmalet crossed. Stop. Very good road. Stop. Perfectly practicable. Stop. Steinès'.

Leaving Barèges, the road tosses its head petulantly and the recorded 8% of the wickedly steep and curveless ramp out of town looks like a serious, even wilful, underestimate. It is shocking. A sign tells you that Sainte-Marie-de-Campan, at the foot of the Tourmalet on the other side, is 28 kilometres distant. Barèges parades its own col signs, duplicating those set up by the departmental organisation.

At 8.5km to the col, the road enters a 'pastoral zone', the Zone Tourmalet, and warns of 'animals at liberty' – sheep and kine. To the left stretches a wide strip of open ground, riverbanks, a ski chalet and, at around 7.5km a left fork dips down into the shallow valley and tiptoes up to the ski station at Superbarège. The right fork enters a short flattish section in the shade of trees, then descends to a bridge over the Escoubous torrent which plunges off the Massif de Néouvielle. There is a sizeable café beside the bridge. A sign: 'Keep dogs on lead', also a small landing strip for mountain rescue.

Approaching the café at the Pont de la Gaubie is one of the defining moments of cycling in the Pyrenees: ahead stand the massive buttresses of the Pic de la Caoubère, beyond them, though not yet visible, the Col du Tourmalet itself. The Pic du Midi de Bigorre is visible, at 2872m towering over the col, the radio mast of the observatory bristling on its craggy, often snow-capped, summit.

Cut into the side of the rock wall which immediately confronts you is what at first looks like a long fissure at about 45°, impossibly steep. This is the road, the first kilometre section of the real climb, the final 6.5 kilometres to the col, 9%. It looks murderous.

A sharp left-hand bend and you are on it, bare rock, no shade from now on. At the top of the first ramp, the road swings right and winds on, hugging the side of the mountain wall, to the left a yawning abyss. The road zigzags out of long straight ramps at gradients hovering round 8.5–9%. The wink of light off car side-mirrors far ahead confirms the tracery of the road but it is some time before you actually see the slight sag in the line of the ridge, the yoke you are heading for.

At 4.5km to go the road swings more sinuously, and at 4km you will see the final two long ramps up to the famous Tourmalet café. This is encouraging.

The terrain all around is harsh and bleak, bare rock, no vegetation, huge cornices of stone to right and left, the antennae masts of the Pic du Midi de Bigorre now prominent. Here in the high place is where the Tourmalet gets interesting. The long approach up the valley is probably one of the more demoralising rides in these mountains, but the reward of getting to these last kilometres, taxing and slow to unfold as they will almost certainly be, is supreme. None of the hors catègorie (too high to be categorised) cols is ever easily won, but the grandeur of the Tourmalet is a very manifest prize. You see it, you get steadily closer, you claim it. There is a puerile diversion in toying with the maths: 8% = 80m gained per kilometre, but by this time you are habituated, somehow, to the severe gradient. Patience and nerve will be sorely tested, as will heart, lungs and legs, but the proximity of the col is a powerful lure and the moment of turning the final left-hand bend, imagining that the last ramp is going to be horribly long and horribly steep, is grand. The ramp is neither as long nor, in truth, as steep as feared and, quitting the 9% you've just cleared, you ride up exultantly to that ecstatic moment on the line of tarmac where the road bends its head towards the descent from the Col du Tourmalet.

Souvenir shop. Ghastly amateurish figurative monument to Jacques Goddet, 1905-2000, director of the Tour de France 1936-86, formidable successor to Henri Desgrange, the Tour's founder.

In the café, a wall-mounted display of photographs, memorabilia, old bikes – 'from the epoch', as they say in France. Roaming the slopes above the col, a small herd of llama introduced in the mid-1990s. Ralph Waldo Emerson wrote: 'The llama that will carry a load if you caress him, will refuse food and die if he is scourged.'

The view back down the way you have come is breathtaking, a favoured panorama for books about the Tour de France, the quintessence of the Pyrenean mountain climbs – the giddy zigzag of bends and the long, long perspective down to the valley floor. It's a bonny sight, and remembering it an indelible proof of what you have just achieved.

Col du Tourmalet *continued from previous page*

Eastern approach

LENGTH: 17.4 KM
HEIGHT GAIN: 1284 M
MAXIMUM GRADIENT: 10%

A steady 12 kilometre climb from Bagnères-de-Bigorre on the D935 up the valley of the Adour to Sainte-Marie-de-Campan and the junction with the D918 to the col.

Sainte-Marie-de-Campan is famous as the site of the blacksmith's forge where Eugène Christophe fabricated a pair of forks to replace those broken up on the Tourmalet when a car ran into him. (The forge is no longer there although a guest house stands on the site. It's a cross between a badly-run Youth Hostel and a boarding school a level, just, above Dotheboys Hall.)

Through the village, houses to either side, the road quite narrow, 5 kilometres of easy gradient, between 2.5 and 4%, flat meadows opening out to the left towards the gently meandering course of the river Adour de Gripp. (Adour is also the name of this part of the region of the High Pyrenees.) [18]

At 3km, the road actually runs downhill for some way before reminding itself of its primary duty, namely to go up. Hay barns, houses with trim curtilages, the familiar big woodstacks of winter fuel, three rabbits in separate hutches next to one dwelling – assuredly destined for the pot – a tranquil rural community lining the road into the hamlet of Gripp (5km) and a number of old step-gabled buildings. This is a much friendlier approach, more welcoming, more accompanied, with the presence of inhabited dwellings, fields that are being worked, a road that has a purpose beyond merely leading to a ski station.

After Gripp, the slopes tighten to a kilometre of 7% and then a steady 3 kilometre progress of 8% to the numerous chalets of Artigues-Campan and its Zone Touristique down to the left (8km). A large number of chambres d'hôtes, gîtes and eateries, principally a centre for mountain walking and horse trekking in summer, cross-country skiing in winter as well as guided tours of the locale and folklore. The road continues past Artigues into trees on the right and 5 kilometres of hard gradients – 9 and 10%. A large bend, the 'Garet hairpin' (10km, some 7.5 kilometres from the col) and the powerful Cascade du Garet. A bit further on another, the Cascade des Arises, a waft of cool air and the happy burble of water helter-skeltering down a rock gully through the trees. It may take your mind off the extreme labour of the climb. Or not.

The road straightens again over a bridge; there are glimpses above the trees of the mountain flanks up ahead, together with a sense that you are getting close to where the road breaks cover and the full challenge is laid down. A long ramp of broad open road takes you into the first snow tunnel (11km), an ugly, gloomy passage, and continues to a more exposed stretch till, at around 12km, the trees peter out and the road loses all pretence at rustic attractiveness. The high ridges begin to show themselves ahead.

Three more snow tunnels, the first supported on steel pillars, across its canopy at the upper end in white paint 'Gino's Aussies', without explanation. A reservoir down to the right in a basin below steep mountain slopes, and three precipitous torrents shooting down from the ridges. A short way on, still at 9%, you ride into the concrete sprawl of La Mongie, (13.2km) the ski station. Plenty of bars, hotels, car parks and festoons of Christmas lights without a shred or glimmer of charm. The road is wide, often commandeered by cattle who, tiring of the bare grass beyond the verges, amble into town for amusement and possibly discarded grub.

Out of town the road is a big fat slob of highway past a string of ugly hotels, no better than a large building site for new developments of chalet villages and apartment blocks.

Some 3 kilometres from the col the road begins to dance – long hairpins and 9%. This is the domain of the Basque fans where the camper vans line the route bumper to bumper when the Tour passes. The col isn't quite visible until the last stretch, but the view back down from that narrow pass in what the Gascons call 'the bad detour', even despite the grim constructional rubbish tip of La Mongie in the foreground, is fine.

---

18 There are a number of 'Adours' – feeder rivers flowing from Payolle, Gripp (below the Tourmalet) Lesponne (further north) which merge somewhat confusingly at Bagnères-de-Bigorre to form the main Adour, which then flows north and then west in a big curve for 335 kilometres into the Bay of Biscay just below Bayonne. The source of the river is held to be below the Tourmalet.

TOUR DE FRANCE 1910-1974

L'incontournable… 'The unavoidable'

The first man across the col in 1910 was Octave 'Curly' Lapize, but he walked part of the way and then famously raged at Desgrange and the organisers. Half an hour behind him but on his bike – around 15kg with 450gm tyres – the whole way came Gustave Garrigou, winner the following year.

As if the cruel effort of getting over the cols were not enough in itself, the rules were draconian: the riders had to carry everything they needed and come in with everything they started out with. They were forbidden any material assistance. Desgrange could do nothing about moral assistance – spectators did get to the cols to stare in wonder at these freaks of nature on two wheels. Special trains from Paris to the south diverted via Lourdes to bring avid fans – men in stiff collars and panama hats, women in gay bonnets and pleated skirts – to the heartland of the Tour.

The oft-told story of the watchmaker Eugène Christophe's heroic refusal to give in when his forks broke on the Tourmalet in 1913 symbolises the courage and endurance which lie at the core of the great bike race. He shouldered his bike, ran 14 kilometres to a blacksmith's forge in Sainte-Marie de Campan, repaired the machine and rode on. The repair took 2 hours and he was docked a further 10 minutes because, having only the one pair of hands himself he asked a young boy to pump the bellows for him. In the early days they rode fixed wheels with a choice of two gears only – uphill and downhill, and changed by swapping the wheel round. When freewheels became the norm, riders pissed on them when they got clogged with mud. They even pissed on their frozen hands for some warmth.

In 1924 Bottechia crossed the Aubisque in a staggering 37min 40sec and, at the top of the Tourmalet, had increased his lead to nearly 11 minutes. Federico Bahamontes, six-times winner of the mountains prize, and overall winner in 1959, led over the Tourmalet a record four times. The Eagle of Toledo announced himself as a magisterial climber in 1954 when, way out in front, he stopped for an ice cream at the Tourmalet café to wait for the others, being a bit wobbly on the descents. In 1961, a little-known regional rider, Marcel Quchcille, who'd won a stage in 1959, entered the ranks of the Tour immortals when he crossed the Tourmalet alone ahead of the race. The applause stunned him. 'I breathed a sigh of relief when I crossed the summit. This Tourmalet frightened me.' In July 1969, on the 17th stage of the Tour de France, as the American space capsule headed for the moon, Merckx attacked just below the banner marking the top of the Tourmalet and kept going. This was folly of superhuman dimension. There were 140 kilometres yet to race. At the foot of the Soulor he lead a small group, among them Poulidor and the 1968 winner Pingeon, by a minute. They gave chase but could not catch him and amid the flurry of eulogy and rapture, one journalist advised an elementary prudence in the use of superlatives 'in expectation of the exploits to come. Economise, therefore, economise.' In 1974, the Tour crossed the Tourmalet twice on consecutive days and Jean-Pierre Danguillaume, not a specialist climber, won both stages.

After Merckx's great solo escape, the veteran Tour addict, novelist Antoine Blondin who once assessed his occupation as 'following the Tour de France', described the Tourmalet as 'planet Merckx'. Nowadays it's planet orange, favoured pitch of the hordes of Basque fans who invest the slopes of the Pyrenean climbs.

Col d'Aspin 1489m

Western approach

LENGTH:	5.7 KM
HEIGHT GAIN:	406 M
MAXIMUM GRADIENT:	8%

The road south from Bagnères-de-Bigorre follows the course of the Adour River. The hot springs at Bagnères were noted by the Greek geographer Strabo (64/3 BC - 21 AD): 'most beautiful springs of very drinkable waters'. The town, known as 'The Athens of the Pyrenees' is less opulent than its neighbour in Luchon and today sports a slightly faded elegance, although it was once quite as popular. The French essayist Montaigne (1533-92) came here, as to other spas, seeking a cure for excruciating kidney stone and gravel (aggregations of urinary crystals) to which he was a martyr. The composer Rossini was a visitor, as were Flaubert and Georges Sand. To the south of the town is Le Cycloscope à Citécycle (www.citecycle.com) an interactive museum devoted to the bicycle housed in a former yarn mill, and a Pyrénées Sport Hôtel which offers massage and various other therapeutic treatments, especially aimed at cyclists. (It's not cheap.)

Through Campan, at 6km. 'Campan' is an Occitan derivation from Latin campus (plain, level country), and designates 'cultivated land' (campanha).

Every summer, the locals plant straw-stuffed dummies of varying sizes, dressed in a range of clothes, male and female, all over their properties – on windowsills and balconies, and in doorways, courtyards, gardens and front rooms peering out onto the street. These altogether spooky mounaques are part of a rather sinister ancient tradition.

In the upper valley of the Adour, the eldest child of any family, male or female, inherited the entire family wealth – land, animals and house. It was therefore considered unacceptable for two heirs to marry and establish too rich a patrimony; better for a younger daughter or son to marry an heir and thus keep the wealth more evenly spread. It was considered particularly reprehensible for an heir to marry someone from outside the village and take the property away, just as village custom looked askance at a widower marrying a young girl or a widow remarrying. If the bachelors of the village disapproved of a betrothal, the affianced man or woman was subjected to the so-called charivari for a month ahead of the wedding: every night the young men mounted what in Suffolk used to be called the 'Rough Band' – a cacophonous serenade outside the house generated by a rowdy jangling of cowbells, kettles and pans beaten with iron bars and the like. In addition, two mounaques, one male one female, were suspended from the wall of the house. From Spanish mona (long-tailed monkey – the local dialect hereabouts has many affinities with Catalan), it also means 'an ugly woman, a fright' and the mounaques were reckoned to portray the faults of the betrothed pair. After the wedding, the newly-weds walked under the mounaques into the house and the charivari would end and the rag-doll taboos be removed… provided the couple paid over enough money to fund a good blow-out for the disappointed rough bandsmen. The tradition of making the Campan mounaques was revived in the early 1990s as a summertime tourist attraction. They are removed in winter. ('Charivari' is a French word of unknown origin, first recorded in the 14th century but certainly of older date in usage.)

Engraved in a stone tympanum above a house in the main street of Campan, this injunction against covetous impatience:

Vous qui vivez en cette demeure
Vous êtes bien et tenez-vous y
Et n'allez pas chercher à midi
Quatorz heures.

You who dwell herein
Remember, life's a boon,
So do not look for problems
Where there is none.

Just after Campan lies the village of Beaudean, birthplace of Dominique Larrey (1766-1842), appointed Surgeon-in-Chief to Napoleon's army in 1805 and one of the first to practise the therapeutic use of maggots for cleaning wounds. He also introduced ambulances for conveying the wounded from the field of battle and a triage system of treatment.

The 17 kilometres from Bagnères-de-Bigorre are easy enough, the worst a sudden steep pitch round a lefthander a short way out of Sainte-Marie-de-Campan which feels worse than it is because it is sudden. It doesn't last long and drops away to restore the balance.

The next 4 kilometres are gentle, through the village of La Séoube and on past the left-hand turn to the Col de Beyrède to Payolle, then the Lac de Payolle (fed by the Adour, here no more than a 'torrent' mountain stream) to the right and, if the horizon is clear, a long view of the domed complex of buildings and radio masts of the astronomical centre on top of the Pic du Midi de Bigorre high above the Tourmalet.

Past the roads to the Hourquette d'Ancizan (right) and the Auberge des Trois Pics (left), the climb proper starts on a big right-hand bend. The road which loops round the Beyrède joins to the left close to the Espiadet quarry which furnished marble columns for the Grand Trianon, a fine miniature palace in Versailles, the Opéra in Paris and the 18th-century palace of Sans Souci in Potsdam, where Voltaire lived for three years (1750-53) as a guest of Frederick the Great of Prussia.

This climb, a relatively undemanding 5 kilometres, kicks off sharply at 9%, but for the rest of the way, on an excellent surface, is nowhere steeper than 8.5% and then only briefly. It's bosky, quiet, secluded, beautiful. Right-hand hairpins are very steep on the inside, the left-handers gentle.

From lower down, the view back across the bracken, broom, gorse and outcrops of rock round and beyond the lake to the Massif de Néouvielle is splendid. The Aspin itself opens up in the final 1.5 kilometres above the tree line, the neckline of the col fully visible ahead. Emerging from a short avenue of trees at 0.5km it eases onto a smooth summit much frequented by cows, (intermittently frisky, even mildly belligerent, in quest of food), from which another grand panorama shows itself southwards across the valley of the Aure, a high dog-tooth battlement of rock marking the frontier with Spain. An exhilarating sight of the switchback descent and the distant valley bottom, too.

Eastern approach

LENGTH: 12.6 KM

HEIGHT GAIN: 800 M

MAXIMUM GRADIENT: 10%

A much more testing climb from this side but a breezy descent.

From Arreau, the ancient capital of the valley straddling a confluence of several small rivers, northwards on the D929 and left onto the 918 which winds through trees at a steady pitch no worse than 5% for 3 kilometres. Here the cover thins out disclosing a large wooded slope across the valley to the right. A sudden flourish of hairpins gets the climb moving but the gradients are mild, 4 kilometres of 5.5–6.5%. At 8 kilometres from the col, the terraces along which the road travels join more closely and the bends get smaller merely presenting a short flick of a turn onto the next stretch. From this point the road is more exposed, generally not masked by trees, but a very attractive ride nonetheless, the longish views of the road ahead actually enhanced by the opening of the valley's wide spaces to the left.

At around 4.5 kilometres from the col, there is a nasty rise in pitch, the 10% of the declared maximum and its abrupt gate-crashing of the more placid gradients without obvious good reason. The slope eases again as the road, clear of the sparse lining of trees, becomes in effect a long shelf along the hillside, crosses a torrent and offers a distant view of the col. At 1 kilometre from the summit trees reappear, and the road swings sweetly to its finish where the border patrols of cattle amble lazily and defecate at will across the bitumen and the loose stones of the car pull-off.

COL D'ASPIN 1938

A humiliating exit

Georges Speicher, born in Paris in 1907, came to cycling late in what at the time was considered to be a droll, roundabout way: via swimming. Not so today.

'I was nearly seventeen years old,' he said, 'and was out of work, then I spotted a small ad for a bike delivery man. I didn't even know how to get on a bike let alone ride one, but, I needed to earn my living and I presented myself. The first few days, I rode next to the pavement, pedalling with my left leg and steadying myself with my right foot on the asphalt.' (France has driven on the right since the Revolution.) A year later he was beating his friends in pick-up races and then joined the Vélo Club de Levallois (on the left bank of the Seine just north of the Bois de Boulogne) and got his first licence. He turned pro in 1932, rode his first Tour that year and came tenth. The following year he trumped that considerable début with a *succès fou*: three stage victories and the overall in the Tour de France.

Very tall with a velvety pedalling action, Speicher was a natural and the team he joined in 1933 was exceptional: in 1930 Charles Pélissier took what was a record eight stage victories,[19] Leducq won overall and again in 1932, Antonin Magne won overall in Speicher's début Tour, Roger Lapébie got his overall win in 1937 and Maurice Archambaud won the inaugural Grand Prix des Nations in 1932.

The 1933 route went east to west and included several cols which hadn't been visited for some time, including the Peyresourde and Aspin. The Italian Martano attacked in the Pyrenees and on the Tourmalet he was in yellow on the road, ahead of Speicher. But the Frenchman would not be shaken off: on the descent he took the overall lead and never lost it.

To that yellow he added the rainbow jersey at Monthléry later that year. He wasn't originally selected to ride the Worlds, but a rider dropped out on the eve of the race and reportedly Speicher was finally located in a cinema and jobbed into the team. He'd done no specific training but, 48 kilometres from the start he attacked on his own and stayed clear for the next 200 kilometres to win. In 1934 he took 5 stages in the Tour – the French team took 20 of the 23 stage wins – and

[19] Later equalled by Merckx in 1970 and Freddy Maertens in 1976.

came 11th overall behind his team-mate Magne. Next year he took the last of his nine Tour stage victories and became national champion for the first of three times (1935/37/39).

Apart from the victory by a German, Fischer, in the inaugural Paris-Roubaix, 1897, French riders dominated the Hell of the North until 1922 when Dejonghe ushered in a string of Belgian wins which lasted until 1944 with only four interruptions: the Swiss Suter in 1923, the Frenchman Leducq, 1928, Speicher in 1937 and the Italian Rossi, 1938. (Contemporary documents say that Speicher was actually beaten by half a wheel by Romain Maes.)

That victory in the doyen of the Classics was the penultimate win of Speicher's curiously imbalanced career. In 1938 he won nothing and, on the slopes of the Col d'Aspin in the Tour de France, he was ejected ignominiously from the race to which he had brought such flair and class. Struggling to keep pace, he had held onto a car and taken a ride. 'Dismissed from the race'. A sad end. (Jacky Durand went the same way in 2002.)

Col de Beyrède 1417m

Three approaches

FROM BEYRÈDE VILLAGE: 5KM & 12.2KM
MAXIMUM GRADIENT: 11%

From Beyrède village (710m), a steep ramp out of D107 (cul-de-sac) to Jumet and a sharp right-hand bend onto the narrow road towards the col; this forks left at about 5km with another approach to the right (12.2km) offering a better surface but a steeper ascent.

FROM PAYOLLE 8KM: 12.2KM
MAXIMUM GRADIENT: 8.5%

From Payolle, a road (the sign says 'recommended route') off the D918 which follows the Adour de Payolle and on up to the Col d'Aspin.

FROM D918: 10.2KM
MAXIMUM GRADIENT: 11%

Mountain bikes only: From higher up the D918 just south of Payolle where a forest track, off which branches other unmettalled forest tracks, joins near the marble quarry. A narrow, fairly good surface, through dense conifer woodland hemming in the route on either side with occasional wider clearings for around 2 kilometres following the nearby course of a stream. At about 2.5, 3.5 and 4.5 kilometres from the col (no km signs so only a guess, could be 2, 3 and 4km) unpaved stretches – no obvious reason why – of 200m, 100m and 200m: loose stones, uneven surface but rideable with no great difficulty, so revisit the conditions of the Tour de France of yesteryear. The second of these two rougher stretches had a big pile of newly-chopped logs to the left and the road was strewn with shards of bark, so maybe they have been chewed up by logging teams and vehicles. The road is frequently traversed by metal drainage gutters, the lips sunk just below the level of the road – easy enough to ride over on the ascent but a potential hazard on the descent when the back wheel takes a hell of a thump. At around 5km, a large clearing as the road takes a big sweep round to the right; a sign announces 'Auberge du Col de Beyrède 3km' and the trees begin to thin a little, which always suggests the summit is near. Straight ahead off the clearing, a forest trail, unmetalled. Very few views on the way up – the tree cordons lower down are so thick, but here now a glimpse of the ranges way off to the left, a veiled blurred outline of the range above which towers the Pic du Midi de Bigorre.

The gradient is fairly constant, around 6–7% with occasional jumps in steepness, particularly at the foot of the climb, but by and large this is a straightforward haul and, just above the clearing and turn, a sight of a ridge to the left, small clumps of trees dotted about a bare hillside. When the road does break clear of the trees it is onto bare moorland, outcrops of rock, with the line of trees way off to the right and receding up the shallow slopes of the surrounding hill to the left. A sudden flattish stretch of about 300m to what turns out to be a false summit, looking down over a deep plunge into the cleft of a gully separating this ridge from another some 2 kilometres further on, which actually looks lower than this rise. A wild spot, bleak and unvisited.

Down a steepish clutch of unsheltered hairpins satisfyingly visible from the false col, some loose

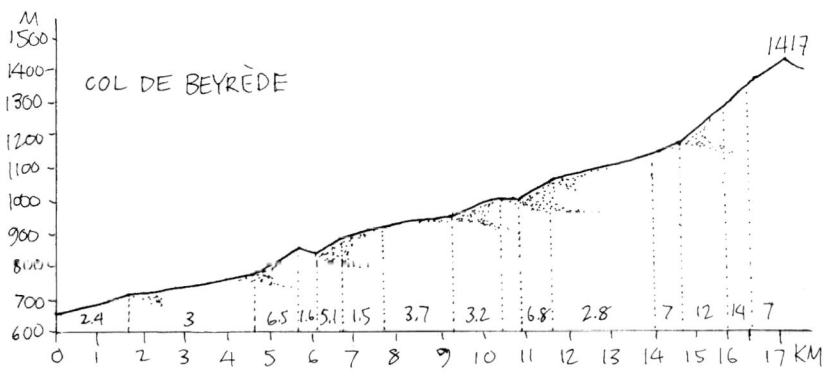

gravel on the surface, to an uphill of no great gradient on a better surface, then through trees to the final uphill which leads over the junction with the road up from the quarry and on to the Auberge (a known visitor who stayed there described it as 'quirky but good value') and the col itself (1417m). A number of cars – obviously a venue for picnickers and walkers – and a fine view both ways across the barren heath and on across the Vallée d'Aure. The alternative route from Beyrède joins just below the col, but the left-hand fork is smoother.

The descent, in truth more of a mountain road than the ascent just described and well-surfaced, shows a generally steeper and longer climb – c.10.2 kilometres as against c.7 kilometres with a maximum of 11% in a particularly hard stretch of 3 kilometres or so near the col – than the one from Payolle. After an exposed top section then through woodland, mostly deciduous, about halfway. Some concrete drainage gutters, less troublesome than the metal grooves, and a cattle grid, easy to see because it's been painted in tricolour – red, white and blue. In a narrow defile of the valley, 4 kilometres down, a series of some six or seven steep-roofed barns, the Granges d'Estupo, none showing any sign of life, no piles of mown grasses anywhere to be seen, but not dilapidated.

A fine winding road which in the wet as I came down wasn't as freewheeling as it would be in the dry – sure indicator of an excellent descent. A sign shows Beyrède at 4km, and about 2 kilometres from town the road passes through a long tunnel of trees before emerging into the open and the final drop to the turn for the nondescript cluster of houses which is Beyrède – a solitary restaurant.

Hourquette d'Ancizan 1560m

Eastern approach

LENGTH: 9.8 KM

HEIGHT GAIN: 810M

MAXIMUM GRADIENT: 10%

This climb makes a very attractive alternative to the Col d'Aspin: wild, remote, tranquil. The word 'hourquette' is Gascon for 'fork', applied to a vee-shaped breech in the mountain wall linking two valleys. A Gascon saying, *lou hourquet de paouso couano,* (the col on which to set your crust), means 'time to pause', that is to put off any thought of the steep climb ahead and the long distance still to go.

From the D929 between Saint-Lary-Soulan and Arreau, the narrow D113 winds nervously up out of the tiny village of Guchen at 9–10% past a stream to the right and a stolid hydro-electric station round some very tight bends, well shaded and onto a stretch with fine views back down to the valley road over Guchen and Ancizan (a short distance south from Guchen).

This is rustic riding at its best – the woodland to the side of the road is home to deer and gaps in the trees give peek-a-boo glimpses of the ridge ahead. There are no signs. At around 5km the shutter on the view-finder opens: the way ahead and up to the distant ridge and the crests of the Arbizon massif, right down to the valley and south past Saint-Lary-Soulan… this is the real-time film reel of cycling a high road not much more than a car's breadth to a lonely col, steep (a couple of kilometres at 7 and 6.5% two-thirds of the way up slacken the more persistent 8–7.5). Nearing the top, some flatter stretches make the average more flattering, but for most of the way this col plays hard to get, masking itself behind the veils of encroaching pine trees and giving little respite in a steady hard pitch of climbing.

Then, quite suddenly, the tough stuff is over and it smiles. At about 300m from the col, the road breaks out onto bare country and so to where the road tips over the summit beside a refuge. A sign on its gate reads 'Donkeys M and F, all ages' – for sale, that is, not a note of residents. The small, stone-built chalet, one room up, one down, is used by the local shepherdess during the summer. In conversation with me in early October, she said she'd be taking the flocks down to the winter byres quite soon – the pasturage was all but nibbled away and 'Ça sent la fin,' (the air has the scent of the [season's] end).

The col itself is part of the Zone Pastorale des Quatre Véziaux and the view is glorious – the descending road snaking away below across a trough of upland heath and moor girded by the heights of the Arbizon and the distant peaks which loom over the Tourmalet to the west.

Western approach

LENGTH: 10.4 KM
HEIGHT GAIN: 477M
MAXIMUM GRADIENT: 7.5%

An easier approach and very different in scenic character, most of the way over open country with some stretches through woodland set back from wide border grassland. The land beside the Adour is known as the Battlefield, commemorating the final defeat of the Aquitani by the Romans, c.28 BC.

The gradients are not so severe either, nothing more than 7.5% about 3 kilometres from the base of the climb where the road crosses a bridge over a stream.

There is a restaurant and Centre de Vacances at Payolle, a popular centre for randonneurs (hikers), campers and one-day out-and-back strollers. The road towards the Hourquette turns off across an open stretch of furze, along and across the course of a small stream and heads into a cordon of trees. For 6 kilometres, marked by yellow-capped borne stones, the gradient is easy enough and the prospect comforting; forest tracks lead off to right and left. Out of the trees and there opens up a long view ahead, the road traversing moorland, its grass cropped close by sheep. A tiny shrine perches on a large boulder to the left. Around 5km there is a sheltering cordon of beeches, after which the road breaks out into the open again and a side turning leads to the Cabanes de Camoudiet, a clutch of summer huts for shepherds tending the sheep and cows moved up from the winter byres, with drystone enclosures for the animals attached. There are predators roaming these high places.

The road dips for a kilometre and a half to cross the Ruisseau (stream) d'Artigou tumbling over boulders and on down the slope, then climbs just over 3 kilometres at between 5.5 and 7% to the col.

5. Bear's Jaw

The principal feature of this region is the massive rock galleries of the Cirques, the unbreached rampart at the southern limit which made the Pyrenees for so long a natural fortress separating France and Spain.

In the local dialect 'Ossau' means 'Bear's Jaw', likening the valley of the Ossau River, at the western end, to the throat of the Pyrenean bear once indigenous, now reintroduced. A graphic description, therefore, of the long oesophageal gorges cutting up into the lower slopes of the mighty mountain rampart wall which so decisively puts its stamp on this central region of the chain. Here the border with Spain straddles some of the most grandiose of all Pyrenean peaks: Grande Fache… Vignemale… Boucharo… Cirque de Gavarnie… Troumouse. Except at the western end where the Col du Pourtalet breaches the wall, the roads peter out into dead-ends of impassable rock and only walkers have access to the high way across.

This area is now dominated by the Parc National des Pyrénées, but for centuries its denizens resisted any form of outside interference, especially from Paris. Feudal lords claimed inalienable sovereignty over their demesnes and the Catholic Church muscled in where it could, bishops being quite as seigneurial in temper and greedy for land and power as any secular grandee. Whether by God or the sword, autonomy was what counted. Paris, in the person of the King's administrators, the Royal Intendants, did eventually impose external governance in 1607, but the law cannot change a mood for independence, while taxes only exacerbate it. The French Revolution sought to homogenise all France with a bewildering system of communal divisions and conglomerating administrative rules, but things are always different on the ground, especially with people who have an atavistic view of their

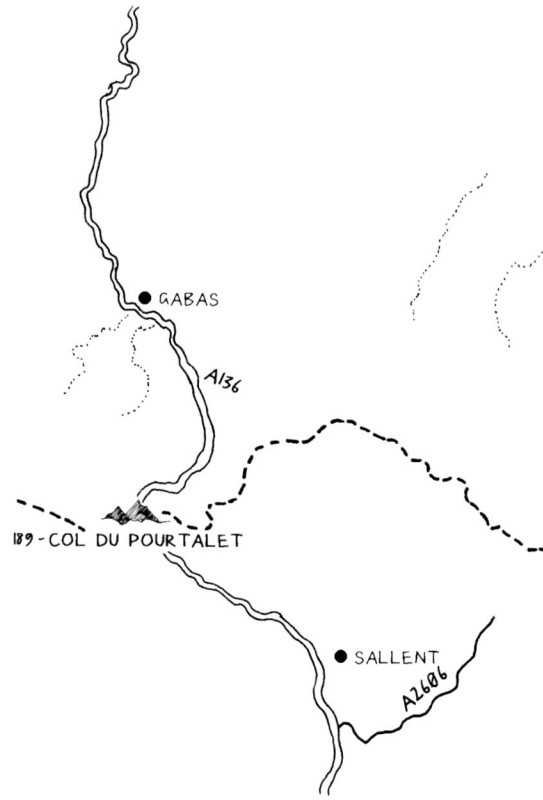

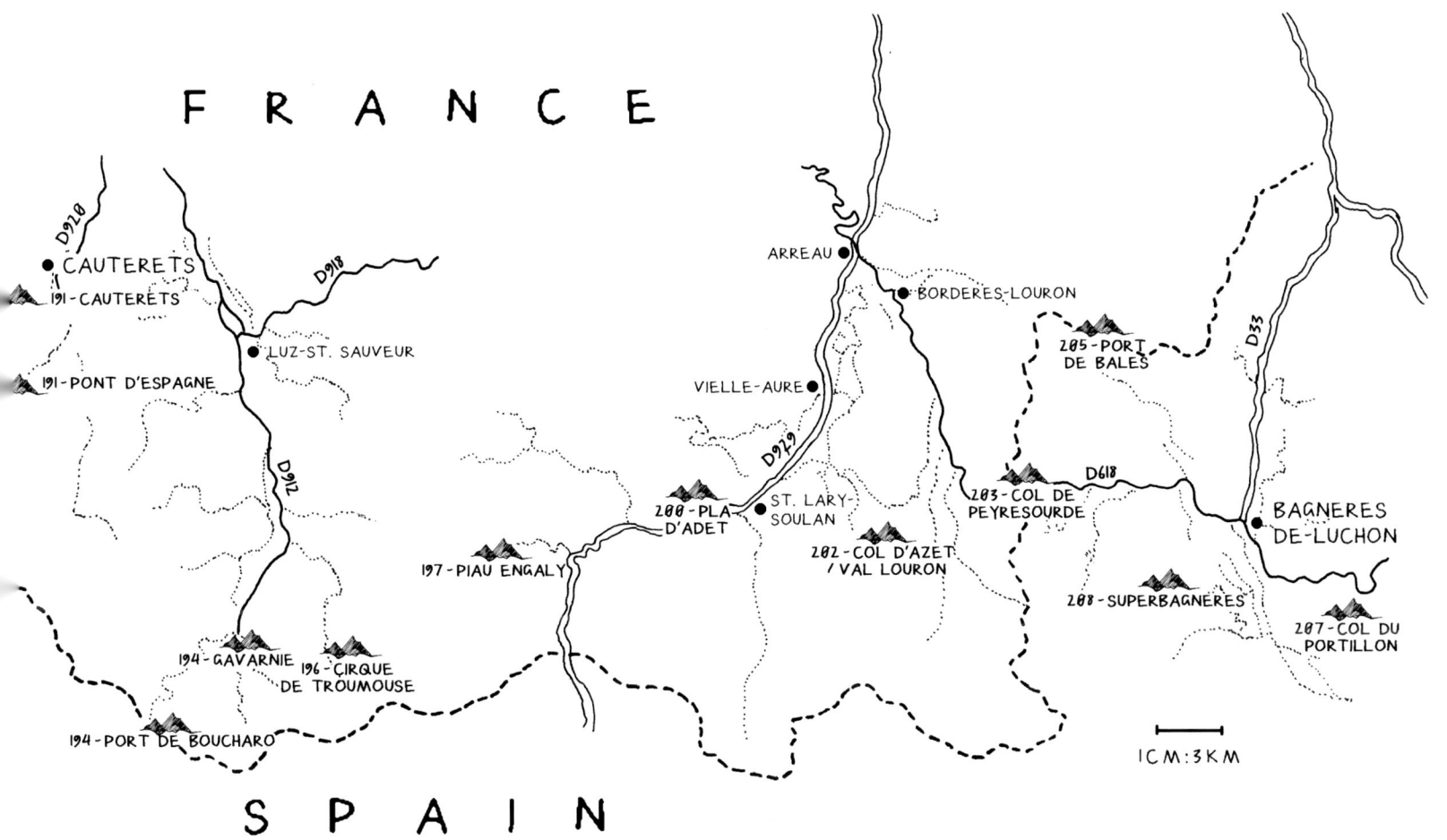

own independence. The Basques were never fully absorbed and the communities of Bear's Jaw, like many others along the chain, scoff heartily at the Marseillaise, Parisian dictate and northern city accents.

A story to illustrate: the men of Massat (in The Four Valleys) have long had a reputation for aggressive pugnacity. Soon after the outbreak of the Second World War, when the news filtered down to the communities of the Bas-Pyrénées that France – Paris – had surrendered and things looked bleak, two men from a neighbouring commune, Seix, were discussing their plight.

'Which side are the Massatois on,' said one, 'French or German?' (Even the question points up the uncertain wider loyalties of these mountain people.)

'Oh,' said the other 'France, apparently.'

'Phew,' replied the first, patently believing that the impetus of the united Massatois, all fifty or so of them, on the wider conflict would tip the balance decisively, 'then we're okay.'

P179 Departmental sign

P180 The western ascent of the *Peyresourde*

P182 A snaky tranquil road heading for the ascent to the *Cirque de Troumouse*

P184 *Val Louron* seen from the heights of *Pla d'Adet*

P186 The imposing ramparts between France and Spain from the *Port de Boucharo*

P188 The Franco-Spanish border atop the *col du Portillon*, the camera is in Spain

Col du Pourtalet 1794m

From the north

LENGTH: 30 KM
HEIGHT GAIN: 1269 M
MAXIMUM GRADIENT: 8 %

The D934 wriggles out of Laruns and continues past the left turn-off towards the Aubisque near a kiosk selling a lively selection of local cheeses and charcuterie. It heads straight into a closely-walled gorge, the Gave d'Ossau, the river which names this area. The surface is chancy, the brooding rock clammy, the air quite chilly. Over a bridge and an easy doddle into the small spa of Les Eaux-Chaudes, a miserable place, the bath-house exuding a distinct air of neglect. Eaux-Chaudes never feels anything better than shut.

A z-bend over the Pont d'Enfer breaks into sunlight and the Pourtalet, now part of the Camino de Santiago, begins to be rather more fun. There is a long drop from just after 5km (700m) and virtually no height gain, to 6km, 710m. 7km rises to only 740m and 8km to 760m. At Miégebat, a hydroelectric station built in 1925, the climb begins to hint at its presence ahead. Around 10km, 900m, the hairpins begin, rounding a curious topiary garden to the left. More gradual descent at 11.5km, the gorge widening to the left, then rolling over a good surface into the village of Gabas (13km, 1020m) – a bar and three hotels. Gabas marks the beginning of the climb proper, though it's more of a change in feel than any heavy hit of gradient.

The road surface deteriorates into Artouste (16.5km, 1110m) – another large hydro-electric plant – and, just beyond, a reservoir, a dam, and a télécabine to the ski station at Sagette, 4 kilometres away. A massive barrage wall a bit further on has been stencilled with red ursine paw prints plus an accompanying legend: 'NON A LA REINTRODUCTION' (No to the reintroduction [of bears]). As the road loses height again, a profile of high peaks appears on the skyline and at 19km, 1280m, a turn-off leads to the ski station and le Petit Train d'Artouste. Constructed in 1924 to carry men and materials the 10 kilometres from Sagette for the building of the barrage at the Lac d'Artouste (1989m) close to the border ridge, the railway line is the highest in Europe and has been a tourist attraction since the 1930s.

For 3 kilometres, the road crosses a flat valley pan, looping apart or snaking in parallel with the river, like skeins of wool. Torrents flow off the rock, the scenery grows wilder, the gradient sets at a hardened 7–8% for a further 3 kilometres through a series of concrete snow tunnels. The final metres ease at 5.5% as the road winds and shimmies up away from the river towards the frontier, dancing and jinking past a parapet wall. This bridge of a pass once did service to donkeys laden with merchandise, across the bare rock of the Pic du Midi d'Ossau's skirts. Although the climb is not hard, it is long and carries an agreeable sensation of inching up to a veritable mountain rooftop. This is confirmed by arrival on the plateau whereon is set the Col itself. Momentous, satisfying, grateful.

The motley assemblage of shops, bars and nick-nack emporia on the Pourtalet is dismal in aspect and the first kilometres of the broad highway into Spain far from encouraging. There is a new ski centre under construction and the access to it, newly widened and resurfaced, is ugly. The vile basura (rubbish) dump it goes past merely underlines the horror that *urbanización* often brings with it. Fortunately this does not extend far and the Pourtalet's southern approach quickly becomes pleasant enough: reservoirs, small towns, easy riding.

After the turn off to the ski town at El Formigal (1510m, c.6km) the road sprouts a verge cycle lane and offers a good fast descent all the way to Biescas, from where Fernando Escartín hails. A tunnel at around 11km is forbidden to cyclists but there is a circumventory path

TOUR DE FRANCE 1991
Changing of the guard

The Tour de France has crossed the Pourtalet (a Languedocien word meaning 'small port or mountain pass') once only, in 1991. Classified as first category, it laid down the gauntlet on the second ferocious day in the Pyrenees over the Aubisque, Soulor, Tourmalet, Aspin and the finish on Val Loroun.

Lemond, the 1990 winner, had abandoned on the 1991 Giro, suffering from terminal fatigue and his showing in the Tour of Switzerland didn't promise much better. Yet on the eve of the Tour, he was in bullish mood. Chiappucci, the previous year's runner-up, was scathing about the American. (He had lost yellow to Lemond in the final time trial.) Asked about his favourites to win, he said: 'Breukink and Induraín, in that order, then Rooks, Theunisse and Bugno.'

'And Lemond?'

'You can't win the lottery every year.'

Lemond was riled.

'Chiappucci just mouths off. He's so damned glib. I'll take care of him.'

He set off well and arrived in the Pyrenees in yellow. But on this overture in the mountains, Pau-Jaca, 192 kilometres over the Soudet and the Somport, the big favourites, the hard men, put him through the mincer. He was obliged to organise the pursuit, working like a lowly domestique (a team member who rides for the leader) with none of the mastery shown in similar circumstances by Anquetil… Merckx… Hinault. He finished the stage in a state of near collapse, his features creased and furrowed with effort. The following day, on the mammoth stage from Jaca to Val Louron, 233 kilometres, Peter de Clerq, riding as a team mate with Johan Bruyneel, took the Pourtalet prime, but it was on the Tourmalet that the dénouement of the drama unfolded. At 700 metres from the top, Chiappucci, now in the polka dots, unleashed a murderous attack. The others followed but Lemond had nothing and the moment for the seizure of power came and went. He had crested the rise of his ascendancy in the Tour and he watched them go. Chiappucci and Induraín eventually rode up to Val Louron in tandem – the Lombard took the stage, the Basque yellow and a firm grip on his first overall victory. Lemond came in, beaten, 7min 18sec down.

Cauterets 934m and Pont d'Espagne 1496m

From Pierrefitte-Nestalas

LENGTH: 19.2 KM

HEIGHT GAIN: 1011M

MAXIMUM GRADIENT: 11%

The 1995 Tour finished on the Crêtes de Lys, the ski station above Cauterets, but has never gone to the Pont d'Espagne. However, the cirque of rock walls marking the frontier barrier, so characteristic of the Bear's Jaw climbs, is spectacular and the ski station is just that, homogeneous as an airport.

The ten or so kilometres into Cauterets itself are fairly mild on a well-maintained road, the D920, up the pretty Gorge de Cauterets topped with rocks that bristle like small fortifications. Nothing worse than about 6%.

Follow the D920 out of Cauterets, and, at the first outcrop of bars and restaurants, sniff deep of the lingering sulphurous odours, the trademark whiff of the Pyrenean thermal station. Water pours in cascades off the mountain too. The road has a lot of swing in it, plenty of tree shade and a satisfyingly steep final section, 4 kilometres of 9-11%. It tops out at around 8.5% for the run-in to the large parking area below the massive rock wall along the frontier and the old stone bridge which names the place. The view of this spectacular chunk of Pyrenean rock alone makes the ride up worthwhile and the descent is a double reward.

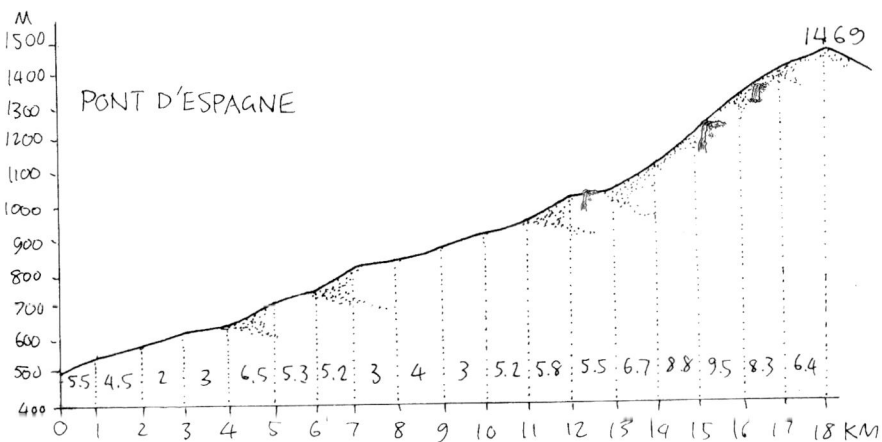

TOUR DE FRANCE 1953

Suicide and low cunning...

The 10th stage of the 1953 Tour, Pau-Cauterets, 13 July, marked the first time that the race arrived atop a Pyrenean mountain, albeit a lowly 934m. L'Alpe d'Huez marked the first ever cul-de-sac stage finish, in 1952.

At Eaux-Bonnes, early on the climb of the Aubisque, three riders went clear: André Darrigade, Umberto Drei and the Swiss Marcel Huber, policing the attack for his leader, Hugo Koblet, overall winner in 1951. A small group of big guns, including Louison Bobet (en route to the first of his three victories) reacted and, a short way on, Koblet himself upped his rhythm. Nicknamed 'the pedaller of charm' Koblet not only had a supple elegance of powering a bike but a classy way with psyching out the opposition: he always carried a comb in his pocket and was wont to ride up alongside other riders on a climb, sit up and comb his hair as if they were on the flat and preparing for a photo call.

Accelerating hard he passed everyone, save for the Spaniard Jesús Lorono who crossed the col alone. Koblet was moving at such speed that it was generally agreed this was suicide and he couldn't last long.

The clouds were low and all morning they rode through a veil of chilly fine rain. To stave off the cold, Koblet applied heat-bearing plasters to his upper body and reins. But, even before the bends leading into Gourette, the road emerged above the cloud cover into bright sunshine; the temperature shot up instantly by 7 or 8° C and Koblet found himself swaddled in a personalised sauna. On the descent towards the balcony of the Soulor, he tried to tear off the plasters but doing it on the move, at speed, was too precarious. He overheated, lost his rhythm, began to zigzag and suddenly, 2.5 kilometres from the top near a small bridge, he pitched headfirst over the bike into the heather and just lay there, insensible. Multiple cuts and abrasions aside, he had broken several ribs.

Even as he was lifted into a vehicle on a stretcher, he whispered to the team mate who had stopped to attend to him: 'Get back in the race.'

Not long afterwards, the young French regional, Guy Buchaille, overcooked a bend and flew head over heels into a precipice. Luckily, he landed on a platform of interwoven branches. His bike kept going, 300m down to the bottom.

Winner of this short (103 kilometres) but dramatic stage into Cauterets in front of the Thermes César, Place du Victoire, was Lorono.

Later that very night, in cloak and dagger secrecy, the directeur sportif of the Breton team, Léon le Calvez, executed a plan hatched by his leader, Jean Robic, to assist him on the descent of the Tourmalet next day. Robic, (overall winner in 1947), being very small in height and slight of frame – five foot nothing – was always at a serious disadvantage on the downhill. Le Calvez packed an aluminium bidon in his attaché case and searched out a central-heating engineer. Money changed hands and, asking no questions, the engineer melted a quantity of lead piping and filled the container with the liquid metal. When it had set and cooled, le Calvez took the bottle, now weighing 9kg, to Robic's room for his approval. One problem: how to effect the swap without catching the hawk-like eyes of the commissaires (judges/referees). But, as Desgrange said, to win the Tour takes head – in some cases low cunning – and legs.

A few metres from the top of the Tourmalet where the commissaires habitually stationed themselves, Robic dismounted and fiddled with his headset as if it had worked loose. The mechanic, complicit in the plot, leapt out of the team car, the lead-filled bottle tucked into his dungarees, and made the swap whilst affecting to adjust the headset. Robic, now fully ballasted, flew down the mountainside like a madman, felt the front wheel wobble and went over. But, he'd got used to crashing, there was less of him to hurt than most: he recovered, made another surreptitious exchange of bidons at the foot of the climb and took the stage into Luchon.

Gavarnie 1365m / Port de Boucharo 2270m

From Luz-Saint-Sauveur

LENGTH: 32.7 KM
HEIGHT GAIN: 1560 M
MAXIMUM GRADIENT: 9%

The 20 kilometres from Luz to Gavarnie up the Gorge de Saint-Sauveur make a very agreeable tourist excursion ride. Saint-Sauveur is an old spa town, small in size, grand in masonry. The patronage of the Empress Eugénie gave it rather top-heavy imperial pretensions and the Emperor Napoléon added to its grandeur with an elegant bridge spanning the Gorge de Gavarnie, complete with flanking narrow columns and imperial eagles, wings part outspread. The word is that he wanted to leave a monument to his illegitimate conception in the town. His mother, Hortense de Beauharnais, daughter of Napoleon I's wife Josephine de Beauharnais, and married to Louis Bonaparte, the Emperor's brother, had a number of affairs and Naploeon III seems to have been the result of a liaison with an unknown lover, in the snug seclusion of a hotel near where the bridge stands. French slang 'faire le pont' (literally 'to make the bridge') means 'to make a long weekend of it'. There may be no connection but one feels there ought to be.

Not far from the bridge, in the rock wall to the left of the road is set a plaque, the engraving rather decayed, commemorating the visit to the High Pyrenees of Jean-Joseph Dusaulx in 1788. Sixty years old at the time, Dusaulx was an academician, famous as the translator of Juvenal, him of 'mens sana in corpore sano... quis custodiet ipses custodes?... panem et circenses' (a healthy mind in a healthy body... who will police the police? bread and circuses – as in 'give the mob food and entertainment and they will keep quiet'). He came to write a memoir of the effect that seeing and traversing these imposing mountains would have on him. His account of crossing a mountain torrent on a bridge made of two parallel beams extends for six pages. During the Revolution, he was a member of the National Convention for Paris and courageously voted against the death of the king: '... blood calls for blood. It is time to stop the shedding of it.' He spent some time in prison as a consequence but survived the Terror to die of natural causes in 1799.

Gèdre (1011m, 11.7km) dominated by the hydro-electric station, is famous as the home of two early Pyrenean pioneers, Henri Cazaux, a mountain guide from Luz, and his brother-in-law Bernard Guillembet. On 8 October 1837, they undertook the first publicly acknowledged ascent of the mighty Vignemale. They made their way to the top up the Ossou glacier, now an established mountain track, bivouacked at the top and came down via the Cerbillona. However, on 2 August 1792 shepherds under instructions from a surveyor, Louis-Philippe Reinhart Junker, had surmounted the Vignemale and set up signals to enable Junker to establish both the altitude and the position of the border. The names of these intrepid mountain men was never recorded, insignificant herdsmen pastorals – in Gray's words 'to dumb Forgetfulness a prey' ('Elegy written in a Country Churchyard') – like the vanished men of the peloton whose selfless, and often anonymous, labours contributed enormously to the victories of the grands seigneurs.

Let not Ambition mock their useful toil,
Their homely joys and destiny obscure;
Nor Grandeur hear, with a disdainful smile,
The short and simple annals of the poor.

From near Gèdre is visible the famous Brèche de Roland – it can't be seen from Gavarnie, higher up. Legend has it that the Brèche, a huge notch 40m wide in the 100m high curtain of rock in the Cirque de Gavarnie, was cut by the dying Roland with his sword, Durandal. Hoping to shatter the blade so that it would not be taken by the advancing Moors, instead he hewed the breach. Since the golden hilt of Durendal contained one of Saint Peter's teeth, a drop of Saint Paul (or Saint Basil)'s blood, a piece of the Virgin Mary's raiment and a lock of Saint Denis' hair, the sword's magical, even divine, properties could hardly be questioned. As he hacked and slashed at the rock, the blade neither broke nor splintered but 'leapt heavenwards'. So to save it, he cast it into a poisoned stream and it is said to have fetched up in Rocamadour in the Lot. This insignificant little town became a pilgrimage destination, for no obvious reason, and was much visited in the Middle Ages by holy men and less than holy monarchs and still draws pious dupes and sundry gullible sentimentals.

Gavarnie is a not unattractive minuscule tourist centre – shops vending souvenirs and mountain gear, bars, restaurants and hotels, donkey rides. The best place for lunch lies just out of town along the Chemin du Cirque following the course of the stream and over a bridge to La Chaumière, bar/restaurant/rooms. Eat at a table by the water and drink in the view of the Cirque, a mighty amphitheatre of rock, with a radius of (about) 6.4 kilometres and 3248m at its highest point, the Pic du Marboré.

From Gavarnie, follow the D923 west towards the Boucharo past a white statue on a small promontory to the right. She's much in evidence hereabouts, Notre Dame des Neiges (Our Lady of the Snows).

The 11.3 kilometres to the Col de Tentes, as far as the cyclist can sensibly go, are hard, the road driving up into the solid mass of the Pic de Tentes up the cut of the Espécières. Non-stop 8-9%, an open bowl of rock covered with scrubby vegetation, the prodigious road to the high barrier between France and Spain. Perhaps you will see marmots scurrying, their little bums shimmying as they scamper – comical, sociable little creatures that do not dwell on the alchemy of gradients and suffering or the fleeting satisfactions of overcoming altitude. They nibble vegetation, sip morning dew and whistle warnings to each other at the approach of humans, including those who do dwell on the alchemy of gradients etc.

The climb reduces in severity towards the plateau from which opens a stupendous view of the neighbouring ranges, 7.5% seeping into 6 and 5%. Here you stand as on a rooftop. A panorama board indicates the names of the peaks in view. The Col de Tentes is no more than a flat stretch of road. It cannot and does not compete with the surrounding sights.

Because Gavarnie is chock-a-block in the season, with walkers, visitors, campervans and sightseers, the best time to ride up to the Boucharo is probably early morning or late afternoon/early evening, thereby avoiding the sun on a completely exposed road. There is no sustenance en route.

From here, the descent, on a pretty good surface, is fast and fun.

Cirque de Troumouse 2100m

From Gèdre

LENGTH: 16.2 KM

HEIGHT GAIN: 1089 M

MAXIMUM GRADIENT: 10%

A short way beyond Gèdre turn left at a fork onto the D922, a serpentine gorge road nosing into the Gave de Héas, the skyline ahead dominated by the huge navel boss of a peak. The climbing is quite hard from the start, 5 kilometres of around 7-8% to a small side road from where you may look down to the inviting still waters of the Lac des Gloriettes at the foot of the Pimené, that peak whereon Junkers observed his shepherd accomplices signalling from the Vignemale.

A flat basin leads to a tiny chapel to Notre Dame de Héas (1500m) - a very popular pilgrim destination during the 18th century - and a maison d'accueil (guest house, literally 'house of welcome') by the Frères de la Prieuré de Notre Dame des Neiges. There is a secular auberge further along the road and a view of the first extremely sharp hairpins taking the road up to the right. Ahead stretches a trackless expanse of land towards more ramparts of mountain.

The hairpins on a narrowing road deliver 2 kilometres of very taxing ascent, up to the maximum of 10% as the land falls away to the left and the road edges up towards the viewpoint from which the Cirque can be marvelled at in its full stature. From the Hôtellerie du Maillet (1850m) the road surface deteriorates but there is less than 3 kilometres of a lesser gradient - no more than 8% - to the great prospect of the Troumouse.

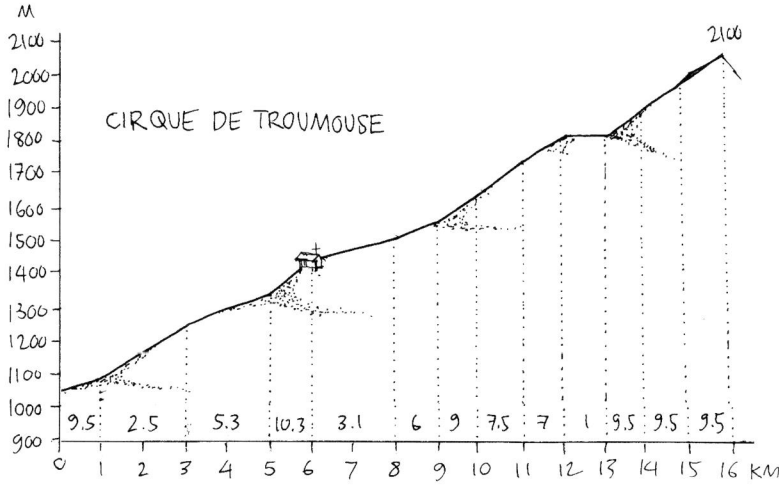

Piau Engaly 1870m

From Saint-Lary Soulan

LENGTH:	20.8 KM
HEIGHT GAIN:	1040M
MAXIMUM GRADIENT:	8.5%

A classic gorge approach: the swirling waters of the Neste d'Aure tumbling over boulders by the side of the D929, the result of a confluence of springs rising in the rock below the Cirque de Troumouse. (Saint-Lary-Soulan is described later.)

The surface is good, there are watering holes en route, the gradient for the first 9 kilometres no worse than 4%, an easy pull past a charming little stone-built chapel in the shape of a flat iron and on to a bridge, Le Pont du Moudang, where the slopes start to bite a bit harder. A rubbish wheely bin is painted with the slogan 'What kind of Love?' Another bridge at Aragnouet (1330m, 11.7km). A short distance on, at Le Plan d'Aragnouet (1340m), the main road swings left and up towards the Bielsa tunnel into Spain, and the D118 climbs right to the ski station. In the triangle made by the meeting of the roads stands a 12th-century Templar chapel with an elaborate, three-step, buttress-style bell-tower. Given its location, and the nature of the Templar order, there may well have originally been a hospice for travellers attached. (There is a fine bar-restaurant just across the border, spit-cooking over an open log fire, and a notable commination on the wall: 'Excommunication reserved against any person who removes, pilfers or in any other way whatsoever makes off with any book, parchment or paper from this library unless they may be absolved, until such time as the said item is entirely restored.')

There is an imposing rugged surround here of bristling peaked ridges as you begin the 7.4 kilometre climb, a largely unvarying gradient of 7–8%, testimony to the fact that it is a purpose-made road for snow-seekers with no antecedent track for donkeys, smugglers or shepherds.

The surface is pretty good, quite exposed, grassy slopes and clumps of trees, a fine view back down the vee of the ravine. At 5km the road flattens out and goes through a snow tunnel – this slight drop in gradient allows a breather before the next lash of hairpin and the up, up, up. This is a road for the circumambient views: the clefts furrowing the mountainside to the right… the torrents hurtling off the upper layers of rock… the approach towards the lesser cirque above… the bare rock and drifts of scree across its neck like the mountain's scurf… the loom of the chalets and ski lifts on the skyline which means that the top is getting nearer and a reminder, perhaps, that this climb has featured only once in the Tour de France and might seem, from this height, a lesser Alpe d'Huez, the hairpins already travelled in plain view below.

TOUR DE FRANCE 1999 STAGE 15
A triumph of self-belief

When Fernando Escartín came to the 1999 Tour de France, his eighth, he had ridden a Giro d'Italia and six Vueltas, but despite coming 2nd in his home tour in 1997 and 1998, 7th overall in the 1995 Grande Boucle and 1st in that year's mountainous Tour of Aragón (ahead of Induraín) as well as 8th and 5th in the 1996 and 1997 Tours, he had never quite matched belief in himself to the obvious talent packed into his legs. Perhaps it was, in part, because this pocket Hercules from Biescas, a town on the western edge of our Lost Mountain area, was not a very alluring rider: hunched over the bars, his body lurching to the right, face twisted in a grimace of pain, his natural speed and strength in the mountains had no panache in it, only kph. And, as he put it himself: 'I am not nasty enough to win.'

But, having been minced up and probably robbed of a stage win on the climb to Courchevel in 1997, by a hostile combine of Festina and Telekom riders, he had had enough and took to heart the sort of credo to which the likes of Pantani and Il Diablo, Claudio Chiapucci, adhere: 'You may blow or you may win but you have to attack.' That is what you say: making it happen takes self-belief.

Stage 15 of the 1999 Tour was reckoned to be the queen of stages, five first-category climbs including the mountain-top finish, Col de Menté for openers, and, between the last four monsters, virtually no recovery time. Portillon... Peyresourde... Val Louron... Piau-Engaly. These were roads which Escartín the carpenter's son knew well, indeed his training ground, 'climbs I knew like the back of my hand'. Always a puzzling simile, that – how well do you know the back of your hand?

Lance Armstrong was being well supported by his team mates Tyler Hamilton and Kevin Livingston but, as they wilted, he took over and only Alex Zülle could stay with him. But Escartín had broken clear on the Peyresourde with Laurent Dufaux. It really was a do-or-die attack, but the Spanish climber was buoyed by the thousands of Spanish fans who had flocked over the border to cheer him on, his father among them. The pair swept up the early escapees on the lower slopes of the Peyresourde, and Escartín, surely sensing that this was his day, dropped Dufaux on the Col de Val Louron-Azet and ploughed on to victory.

Zülle passed Dufaux and came 2nd at 2 minutes 1 second, along with Virenque and Armstrong, who had taken the yellow jersey with an imperious show of strength on stage 9 to Sestrières (destination of Chiapucci's legendary solo ride in 1992).

The change wrought in Escartín that day was profound. He had moved into second place overall, at 6min 19sec on Armstrong. Next day, as his Kelme directeur sportif Alvaro Pino remarked, 'he attacked on the Aubisque and never looked back, not once. He never cared who was or wasn't following him. That's a real change.' He didn't win, but he came in with Armstrong and Zülle, thinking now of the podium in Paris. He lost time to Zülle in the final time trial but came 3rd overall.

Of his ride that first day in the Pyrenees, Armstrong said: 'Where I suffered the most… was when Fernando Escartín attacked. It was very tough to follow him.'

Pla d'Adet 1680m

From Saint-Lary-Soulan

LENGTH: 1.6 KM

HEIGHT GAIN: 870 M

MAXIMUM GRADIENT: 10%

The D19 leads north out of Saint-Lary for 1 kilometre to Vignec (819m), where the D123 turns left up to the winter sports station. After little more than a kilometre, round a left-hand bend, the game is on. This road is built for big gear boxes, clutches and multi-horsepowered engines. Three straight kilometres cut with thoughtless savagery into the side of the mountain at 10%, a cruel exposed ramp which, from below, looks quite as bad as it feels when you are on it. The view of the valley stretching out beneath this climb to the snow kingdom is stupendous, the satisfaction in store at the top a further bonus but there is no masking the difficulty of this climb.

After 3 kilometres, the gradient slumps to around 9% and, 1 kilometre on, to a childish 7% through the village of Soulan (1275m, 6km), before it wakes up to its adult duty once more and grinds back into 9% at minimum. A left-hand hairpin and a bridge at the Granges d'Espiaube (1485m, 8.8km), comes just before the turn off right to the Col de Portet (2215m), the higher of the two ski stations served by this approach. (It's another 8.9 kilometres if you're interested and you like suffering that much.) The last 2 kilometres are a mere 6–7%, a doddle by comparison with what you have just done and the view is splendiferous, a majestic panorama back down where you have come from. Hurray.

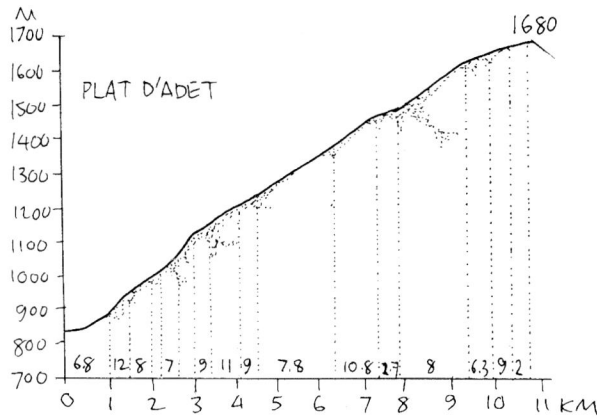

TOUR DE FRANCE 1975

Merckx on the ropes

This was only the second (of eight, so far) inclusions of the Pla d'Adet in the Tour de France. An elite group of six riders arrived at the foot of the climb, Merckx and Thévenet among them. At 50 seconds came a larger group, led by Poulidor, shelled out on the Tourmalet and Aspin.

Thévenet was in good form. He looked strong, imperturbable, confident. By contrast, Merckx's dominance of what he called 'this most beautiful race' was beginning to look vulnerable. There was a certain circumspection about him and a suspicion that he was riding to consolidate his lead, plugging gaps rather than asserting full authority. When Thévenet launched the first attack with a crushing burst of acceleration, it was clear that he was carrying the fight to the Belgian. Gimondi and others, hanging on for dear life since the Aspin, had no answer. Merckx responded however, and soon caught him, in company with Ocaña of Spain, Van Impe of Belgium and Zoetemelk of Holland. No sooner had they rejoined than the nervy Dutchman in his turn attacked. Merckx held back. But Thévenet went again. Merckx forced himself to follow, dropped Ocaña, and only Van Impe could stay with him. Thévenet, meanwhile, was in full cry behind Zoetemelk, pounding up the slopes, winning time. Behind them, Merckx was working like a fury, ceding ground with the avarice of a miser, surely aware that this Frenchman was beginning to get his measure.

At the finish, Zoetemelk took the day by 49 seconds over Thévenet and 55 seconds over Merckx. The Belgian had lost nearly a minute in 10 kilometres of climbing.

Zoetemelk said that, at the foot of the climb, he had looked round at the others and could see that neither Merckx nor Ocaña were in good shape. Thévenet looked very strong though, in firmer control than he had been in that year's Dauphiné Libéré, which he won.

'He is my favourite for the Tour,' Zoetemelk added. And so it proved.

Col d'Azet / Val Louron 1580m

From Vallée de Louron

LENGTH: 8 KM
HEIGHT GAIN: 635 M
MAXIMUM GRADIENT: 10%

From the D25 the road turns into the village of Génos, an up and a down before crossing a bridge over a cascade tumbling down the hillside to the left. A sharp heave up onto the first viewpoint up the valley to the right. The houses give way to more bucolic surroundings and the climb, to the Station Touristique de Val Louron, is on. The road widens and shows its teeth: 6km, 1095m, 10%. There are plenty of Tour de France graffiti scrawled and splashed on the tarmac. Broad hairpins, a fine shot of the lake by Loudenvielle below. This climb is much blessed with panorama and at 5km another 10% warning, when you do feel that you are climbing to a high vantage point somewhere up the road ahead, a silent attendance of mountains to the left to remind you just where you are, frail mortal, on this narrow ribbon of tarmac edged with long drops, and a sign announcing 'Troupeaux en liberté' (sheep on the loose). They are not belligerent.

The gradients begin to slacken – 8% at 4km and, just beyond, a view of the buildings in the tourist complex. As if sketching a low bow, the slopes weaken to 7% at 3km and a graffito reads 'Virenque, come back'. It does not add 'all is forgiven'. If the sheep are not violent, apparently the cattle can cut up rough – a 'Danger' sign at 2km, 8%, warns you not to approach them. The terrain is more exposed, the road more sinuous now past the turn left, flat and then downhill to Val Louron, barely worth a visit; far more interesting to press on through the remaining kilometres at 8% to the Col d'Azet from which the views are stunning, especially a grand aerial shot of the resort town of Saint-Lary-Soulan, destination of the descent. Way across to the north, the road which goes up to Pla d'Adet and Col de Portet is clearly visible, cut into the lower skirts of the Arbizon.

From Saint-Lary-Soulan

LENGTH: 9 KM
HEIGHT GAIN: 780 M
MAXIMUM GRADIENT: 9%

Saint-Lary-Soulan is a bustling summer and winter resort town, a celebrated ski and mountaineering centre, well stocked with bars and restaurants, a good bike shop.

A gentle pull to the bar/restaurant Chez Lulu in Sailhan, at 9km from the col, whence the gradient ups to 4%, but at 8km it gets tougher – 9% – and most of the rest of the way it will not drop below 8%. Round big swishing loops of road on open hillside into Estensan, a well-groomed hillside village (7km) and, 2 kilometres above it, the village which names the col. Azet (5km, 8%), a hilltop village, boasts a very grand Mairie, rectangular lantern atop its new roof, and the road twists cautiously through as if paying its deference and civic respects. An Auberge du Col at 4km then a grinding back to 9%.

From 8% at 3km, the final 2 kilometres on the narrow, well-surfaced road are rather friendlier – 6% – and at this height the verges are more cushioned than on the other side of the climb.

Col de Peyresourde 1569m

Western approach

LENGTH: 7.7 KM
HEIGHT GAIN: 594 M
MAXIMUM GRADIENT: 10%

The 9 kilometres from Arreau along the D618 to the junction with the D25 towards Loudenvielle and beyond to the head of the Vallée de Louron, are negligible, an easy pedal along a newly flint-chipped road on which I punctured during the Raid Pyrénéen in June 2005. After the fork, there are a further 2 kilometres of rolling road, only slightly tighter than flat, before the first bit of serious uphill just short of the right-hand turn and drop into Estarvielle. You also pass one of a small number of biker-friendly restaurant/hotels in the Pyrenees. The Hôtel des Cîmes extends a cordial 'Bienvenue aux Motards' (motorcyclists welcome) and bids all passing leather-jacketed easy riders pull over to sample the specialities of the house: raclette, (toasted cheese usually served with potatoes and cornichons – gherkins), fondue and garbure (thick vegetable soup).

The lake at Loudenvielle and a big tourist centre for sports and randonnées (mountain walks) in the Vallée de Louron sit below the long escarpment off to the right.

There is fair cover for most of the way but 3.5 kilometres from the top the road pulls clear of the trees and settles into a rhythm of long straights and shallow bends at a steady 7.5%. A sudden dip after the road flattens a bit and now, although the col isn't immediately visible, the vee where the slopes of the two adjoining peaks meet is: the right-hand flank, on top of which sits the Peyragudes ski station, bare, the left thickly wooded. (The forest was planted at the beginning of the 20th century to impede avalanches and mudslides.) At 2km, the col does creep into the picture and it's a powerful lure drawing you on round the last broad sweep of the approach to it which has a real frontier feel about it. (It actually marks the boundary between the départements of the Haute-Garonne and Ariège.)

On at least one Tour de France, the 1926 edition, it served as the site of a secret control, a makeshift shelter made of tarpaulins weighted with stones and tied to poles. A sign commands riders to 'dismount and sign'. The commissaire, in oilskin waterproof and flat cap, poses opposite a rider in long socks and what looks like a waist-length poncho made of sackcloth. He scowls as if he does indeed have ashes in his mouth. A knot of spectators with and without umbrellas look on…

Before the race that year Desgrange had accused the riders of being lazy, the directeur sportifs of weakness, the press of being needlessly hypercritical. The riders argued that there was no point in wearing themselves out unless it was absolutely necessary. 'The Tour de France lasts a month, we won't shorten it by a day by riding like madmen on every stage as we have to do in the Alps and the Pyrenees.'

Desgrange responded: 'Take note, the Tour de France only became the Tour de France when we sent the riders into the mountains. If we'd left them in the plain or if our country didn't have Alps and Pyrenees, very well, we would have taken part, over seventeen stages, in administering seventeen sleeping pills and no-one would ever have started the racing.'

The temporary secret control booth has been replaced by an excellent contemporary café offering crêpes at 1.40€ apiece, 12 for 4€. One Raid rider of my acquaintance coaxed himself up the Peyresourde by counting the pedal strokes '10, cheese omelette… 1…10, cheese omelette…'

The view out into the Ariège is not spectacular but the pleats of distant ridges make a copybook aspect of mountains. The descending road flicks round three mighty hairpins before opening out into one of the fastest downhill runs in the Pyrenees, a hearty encouragement to 'switch the brain off and let it roll'.

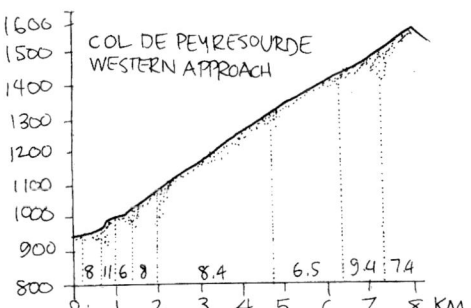

COL DE PEYRESOURDE *continued from previous page*

Eastern approach

LENGTH:	15.3 KM
HEIGHT GAIN:	950 M
MAXIMUM GRADIENT:	9%

Bagnères-de-Luchon is known as 'The Queen of the Pyrenees', noted for its thermalisme, climatisme, sports d'hiver (thermal baths, beneficial climate, winter sports) and twinned with Harrogate, 'Queen of Yorkshire, city of flowers' (Luchon has its own summer Festival of Flowers) and Sitges 'Queen of the Catalonian beaches'. Others call Luchon 'Capital of the Empire of sulphur'. The Romans first exploited the sulphurous and radioactive springs – sovereign for rheumatism and respiratory complaints – and built a bathing resort in the town they called Lugdunum but the springs, 60 of them, were not developed again on any scale until 1759. The royal Intendant of Gascony and Béarn, Baron Mégret d'Etigny, decided to develop the town. These officials were not popular. D'Etigny forcibly acquired land to make way for three avenues linking the town to the springs. Local opponents to the civic aggrandisement hacked into the road surface and tore up the trees. D'Etigny had the road repaired and more saplings planted. The wreckers moved in again. D'Etigny repaired and replaced a third time and posted a military guard. This time the avenues survived and Luchon became a fashionable spa town, one of its main streets dubbed Esplanade des Oeufs for the faint whiff of sulphur that often pervades the air.

The spa thrives and the town retains the grace and elegance of its heyday – shaded walks, municipal gardens, fountains, the baths housing the unique Vaporarium, (a natural warm vapour bath in 150 metres of subterranean galleries), the grand tree-lined avenue through the centre named for D'Etigny, restaurants and hotels. The most recent addition to Luchon's list of therapeutic programmes is a cure to wean smokers off the weed. On the east side of town, Montauban de Luchon, there is a Jardin des Cascades.

There are two bike shops in town. Opposite the cemetery on the way to the Peyresourde is a sign for the Abattoir.

The first 3 kilometres out of town follow the cleft of the deep One gorge along a broad open highway flanked to either side with parapet and high wall. An easy 3%, a harder 6.5 and another 3% average. At 3km the trees begin to crowd in and the gradient establishes itself at 6%. The road is wide most of the way, narrowing through several villages en route, with not a great deal of movement in it. This adds to the difficulty of what is a comparatively long and unvarying ascent.

At around 5km from the col, the road flattens briefly at 4% past the village of Garin – an apt name for one of the iconic climbs of the Tour de France but in fact no connection with that Maurice Garin of Lens in the Pas-de-Calais, winner of the very first Tour de France in 1903. To the left, across an open sward, stands a rough-hewn stone stele in memoriam of Pierre de Gorsse, 'writer and protector of the Pyrenees', born in the year of Garin's win, died 1984, and also the tiny Chapelle de Saint Pé (the French seem to have made their own choice of saints without reference to the Catholic hierarchy). An avenue of limes shades the road for a short distance but this climb is otherwise very exposed and generally quite busy with traffic. There are no separate kilometre and gradient signs although several direction markers do give distance.

Villages appear in the hollow across to the right and the big bluffs to either side of the col hog the central horizon from around 3km at 1330m. The last stretch is dramatic indeed, hitting those three large hairpins, the road slanting acutely, the air thinning and the col, hidden up there, a tantalising prize for what is a very gruelling ride. The surface is newly asphalted – a new page, tabula rasa, for the Tour de France visitors' book.

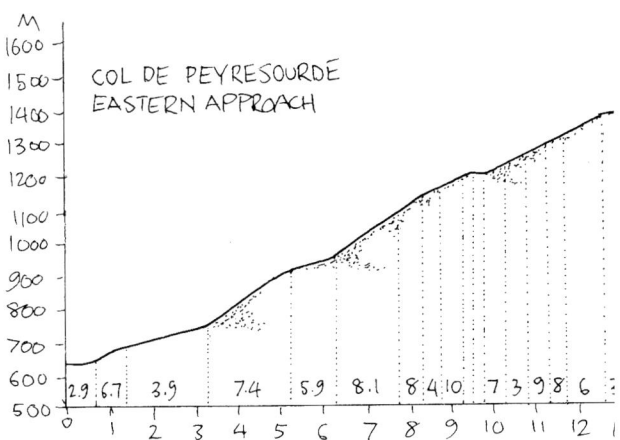

Port de Bales 1755m

Northern approach

LENGTH: 19 KM
HEIGHT GAIN: 1185 M
MAXIMUM GRADIENT: 14%

You have the Tour de France to thank for this one. Originally the southern approach ended at Bourg d'Oueil, but as the Tourist office in Luchon assured me, the Tour organisation had had its eye on this by-road for some time and, in July 2006, they linked the northern approach south with 5880km of brand new tarmac laid over the old mountain path.

The impressive abbey and bastide of Saint-Bertrand-de-Comminges, 8 kilometres north of Mauléon along the D925, is worth a detour and a 62 kilometre cycle track, following the old railway, links Saint-Bertrand with Boussens, to the east. In Saint-Bertrand, the friendly Chez Simone restaurant offers good plain low-cost fare.

From Mauléon (bar and restaurant), the road winds up the leafy Ourse valley at easy lifts to Ferrère, (680m, 3km). The word 'Barousse' appears to mean 'the mountain where the water springs' and a short way along from Ferrère stands the mineral water plant named for Saint Nerée, the holy man credited with discovery of the source. The original thermal springs in which he may have luxuriated – or, conscience-pricked, felt he ought not to – now supply the bottled water 'des hadettes', namely those tiny fairies (local name hadas) who inhabit the Pyrenean grottoes and are here charged with the protection of the Barousse springs.

The way is easy, shaded with overhanging trees and steadily marching in closer concert with the stream bed as the valley straitens into the cleft of the gorge. At 6.5km, the Chalets Saint Nerée (770m) a cluster of impressive wooden mansions, form a *colonie de vacances*, a holiday centre for walkers, climbers and families seeking rural retreat. Round a large bend the road moves onto a bridge by the Granges de Crouhens (828m, 7.5km) and a rustic side road leading to a cross-country ski area. When I stopped to quiz two people in Ferrère they told me that there had been a cycle race up to, but not beyond, the Port de Balès, that very few people came skiing here any more – not fancy or well-provided enough, one assumes – and that there are very few cuckoos in the valley these days (I'd asked about the famous springtime late fall of snow, the 'neige de coucou')… 'It's all helicopters now' said the old man with a wry smile.

From the bridge, the climb proper begins through the Forêt de Barousse and hereon the difficult or dangerous route warning of the Michelin map is amply justified. The road is uneven, very taut – in places barely enough for a single car – twisting, crowded upon by trees and, worst of all, liberally littered with rocks and even boulders. The gradient kicks up immediately too, and the remaining 11.5 kilometres to the pass are a serious passage of steady 8–10% average with intermittent short stretches of very punishing steepness, some 14%, possibly.

At about 7.5 kilometres from the pass, the head waters of the river Ourse de Ferrère tumble off the side of the mountain in a rush. This ride, hard, very pinched for space and hazardous as it is – a fiendishly tricky descent, too, with little view ahead – does, however, boast a stark, untrimmed, untailored beauty… one of the more rugged mountain passes indeed, a road not much travelled, a throwback to the distant past when these ranges offered summer grazing and the occasional passage from one valley to the next, barely for social reasons, or even hot commerce.

At 6.5 kilometres from the pass a passage Canadien (cattle grid) fronts a sign warning of falling rocks for 5 km. Hmm.

There is no habitation anywhere, apart from the very decrepit refuge de Saoubette (1250m), animal stalls attached, 6 kilometres from the top. Inside: a table, chairs, rusty iron bedstead with manky mattress, outside: a wood-planked nettie with a hole in the crude floor for excrement.

Southern approach

LENGTH: 20.2 KM

HEIGHT GAIN: 1130 M

MAXIMUM GRADIENT: 9%

Head towards the Col de Peyresourde out of Luchon on the D618 and 4.2km along, at 824m, as the road swings left, turn right onto the D51. The approach to the Balès up the course of the Neste d'Oueil, the river which names the basin, is narrow, exposed, beautiful. A series of small villages lie en route, the D51c leads left to Benque – 'bonk'? – with a 12th century church and fine 13th century frescoes. The broad valley looks well-worked, thoroughly nibbled leas cover the foot of the western mountain slopes with a noble green sward, the upper slopes draped with waist-length conifer plantations. The view ahead up to the bare ridge below Mont Né is striking and, gradually, the magnificent panorama to the big ranges around Superbagnères looms above the horizon south, too. This old road, its surface quite well worn but unpitted, hits you hard at first with a 10% fist in your nose but relents with 8 and 7% into Saint-Paul d'Oueil (1123m, 8km). The rest of the way to Bourg d'Oueil at the head of the valley, gateway to the high Port, is an easy ramble.

Out of Saint Paul the road dips and bends, isolated houses dot the sides of the valley and only the minimal kilometre stick posts mark the way. In Mayrègne (1195m, 10km) the Hôtel du Pic du Mont Né looks tired, shut and unvisited. The village of Caubous (1255m, 11.8km) doesn't last long and, a hundred metres on, the community of Cirès (1250m) swaggers up, with a flourish. This marks that strong distinction which villagers everywhere like to stress: you may be Caubous people, but we are from Cirès. Cirès is very full of itself: copper-capped hanging street lamps… a substantial Mairie… assertive and very top dog. Gîtes rurales, a restaurant/bar which brags that it opens 7/7 but seemingly not in winter, a steep road up to the church and what is most emphatically Cirès, 'Centre'.

From Bourg d'Oueil (1340m, 14.2km) runs the 5.88km of spanking new tarmac, lined with a cream-white concrete gutter up to the Port. The former mountain path is very tight in width, its open side giving onto precipitous drops, nor are there barriers…this is a truly hairy descent. Sharp bends here and there remind you of where the mules once trod and there's a glorious open view back down the valley from a long wiggly stretch, like a corniche, above Bourg d'Oueil. A placard indicates that isards have been reintroduced, their movements tagged by blue- and yellow-coloured collars. The gradients are a steady 6% average with no great surprises, mostly exposed but a copse of firs does straddle the road in one point where the old track snaked through.

A stick post at 5km announces the approach of the col, the saddle almost in sight as the road sidles onto an exposed ledge which makes this higher reach very cold when the wind blows and very hot when the sun is out.

Here is the open col, the last few metres spooling out the relief of getting there. It's a hump of a col by a car pull-off marred by an unseemly clutter of signs: no coaches allowed to go on down towards Bourg d'Oueil, as if any charabanc would have made its way up here from Mauléon… weight limit 19t… 'aires de croisement' (passing places) at every 300m… 8% average over 12 kilometres of descent to the south… a new col sign and an old stone cairn too with sign atop. The D925 swings west off what was the track up from Bourg to the Lac de Bordères, and a mountain refuge near the Port de Pierrefite (1855m) just below the peak of Mont Né (2147m).

Col du Portillon 1293m

Western approach

LENGTH: 9 KM
HEIGHT GAIN: 633 M
MAXIMUM GRADIENT: 10%

The Portillon makes an obvious and very agreeable passage into Spain and immediate access to the Porta de Bonaigua and the cols of The Lost Mountain.

Out of Luchon, follow the D125 towards Superbagnères and turn left on the D618, the old coaching road, to Saint Mamet; a few hundred metres on, turn right again at the 'ESPAGNE' sign. A fine perspective of the interlocked fingers of the valley sides framing a large conical peak recedes into the hazy distance which is Spain. There are only two signs, standard practice it seems in the Haute-Garonne which has but recently introduced them: at the start of the climb and another at 3 kilometres from the summit.

This road is well-surfaced, thanks to the Tour's visit in 2005, and plenteous trees give ample shade most of the way along a road which alternates long straights with an easy flow of bends. A cooling cascade tumbles off the mountainside to the left at 2.5km and the Cascade de Sidonie follows 500 metres further on. The surface is fairly good.

The middle section of the climb, 4.5–6.5km (with a phone at 5km) is exposed and seems a lot steeper and more punishing than the statistical evidence (no worse than around 8%) suggests.

Three kilometres from the summit a sign marks 1000 altitude. This means that the final stretch runs at around 10% average but, as with the middle section, this is misleading: somehow this 10% has blunt teeth. Now the road narrows, the trees crowd in and the bends twitch more sharply as the jaws of the gradient close. A steep right-hand bend past 2 kilometres from the col marks the real urgency of the climb and a succession of hairpins. At around 1 kilometre from the top there is a stretch of new tarmac. Crossing the summit line in a glade, dappled with light, is always sweet. The frontier is marked by two small masonry obelisks to left and right of the road. Smugglers made this traverse to and fro in years past, the forest giving welcome cover, and the journey was comparatively short. This is ripe contraband country, for those who knew (know) the terrain and the mountain's moods.

Eastern approach

LENGTH: 8.5 KM
HEIGHT GAIN: 600 M
MAXIMUM GRADIENT: 8%

From Bossost, a busy town on the main route to Viella which follows the course of the Garona (the road crosses the border at the Pont du Roi, 582m, one of the easier traverses of the Pyrenean range), the climb is quite different in character. (Note the excellent, cheap, friendly Hostal Restaurant Tina on the right just before the Portillon turn off.) The road is broader, more exposed, less interesting but a great descent. However, just above 4km a belvedere to the left affords a great panorama of the high peaks to the south, (all named on an information board) among them the Pic d'Arrès below whose crag sits the Hospice de France (see overleaf). At 6km, a new complex of buildings to the left (sizeable interchange of main road and access road) houses a centre for the 'observation of autochthonous (i.e. native to the area) wild life'.

At 7.5km the road winds into the trees and the final kilometres are a delight, a woodland ride through the fragrances of leaf, mulch and bark.

Superbagnères 1804m

From the north

LENGTH: 19.3 KM
HEIGHT GAIN: 1200 M
MAXIMUM GRADIENT: 9%

Leaving Luchon on the D125, the road follows the course of the river Pique south. The gradient hovers around 4% with a 7% snarl between 3 and 4km. The surface is good, the ravine close to and green, the undulating road has swing and the view ahead is fine – a grassy-sloped craggy ridge with a beard of trees. A bridge, the Pont de Lapade, crosses the Pique at 5.2km and at 6.1km the road forks: the D46 right towards the climb, straight on to the Hospice de France. This mediaeval mountain refuge was built on a much-frequented trading route between France and Spain, a 3-hour walk away in good weather. It's now very dilapidated and all but falling down. It's 7.4 kilometres from the junction, a height gain of 760m, therefore an average nearly 10% with 12% at the top.

The Pont de Ravi crosses the Lys River whose waters flow on to join the Pique and 3.4 kilometres on (5.5–7.5%) the D46 swings round a right hand hairpin past the approach to the Gouffre d'Enfer ('Abyss of Hell') the Ru ('small stream') d'Enfer and the Cascade d'Enfer which, presumably, cools the heat of the fire and brimstone issuing from Satan's subterranean parlour. He stinks of sulphur, like parts of Luchon.

As on any cul-de-sac climb which has featured in the Tour there is a stir in the imagination, a frisson of that day when the slopes were packed with fans watching the final drama of the stage. This mountain, first included in 1961, has been visited six times in all, most recently in 1989 when Robert Millar won the stage, and twice as an individual time trial: 1962 stage 13, Bahamontes: 18.250km in 47min 23sec and 1979 stage 2, Hinault: 23.870km from Luchon in 53min 59sec.

The gradient oscillates between a fairly gentle 6 and two pitches of quite savage 9% (14–16km) but the views distract – back down the valley and up to the curtain-wall of rock beyond which lie the monster peaks on the French side and the Maladeta range in Spain. For an aerial view of this cluster of Pyrenean eyries alone the climb of the Superbagnères is worth every ounce of effort.

There are no signs; the surface is smooth.

At 14km, on the 9%, La Carrière, ('the quarry'), a recess hacked out of the bare rock of the mountainside offers a giddy view to the left of the folded slopes of the far ridge and, above to the right, the winding gear of the ski lifts on the skyline. A sharp right-hand bend reveals the final ramps cutting up to the right (they always look impossibly steep, but do not be intimidated). The way is barren from here, the summit scraped to the bone by wind and frost and, after two mild kilometres, the notional red kite (the first red flag indicating the final kilometre was raised in 1906) unleashes another belt of 9%.

The Grand Hôtel, which dominates the hump of the ski station, is a massive squat oblong Schloss, a blockhouse more elegant inside than its ugly exterior promises, open most of the year. A crowd of chalets and a chapel perched on a spur away from the road. The cafés of the resort were firmly shut when I was there in July, their offer of un croque vite, (a quick bite), a needless hypocrisy. The vast 360 degree panorama, by contrast, was open to the wide heavens – a magnificent perspective: the twelve peaks of the 'cursed mountains' (Maladeta), many of them snow-capped all year round, to the south; the massif from which springs the Neste d'Oô and a line of glacial lakes to the west; the long vista of the valley down towards Luchon and beyond. Truly stunning. And… an exuberant, fast, 20 kilometre descent in store.

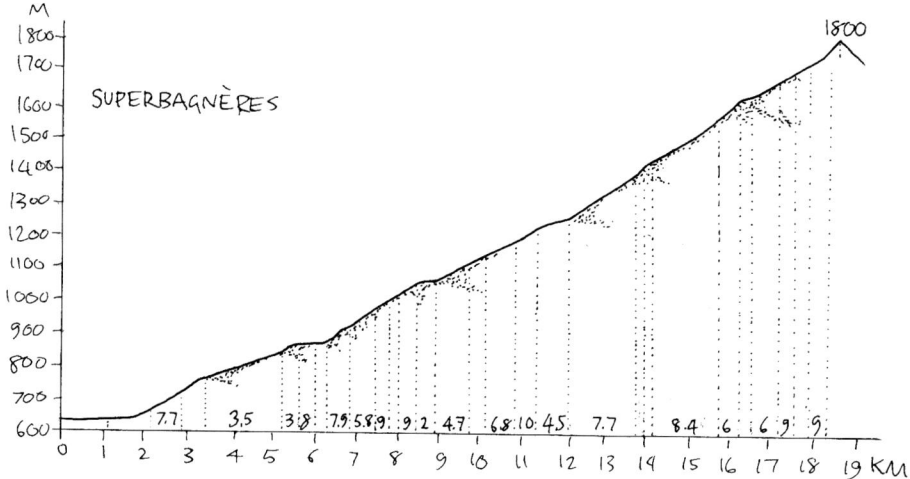

TOUR DE FRANCE 1989 STAGE 10

Failed wheel-sucker

Laurent Fignon and the re-emergent Greg Lemond were eyeing each other nervily and Lemond, in the relatively weak ADR team, was sucking wheels unashamedly. The day before he had sat on Fignon all the way to Cauterets, thereby gifting the 1998 winner Pedro Delgado a handsome win. Delgado was chewing away at the deficit he'd shouldered since turning up late for the Prologue.

This second Pyrenean stage crossed three mighty cols, Tourmalet, Aspin and Peyresourde en route to the high finish. When Robert Millar and Charly Mottet attacked on the Tourmalet, Fignon either had or offered no answer. Perhaps, like Anquetil with Poulidor, he was watching only Lemond. As Millar and Mottet went aways, Fignon struggled but got no help from the others. Angrily, he demanded more resolute help from his team mates Pascal Simon and Gérard Rué. Lemond did nothing.

The Millar-Mottet tandem thrived, Delgado attacked on the Aspin and joined them. The pursuit, aided by the PDM riders Stephen Rooks, Sean Kelly, Raúl Alcalá and Gert-Jan Theunisse, hammered on but still Lemond sat on them, despite furious rebuke from Fignon. They arrived at the foot of the Superbagnères fully three minutes down on the Millar-Mottet-Delgado escape. Since Delgado had put over half a minute into Fignon and Lemond the day before, this was unsettling if not critical. Lemond's self-interest was harming them both.

Suddenly, the American attacked. Fignon, albeit weakened by the hard work of chain-ganging, countered immediately with astonishing power. Lemond responded, caught his wheel but faltered. On the line he had ceded 12 seconds to the defiant Fignon – the time gain hardly less important than the psychological blow – and the Parisian took yellow over his rival by 7 seconds.

Millar won the stage in a final battle with Delgado, the two of them dropping Mottet on the run-in to go clear by 19 seconds.

6. The Four Valleys

The verdant, well-watered valleys and the upland meadows of the Couserans, split by the high ranges of the Lower Pyrenees, are like the outer defence works of the mighty central spines, merging with the plain to the north.

The Four Valleys of the sector's title at its western end – Bellongue, Bethmale, Biros and Balaguères – are part of a lacework of some eighteen greater and lesser furrows cut into the terrain by waterways irrigating the ancient region of the Couserans (from 'Consoranni', the Roman word for the local Aquitanian tribe and the later Gascon 'Coserans'). The area, once quite rich in iron (most of the mines were exhausted a long time ago), is generally poor these days, the population sparse, the agriculture mostly confined to smallholdings and the production of a tasty range of cheeses (ewe, goat and cows' milk), honey (of various perfumes, notably chestnut – very strong) and charcuterie. The Ariège, the name of the region as a whole – roughly from the Four Valleys east to Ax-les-Thermes, north to Toulouse and south to the Pyrenean border – may be one of the poorest départements in France but its people enjoy, per capita, the greatest longevity. The answer? A staple diet of garlic, red wine and duck fat spread as dripping on bread. Medical research has shown that this claim is not wild: duck fat is an excellent counter to a build up of bad – low density lipoprotein LDL – cholesterol. Red wine and garlic we know about, of course.

One of the Ariégois specialities worth investigating is a dark, aromatic drink called Hypocras, a concoction of sweet wine, mountain herbs and plants, based on a mediaeval recipe, used as a coulis (purée) to accompany grilled goat's cheese, puddings, or drunk as either an aperitif or digestif.

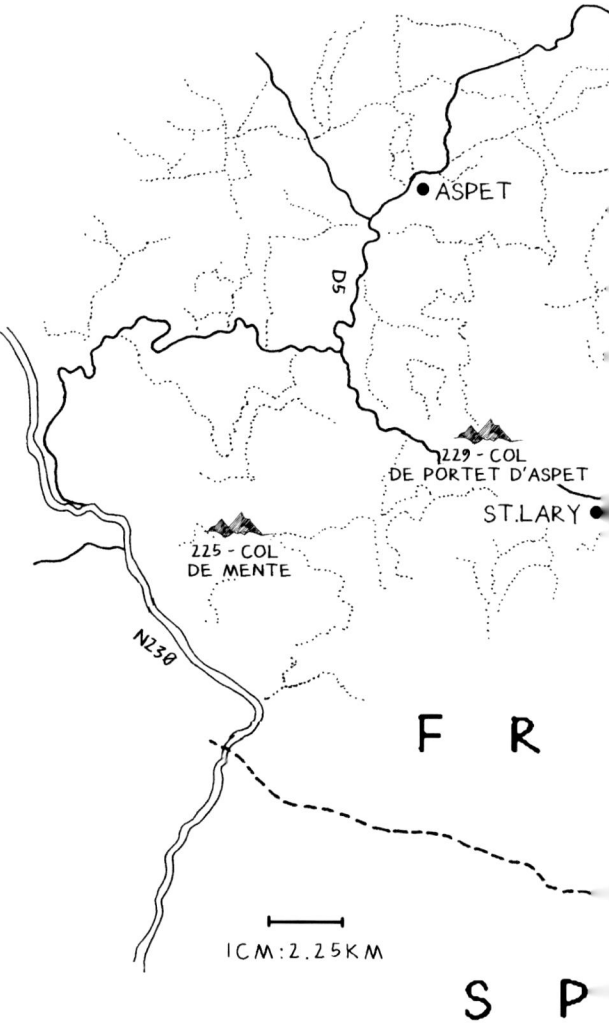

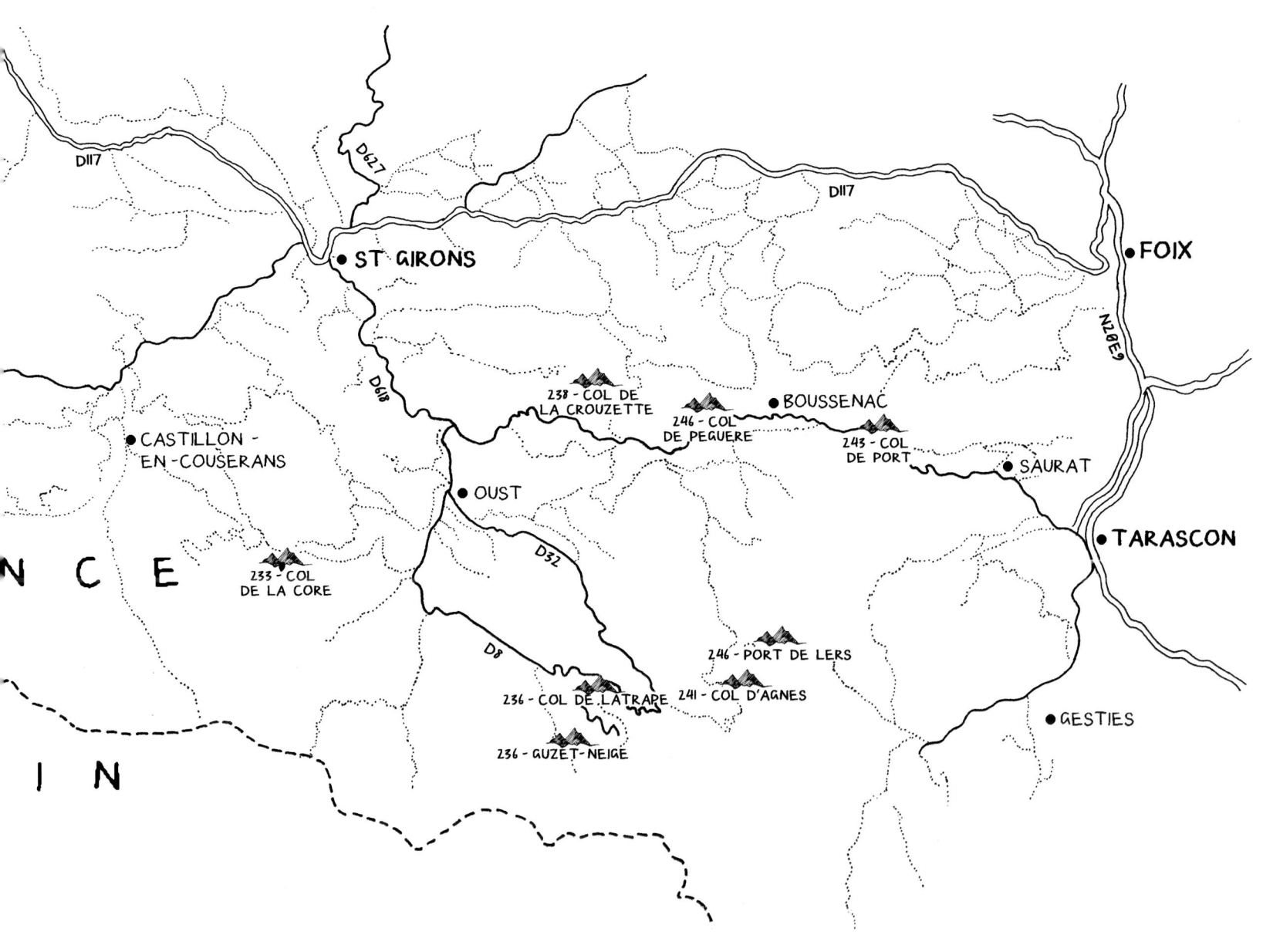

Local butchers will often mark up on a slate the origin of the animals whose meat they are offering for sale: farm or tiny homestead. It's gastronomically encouraging, if offensive to the pernickety foreign townie sensibility. Tough.

The Ariège is also famous for its cassoulet and local chefs will argue strenuously for the absolute essential in their particular recipe of the exact right type of haricots, and there are many – for fatness, size, texture…

Cycling in the mountains of the Ariège is wonderful: many of the cols are remote, rustic, joyous to ride and the views, over the wild splendour of the Lower Pyrenees, magnificent.

P213 The house in *Oust* of a Catalan expatriate, still proud of the country of his birth

P214 A long view west from the *col du Menté*

P216 Tarmac visitor's book on the northern slopes of the *Agnès*

P218 Plaque marking the site of Fabio Casartelli's fatal crash

P220 The north descent towards *Aulus-les-Bains* from the *col d'Agnès*

P222 The corner on the *Menté* where Ocaña fell in 1971

P224 Goats…'Who are you staring at?'

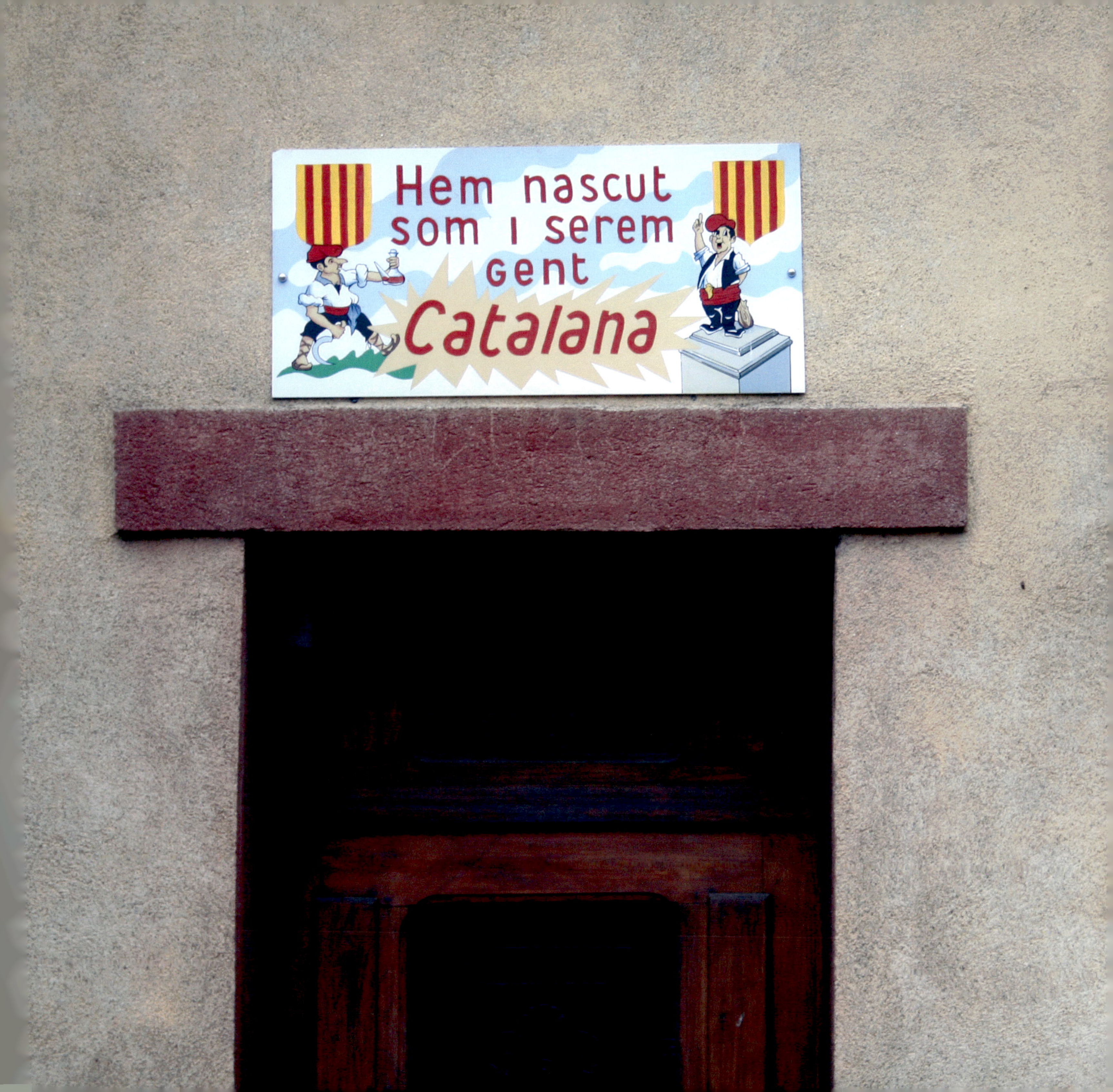
Hem nascut
som i serem
gent
Catalana

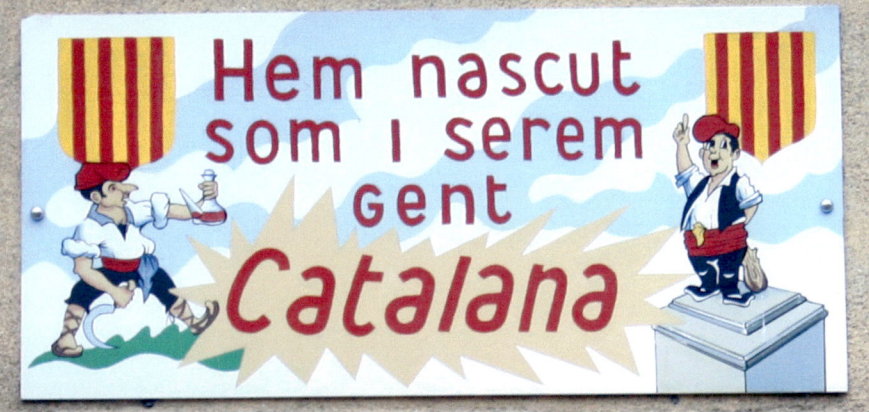

Col de Menté 1349m

Eastern approach

LENGTH: 11.1KM

HEIGHT GAIN: 750M

MAXIMUM GRADIENT: 11%

Just south of Laubague at 633m turn right off the D618 onto the D85. The D618 continues up the Col de Portet d'Aspet. Follow the D85 along the valley of the Ger south. At 3.5km, through le Couret, and a right turn onto the D44 at the start of the climb, 780m, and on into the picturesque village of Ger le Boutx (885m, 5.3km). The road twists steeply out of Ger and climbs through woodland to the col. If you aren't satisfied, there's a road up to the ski station at le Mourtis (1450m) and a forest path down into the valley via the Col d'Artigascou (1351m).

From the meeting of three ways at the foot of the Col de Portet d'Aspet near Henne Morte, the col road climbs for a short distance initially but then flattens out and drops some way round the mountain wall to the left into a small hamlet (a gîte nearby) and round a big right-hand bend to the first real steep uphill, at 3.5km. The road surface is good. The rise and fall of this section of the climb makes nonsense of the average gradient, given as 7% on the sign at the crossroads, the prime reason why this Rapha guide prefers to register maximum steepness.

Further along this fairly tight valley entrance well-shaded with deciduous trees, another very sharp, twisting drop leads into the village of Ger de Boutx (885m, 5.3km) and a junction with the D85 leading up the fissure of the re-entrant cut by the river Ger to the forest track of the Col d'Artigascou.

The final 5.8 kilometres of the ascent varies in degree with several sections hitting the 11% maximum. A number of cyclists riding the Étape that hot day in July 2007 surrendered to heat and gradient and stopped to rest awhile in pockets of shade – tree cover gets scarcer above Ger de Boutx. The road rounds a tight right-hand hairpin onto a steep ramp out of the village, offering a clear view across the ravine of the church on the hillside. A slight easing into Soulan, just beyond Ger, and then the pressure resumes. A sign at 1089m gives the col at 3km which means an average of around 8.7%, parcelled out in variants of worse and milder. Those changes in rhythm make this a tough climb, the second half more exposed and demanding.

Two kilometres from the col the road is once more wooded on both sides and, as if flexing its own cramped back, flattens slightly towards the clearing at the summit – a high crag up to the right, a grand vista through the open curtain of trees straight on, the D44 up to the Col d'Artigascou and the ski station at le Mourtis to the left as well as – and, welcome indeed – the café/restaurant 'Halte Moto', another establishment which extends a special welcome to the motorbikes.

A memorial stone and plaque sits on the hillside below the crag to 'Serge Lapébie Route du Sud, 1948-91'. The son of Guy (3rd, Tour de France, 1948) and nephew of Roger (winner, Tour de France, 1937) Serge's own palmarès (career wins) have not, so far, come to light though he was 40th in the 1970 Critérium National, behind Cyrille Guimard, Raymond Poulidor and other stars of the peloton. Father and son lend their name to a cyclosportive event each summer – three circuits of varying length and difficulty in the area.

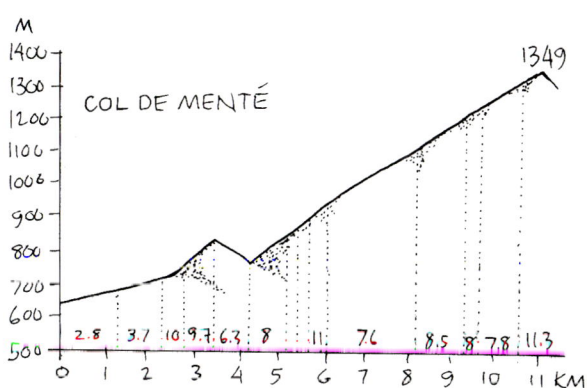

Western approach

LENGTH: 9.8 KM
HEIGHT GAIN: 850 M
MAXIMUM GRADIENT: 9%

From the main N125 heading south into Spain, the D44 leads out of Saint Béat (505m) and climbs hard up from the overspill of the town. At 2.4km, largely in a hollow to the left of the road, the village of Boutx, (700m and a church with a fine, imposing cupola). From here, a steady ascent up the valley wall and into the trees to the Menté.

Saint-Béat on the river Garonne used to guard the valley route into France from Spain. The castle, built in the 14th century, commands the road from a terrace above the town. Look out for the old-style pharmacy in the main street – apothecary's bottles inscribed with gilt Latin abbreviations of drugs, powders and simples. General Joseph Galliéni (1849-1916) was born in Saint-Béat, one of three First World War commanders hailing from the tonics in the air and soil of the Pyrenees: Ferdinand Foch, (1851-1929) Allied Supreme Commander from April 1918, was born in Tarbes, and the ancestral home of his family was in Argelès-Gazost; Marshall Joseph Joffre (1852-1931) came from Rivesaltes, famous for its white Grenache wine, in the Roussillon at the eastern end of the Pyrenean chain below the Pic du Canigou.

Just out of town on the D125 south from Saint-Béat, the D44 crosses the Garonne and immediately gets stuck into the hard work of climbing from 505m to the col 9.8 kilometres away. There are no signs, save, below the hamlet of Saint Boutx at 2km in, a panel welcoming you to 'Haute Garonne, Montagne Sauvage, Pays de l'Ours' (High Garonne, Wild Mountain, Bear Country). The gradients are sharp, none less than around 8% and a few injections of around 10%. The valley floor is spread with a beautiful plantation of poplars and Saint-Boutx is a friendly, shoulder-rubbing community of houses overlooked by a largeish church with a distinctive hexagonal domed tower, the six ribs sprouting from arched pediments. Just beyond the village, a huge molar of rock rears up to the side of the road, its base eaten away in the sort of cavity that speaks of years of chomping on far too many sticky and corrosive confections.

PAUL KATZ

'The Pyrenees this day were prisoners of a sombre shambles'

Some 3 kilometres from the top of the Menté, set high into the sidewall of rock on the angle of a right-hand bend, a plaque reads:

> "*Lundi 12 juillet 1971. Tragédie dans le Tour de France. Sur cette route transformée en torrent de boue par un orage d'apocalypse Luis Ocaña maillot jaune abandonnait tous ses espoirs contre ce rocher.*"

> Monday 12 July 1971. Tragedy in the Tour de France. On this road, transformed into a torrent of mud by an apocalyptic storm, Luis Ocaña, the yellow jersey, abandoned all his hopes against this rock.

In the Alps, Ocaña had crushed Eddy Merckx. Having taken a little over a minute out of him into Grenoble, on the next stage to Orcières-Merlette, the Spaniard launched an imperious attack and shelled out all the big hitters. Merckx chased furiously but lost nearly 9 minutes – and the yellow jersey. He clawed back some time in the next two stages, but on the morning of the first sally into the Pyrenees, Revel to Luchon, cols de Portet d'Aspet, Menté and Portillon, Ocaña still held a daunting advance of 7 minutes 23 seconds.

His father had crossed these mountains as a refugee from Franco's armies during the Spanish Civil War and young Luis (born 1945) spent part of his childhood in the Vall d'Aran across the river, east of the Portillon, before settling in Mont-de-Marsan, north of Pau. The Pyrenees were on his doorstep, he knew them well, particularly the Portillon near where he had spent his childhood. He decided it was there he would attack, intending to 'casser la baraque', to blow the race to bits for good.

On the Portet d'Aspet, Merckx set an infernal pace but Ocaña contained him, apparently quite at ease. Six times Merckx accelerated fiercely to drop his Spanish tormentor without success, and then the capricious weather systems of these inscrutable mountains intervened. The skies turned black and unleashed a storm of apocalyptic force. Ocaña detested rain and stuck to Merckx's wheel. Merckx was seemingly indifferent.

On the Col de Menté, the storm worsened. The black sky rent with gashes of electric glare from lightning. Hail battered road and riders, the road itself was awash with liquid mud which rendered the tiny brake pads on the bikes useless – better to use the soles of shoes – and visibility was near nil. The vertiginous descent was dangerous in any conditions but, in this Stygian obscurity, potentially lethal. The gloom was lit only by a haze of amber from the car headlights, filtered through veils of rain and hail. Explosive cracks of thunder reverberated deafeningly off the amplifying reflectors of the mountainside rock. The black torrents in the drainage gutters overflowed to make the road no better than a ski pad. It was about 4.30pm.

Into the bend marked by the plaque, a tight left-hander, Merckx, always a reckless descender and riding at a crazy speed in such awful conditions, aquaplaned and very nearly lost his wheel in a slip of gravel, but stayed upright. Behind him, Ocaña lost control, his front tyre punctured and he went down. As he stood up again, Joop Zootemelk ran into him, then Lopez Carril and the Portugese Joachim Aghostino, a great bull of a man. Ocaña was done for, sprawled on a bed of loose stones in terrible pain, his Tour finished, the yellow jersey soaked through, streaked with blood. A helicopter air-lifted him to a clinic in Saint-Gaudens where the nurses had to cut the jersey off with scissors.

The Tour went on. Down in the valley, the sun shone.[20]

Next morning, Merckx, once more race leader, refused to wear the yellow jersey, just as Ferdi Kubler had refused to put it on after the wholesale abandon of the Italians in 1950 in protest at crowd violence.

'The honour of wearing the yellow jersey ought to be Ocaña's,' he said. 'I have no right to take something which does not belong to me.'

---

20 One of Merckx's team mates, Marinus Wagtmans, descending at 80kph, shot off the road into a field.
Whether it was a wall he hit or a tree, his Tour was over, too.

Col de Portet d'Aspet 1069m

Western approach

LENGTH: 23 KM
HEIGHT GAIN: OVER 1000M IN TOTAL
MAXIMUM GRADIENT: 17%

Two routes on offer from the west: over the Col de Menté [see separate entry] or via the minor Col des Ares (797m) and Col de Buret (599m) – minor in difficulty but a very attractive crinkum-crankum road threading its way, dappled with light, through quiet Pyrenean woodland. From the main road north of Bagnères-de-Luchon the D then N125 followed by the D618 leads to an exceptional viewing point at Antichan-de-Frontignes. A sort of balcony looks out over the river basin and the far ranges, a truly splendid vista. The descent from the Ares – 6.3 kilometres into Cazaunous – and the 3.8 kilometre slope up to the Buret are as pleasurable an interlude as you will find in the far more strenuous blistering of body and mind on the big cols and the climbs they lead to, the Portet d'Aspet in particular.[21]

From the Buret pass (3.5km) drop into Sengouagnet, right turn, easy uphill of 3 kilometres to Laubague and a flattish kilometre to the base of the climb proper from Henne Morte and a bridge over the river Ger, the Pont de l'Oule. There remain 5 kilometres of extremely severe gradient – 17% for one longish stretch.[22]

About 500m up, a plaque marks the place where, on Tuesday 18 July 1995, Fabio Casartelli fell during stage 15 of the Tour de France. Descending from the opposite direction, he lost control of the bike and came off. The impact when his head struck the road was fatal; he was airlifted to hospital but pronounced dead on arrival. (This descent is particularly unpleasant because of the blind corners and variable camber – often it tilts out towards the open side where stretches of the verge are lined with small sharp-edged granite blocks.)

A short way further up from the plaque stands the memorial to Casartelli, the Olympic Road Race champion in 1992, in a small clearing to the left: a finely-sculpted disc wheel merging at the back into wings, rough-etched to suggest wing feathers, with the leading rim swathed in a banner streaming back as if caught by wind.

It is indeed a blighted col. On the 1956 Tour, Camille Huyghe crashed into the stone parapet on the eastern descent and sustained grave injuries but rode on. In the '70s an English speleologist disappeared on the flank of the mountain and in 1973, Raymond Poulidor plunged into a ravine and, though his injuries looked worse than they were, he was badly concussed.

'What's happened?' he asked. 'Can I get going? Tell me.'

'Come on, Raymond, better if you stop…' replied Louis Caput, his directeur.

The climb continues at around 9 and 10% – new green Haute Garonne signs mark the distances and altitude – but at 2 kilometres from the col, an interval of about 600m of 17% begins. It's horrible, mercifully not too long and it makes the 9.5% average of the long bends to the finish feel almost mild.

The road is well shaded most of the way until it opens out onto the approach to the col: a modest café and an ever-flowing source of delicious cool spring water to the side.

---

[21] Sound both 't's in Portet, 'e' is short as in 'bet'.
The 't' in Aspet is *not* sounded, thus 'aspay'.

[22] Just to the north, the subterranean complex of caves known as the Coume Ouarnède, also Félix Trombe-Henne Morte, has 104km of galleries, shafts and chambers at a depth of some 1,000 metres, with 45 separate entrances, the longest network in France and one of the most complex anywhere in the world.

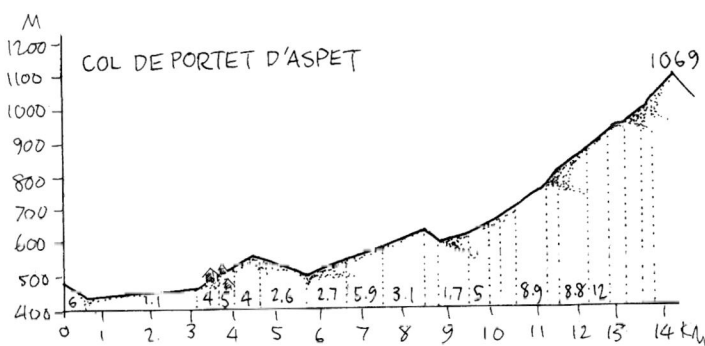

Col de Portet d'Aspet 1069m *continued from previous page*

Eastern approach

LENGTH: 5.6 KM

HEIGHT GAIN: 382 M

MAXIMUM GRADIENT: 11%

The D618 from Saint-Girons is no more than a fast uphill most of the way to Saint-Lary (687m and 5.6km from the summit) with occasional jerks of gradient to make the average look fiercer than it is. A fairly busy road for the first 12.4 kilometres to Audressein where you turn right onto a steep descent into the village – the road continues straight on as the D4 to Castillon-en-Couserans and the Col de la Core. On this quieter, undulating stretch, it's very pleasant riding through well-tended farmland.

In Audressein, a highly recommended restaurant to the left (Auberge d'Audressein) on the bend at the bottom of the hill; on through a number of villages, Argein, Aucazein and, in Orgibet (649m, 9.6km) one of the friendliest country restaurants I know, the 'Aux Deux Y', good food, excellent service, very reasonable prices. Say that you have read this book and mention 'the English cyclist who brings people every year to watch the Tour de France go through'.

More ups and downs, a gentle roller coaster, into Saint-Lary (bar and restaurant) where the gradient bares its teeth and snarls at you. From the village of Portet d'Aspet itself, (860m, 2.5km) the sweeping hairpins arrive and the going is moderately tough with a maximum, on the last ramp, of around 10 or 11%. But the restaurant on the col is clearly visible from some distance off, which is a powerful incentive.

In large white letters daubed on the packed earth of the bank to the left-hand side of the first major bend, Portet d'Aspet always advertises its summer fête, knowing that the cameraman in the helicopter following the Tour will focus on the legend as the race passes and give them some free air time.[23]

The climb in this direction is really of no great account, but the descent – 30.5 kilometres mostly downhill all the way to Saint-Girons – is one of the fastest, safest and most exhilarating in the Pyrenees.

---

23 *Portet* is a local dialect word (the Langue d'Oc being a close cousin of Catalan) for 'doorway, gateway, entrance' akin to modern French *porte*, and its Spanish equivalent *puerta*, corresponding exactly to *puerto*, the common Spanish word for 'col' or 'mountain pass'.

TOUR DE FRANCE 1934

Vietto's sacrifice

The morning of 3rd July 1934, 8am. The courtyard gates of the building in Paris where L'Auto, sponsor of the Tour de France, has its offices, 10 Faubourg Montmartre, swing open and the 60 riders signed on for the race emerge in front of a huge crowd. Along the Grands Boulevards, left down the Rue Royale onto the Place de la Concorde, up the Champs Elysées and on to the start proper at Le Vésinet in the western suburbs...

Antonin Magne, leader of the French team, recalled: 'What a memory that was, riding up the Champs Elysées... the crowds were denser than those which turned out for the Armistice in 1919.' Another member of the French team and a newcomer to the Tour, the 20-year-old René Vietto, had announced himself as a climber of sheer brilliance in races in the Alpes Maritimes.

His machine was tailored to suit his fluent riding style, modelled on that of the great Italian Alfredo Binda. The rear of the frame was reduced in size, the saddle very narrow, the bend of the handlebars quite shallow, the ends sawn off short. Prefiguring the heels-up action of Anquetil, he seemed to push the pedals with his toes and, even on severe gradients, he hardly rolled his hips, his whole frame steady, a perfect economy of effort. 'Purity. An artist. Poetry in motion on a bicycle,' as he himself described his hero, Binda.

He won the 7th stage into Grenoble over the Galibier, arrived in Gap the next day with an advance of 6min 28sec over his leader Magne, won the next stage from Gap to Digne over the dreaded climbs of the cols de Vars and d'Allos, and the 10th between Nice and his home town, Cannes. Having started the race quietly, in the mountains he had, quite simply, crushed the opposition and worked his way up from 16th to 6th overall. Magne was in yellow.

On stage 15, Perpignan to Ax-les-Thermes, Vietto, now 4th overall, flew up the Puymorens at unmatchable speed. On the summit, he lost some time in changing his back wheel round for a higher gear and the yellow jersey group, following him in Indian file, caught him up on the descent, near Hospitalet. Suddenly, Magne took a bad line on a bend and went down like a toppled log. He got up, unhurt, but the wooden rim of his front wheel had broken. (Wooden rims did not overheat from the friction of braking as readily as metal.)

He told Vietto to give him his bike. 'No, take the wheel,' came the reply.

Some sources record that this proved impossible because Vietto's axle was 9cm long, Magne's 8cm: the forks wouldn't take the wheel. But the picture shows Vietto in tears, sitting by his bike, number 38, minus a front wheel.

Meanwhile, a team mate Roger Lapébie flew past, averting his eyes, hot on the wheels of the Italians Martano (seen as the big threat) and Cazzulani. He took the win in Ax. After a frantic chase, Magne lost only 45 seconds altogether. The big loser was Vietto who lost 4 minutes on the day and the chance of moving up to 3rd overall.

The following day, Vietto agreed not to attack on the cols. At the start of the tricky descent of the Portet d'Aspet, Vietto slowed up so as to protect Magne. Some way down, Magne heard ominous cracking noises from his transmission then his chain snapped. This was disaster. Vietto, unaware of what had happened, was pressing on down the descent and the rest of the French team were some way behind.

However, the German rider Geyer overtook him and told him: 'Magne kaput.' Vietto, however, like Ariel, 'correspondent to command', turned round at the bidding of team loyalty, rode about a kilometre back up the slope and surrendered his bike to the yellow jersey. Magne rode off on the machine which ill fitted him, while Vietto sat miserably on the parapet wall to wait for the service vehicle. In those days, the lorry with spare parts and mechanic drove at the rear of the race. Any unfortunate whose bike was unrideable therefore had to wait for the entire field to go by before being rescued. On a flat stage this might not entail much delay; in the mountains, the loss of time could be crippling.

Vietto waited and waited, in tears, his ambition dashed, the glorious promise of his dominance in the mountains unrealised. He slumped to 6th overall and reached Paris winner of the Mountains prize (inaugurated in 1933) and 5th overall, only an hour down on Magne who took his second win.

Of the sacrifice of his wheel on the Puymorens, Vietto later said, perhaps sardonically: 'I didn't give it. They took it. It was a stick-up. I should have lodged a complaint.'

Col de la Core 1395m

Western approach

LENGTH: 14.5 KM
HEIGHT GAIN: 920M
MAXIMUM GRADIENT: 9%

From the junction with the D618 which continues into Audressein, the D4 finds Castillon-en-Couserans (550m) 1.4 kilometres further on. At Les Bordes-sur-Lez (580m, 3.5km) turn left on the D17 towards Arrien (6.6km) and the village of Aret (710m). At 8.6km, the narrow D417 tumbles away to the right and the road up to the col grows steadily more exposed. The views are glorious.

The road winds along the lower slopes at an easy gradient; round the first bend a good view down into the Vallé de Bethmale and the wooded slopes sweeping up from the riverbank. A 1 kilometre sign is at 630m and reads 5%. More bends, a very attractive ride, a lot of movement in the road into a small village, Arrien-en-Bethmale, well-tended gardens, vegetables and flowers. 2km, 5.5% and 680m, the road tops out once more with a fine panorama down to the right. This is like a long viewing platform. The tiny village of Aret with a war memorial; a French soldier – known colloquially as a poilu (hairy) from the moustache favoured as a sign of toughness – in a pale-blue greatcoat. Every community records the names of their war dead, Morts pour la Patrie, many of them showing a list containing several men with the same surname, possibly related. In a hamlet, the lists are poignantly short, but what a crippling proportion of their able-bodied does that represent? The majority of these dead were lost in the appalling slaughter of the First World War, many of them in the bitter fighting round Verdun.

The villages strung out along the road, six in all, add interest and welcome, deflect the obsession with percentages and distance and height gained. Not much cover, occasional banks of trees, a good surface, and the satisfaction of a long look down to the valley road – the more down you look, the more up you feel. Possibly.

Samortein off to the right as the road sweeps down a long bend and a very flat stretch to relieve the legs, into a small community, Ayet, a block-built church to the left and a tumble of terracotta pink-tiled roofs to the right. The road, two lanes in width but not much used by cars, continues to swing in a pleasing rhythm and the valley narrows as it funnels towards the head, 6km and 5.5%.

Some shelter, always agreeable, and the gradient is easy, tightening slightly to 7.5 at 7km, a long ledge by the mountain wall to the left, and now the bends become crankier, less friendly, one of those climbs which has a middle patch – between the happy-go-lucky approaches and the exposed business at the top – when it doesn't quite know what it's doing with itself, or whether it's fundamentally sweet- or evil-tempered. 8km, 960m, 7.5%, meandering along the side of the mountain, then round a big sweeping bend at around 8.5km by a cordon of tall pines. There is no sign, yet, of where the road goes higher up, though a fine view back down the valley and a long vista of the knuckles of the interfolded hills and mountains in the distance. 9km 1035m, 6%, a big left-hand bend and another long cordon of pine trees shading you from the right.

At a car pull-in, near the Lac de Bethmale and a maison forestière (forest lodge), a byway goes off to the right, the road becomes quite sinuous and the hairpins are a clear indicator that here begin the upper reaches of the climb. Also, a long view of the ridge up to the left, a large bluff of rock, bare and scratched across with what must be the continuation of this tarmac. Scattered dwellings up

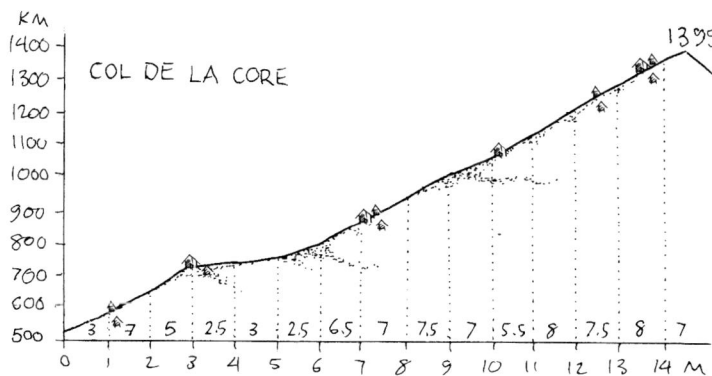

THE FOUR VALLEYS 233

and down the slopes, spinneys of pine, and now we can see what surely is the road. Whether this is comforting or not is a moot point. At least the kilometres are disappearing under the wheels and the col is being reeled in.

Grazing land to the left, cordoned off with drystone walls, as the gradient hits 9% into the valley head, and up above a huge mass of rock. 11km 1160m, 7.5%, from where the road you've ridden is clearly visible, the sight of it propelling you on: so far so good and so far and always on.

The road ahead shows itself, carved out of the side of this bowl-like re-entrant. An easy pull. Wonderful views both down the valley and up to the narrow yoke of the col and the high knoll called the Cap de Boureix. 12km 7.5%, cars descending reveal the course of the climb ahead and, as ever, the angle always looks worse than it proves to be. Steep hairpins, the col standing out up to the right, a little dip between the big shoulders of rock. 14km is 4% and we're at the col. (No 13km sign.) A commemorative plaque marks 'Le Chemin de la Liberté' (The Road to Freedom), in honour of the passeurs of the cantons of Castillon, Oust and Saint-Girons, who crossed this way, 1943-44. Stunning views west, where the valley sides are fairly shallow, around 45°, east towards steeper-sided flanks, 60°, and over three of the valleys which lend this sector its name; the Forêt de Seix on the mountainside to the right, the town of Seix way below. The col stands at the same level as most of the adjoining ridges. A caravan which calls itself Buvette ('drink stall') Col de La Core serves hot and cold drinks. A red and white wind sock up to the left, presumably for the benefit of hang gliders. A view of the road down into Seix for quite a long way round a series of tight hairpins. A sign on the road marking the entry from Haute-Garonne to the Ariège.

Eastern approach

LENGTH: 14.25 KM
HEIGHT GAIN: 835 M
MAXIMUM GRADIENT: 7.5%

From Seix (510m), the D37 climbs out through the top of the town to Sentenac d'Oust, 656m at 2.6km. Here the D37 leads right to the Col de Catchaudégué (christened, by a visiting clubman, the 'Catch a Dago') and another hour or so's riding to the col.

The road winds through the narrow street of Seix onto a broad long stretch of highway that is no pleasure to ride: a charmless urban exit. The climb gains in character the further it progresses. 1km says 7% but it feels a lot harder. Road surface smooth. The side of the valley to the right quite close, houses to the left. 2.5km, a turn-off to the right, the road swinging quite amply through an umbrageous overhang of trees. 3km 6.5%, 735m, long, hard ramps here, a wide unfriendly road on the climb out of Seix, altogether better for descending. At around 3.5/3.75km, Sentenac d'Oust, a cluster of houses, nicely tonsured meadows, on a very steep pitch that rears up abruptly, a road to the right leads to La Soumère and Alos, the southern approach to the Col de Catchaudégué. A good view of the Guzet range. 4km 6.5% at 785m, a large hayloft by the side of the road to the left. At about 4.5km a dense forest to the right and a line of larches to the left, fragrance of pines. This route is very handsome, the deep valley rarely far from sight. 5km 7.5%, and just beyond the sign, a sharp right hand hairpin onto the next level of gradient. 6km 6%, a long stretch where you can see way ahead, scarcely a kink in the road. 7km 3.5%, quite gentle, shaded, a welcome breather before a sterner test ahead and great views down in an arc of about 45° across the abyss behind, and a number of communities dotted about the junction of valleys. A waterfall on the right. 8km 6.5%, what this climb has that the other side does not have is the sense that you are getting to grips with the mountain from quite low down, tackling the height and gradients on a snaking road. Between 8 and 9km the road has the aspect of a corniche, hugging the mountainside and a precipitous drop to the left. This makes the descent tricky.

Beyond 9km (8%), where the trees have thinned out, a hard stretch – steeper and long straights with the airy space of the valley beyond the strip of tarmac. Then, a large cluster of deciduous trees, poplar, oak and birch, to the right. The ridge looks a long way off and that can be demoralising, a constant nag when you seem to be making so little ground.

At around 10.5km the road, quite serpentine here, suddenly becomes exposed, a yawning drop to the left, and, just before 11km (6%) a route forestière branches off and a torrent falls down the mountainside to the right – a rush of water and cooler air.

12km 7% brings a clear sighting of the col above at the notch of this deep re-entrant. The road is quite shaded and more enclosed than the western approach, the treeline reaching very close to the summit; as is very often the case, one side of a climb is densely afforested, the other rather barer. These trees are nourished by the wetter weather systems that come in from the north, the southern slope being more subject to sun and desiccating heat.[24]

24 The Col de Cachaudégué (893m) is well worth a detour. It tops the narrow road between Lacourt (on the D618 south of Saint-Girons) and Seix and threads through what feels like a lost valley, tiny hilltop clusters of houses en route, down to the course of a river and up again. A wonderful ride. Aptly, perhaps, rather stiffer from the Seix end.

TOUR DE FRANCE 2003

From the roadside... Cor! Lovely!

Riding the mountains is where you can get closest to the epic heart of the Tour de France mystery; watching it go through the mountains is where you truly experience the indelible thrill of seeing the race from the roadside and, although the pros never go what you might call slowly, the pace is trimmed a bit on the climbs.

   In 2003, the Col de la Core had a heavy presence of spectators lining the route, many of them having driven up the night before to be sure of a good vantage point. One of the campervans belonged to a young couple from Colorado. Two American cyclists rode up to the col and, happening on the folks from home, got into conversation. The young woman, fixing lunch, dropped something just as the first motorbike outriders with press cameras aboard raced up and, as she leaned down to pick up what she'd dropped, she displayed a perfect callipygous view of her sumptuous rear end. She was, the personal archive assures us, 'an exceptionally hot-looking chick'. A few minutes ticked by and suddenly the Colorado couples' cell phone rang. The husband answered, listened, suddenly beamed and began to laugh and shout into it like crazy. He handed the phone to his wife, who listened, blushed and, in her turn, burst out laughing, if rather self-consciously. It transpired that when she bent over and fulsomely displayed her tuchis, a camera moto swooped and the striking image was almost instantly flashed all over the television coverage of the race, Stateside. The folks back home were phoning to tell her how much they'd enjoyed seeing her on nationwide TV.

   'Man,' said the provider of the archive details, 'did she go pink. It was wild.'

Col de Latrape 1111m and Guzet-Neige 1520m

Eastern approach

LENGTH: 11KM
HEIGHT GAIN: 850M
MAXIMUM GRADIENT: 9%

From Seix (510m) the D2 follows the course of the river Salat, which rises in the ridge dominating the skyline south. At Pont de Taule (567m) the D3 continues towards the ridge and the border with Spain on its crest, as a sharp left turn becomes the D8 up the Ustou valley along the course of the Alet River. A succession of villages for no great gain in height: 6.7km La Pomarède, 8.3km Le Tourté, 9.1km Escots (654m), 11km Le Trein d'Ustou and 600 metres beyond to the right, the narrow-hairpinned D38. Across a bridge at Sérac d'Ustou and onto the climb. The road to Guzet swings off right at 17.2km, 1030m. The Col de Latrape lies 1.2 kilometres further on, Guzet 6.7 kilometres.

The eastern approach from Seix comes up the narrow valley of the Ustou, a gentle, undulating uphill of 12 kilometres via Pont de Taule and a sharp left turn; the road continues straight ahead south through Couflens and peters out just beyond Salau on the flanks of Mont Rauch. The Auberge de Myrtilles in Salau is recommended. From there you can continue on foot over the ridge via the Port de Salau – a ruined gendarme post and warehouse (for confiscated contraband) – into Spain. Sheep tracks on the far side lead, eventually, to grassy roads and long hairpins down to a grit road and finally onto tarmac and Esterri d'Aneu, at the foot of the Puerto de la Bonaigua [see page 114].

In 1813, Napoléon Bonaparte ordered the construction of a road across this ridge through the Port d'Aula, a few kilometres west of the Salau, to link the French Salat valley with the Spanish Vall del Noguera Pallaresa. (Since his brother Jerôme was installed on the Spanish throne, this posed no diplomatic problem.) The project came to naught but was revived in the mid-1960s when Spanish authorities considered the possibility of constructing a road as an additional trans-Pyrenean route for commercial vehicles which would also open up their valley for tourism. Once again, the project stalled.

A very pleasant ride (D8) all the way to Ustou and over the bridge at Le Trein d'Ustou ('Beyond Ustou') where the climb proper begins. 5.6 kilometres to the Latrape, 11 kilometres to Guzet. The Latrape is fairly mild, a broad well-surfaced road with long straights and generous bends which make it one of the fastest, most exhilarating descents in these mountains, all the way, (promisingly), to Seix. Gradients at 6.5, 7.5 and a short flattish stretch to 3km and 8%. At 3.75km a sign warns of 'Couloir d'Avalanche' (avalanche corridor). 4km gives 8%, the maximum steepness on this part of the climb which is fairly well shaded lower down. At 4.4km, the D68 for Guzet-Neige joins from the right.

A short downhill onto what is one of the most agreeable of all ski station approaches. It swings well in easygoing movements, a road with a longer pedigree than the hackwork of roads laid down for the sole benefit of the snow crowd. The gradient never tops 9%, there is ample shade from the pine trees skirting the road and the surface is smooth. (About 500m of new gravel at the start of the climb made the descent tricky in July 2005.) Signs read 6.5, 6.5 and, at 7km, 8.5%, where a big left-hand bend gives onto a long view of the spindly outline of a drag-lift gantry atop a big bluff way to the right. It might be a gallows. Beyond 8km at 8%, you catch sight of chalets part-obscured by trees on the hillside below the ski station and after a harder pull of 9% at 9km, the road flattens by a large car turn-off for the Hameau du Pas de Loup ('Wolf's Track Hamlet') and a sign 'Bienvenue à Guzet 1400'. A bar and restaurant perch above the car park. A fine view back down the Vallée d'Ustou. Just past the angle of the bend, the 10km sign reads 1450m and 7%. Long ramps to the bald summit of the mountain, plenty of food and drink and a splendid view across the peaks which mark the Franco-Spanish frontier.

After the descent to the D8, the 5km sign (which shows no altitude) reads 4.2% – so a fast run-in to the Col de Latrape and a couple of restaurants. The Champs des Neiges set back from the road is recommended. Excellent menu du jour and, always a good sign in France, frequented by local workmen.

The climb to Latrape eastwards from the spa town of Aulus-les-Bains is a regular 6.5–7% on 4 kilometres of wide road and long straights, a great view of the town from the lower ramps.

TOUR DE FRANCE AND ROUTE DE SUD
Memories of Millar

The climb has featured in only three Tours: 1984, 1988 and 1995.

In 1984, on a day of suffocating heat, Robert Millar rode to a memorable victory here. On the long climb to the summit he shook off both Jean-René Bernaudeau, who'd led them over the Col de la Core, and Gérard Veldscholten to take a win reinforcing his claim to the polka-dot jersey. This he won outright in Paris, having come 4th overall. Three kilometres from the top, Laurent Fignon made his own decisive move and tightened his grip on the race: he attacked, dropped Hinault and took 52 seconds out of him. He eventually led home his former boss into Paris by over 10 minutes.

A minute behind Millar as he broke free and went on alone to Guzet, the diminutive Colombian climber Luis Herrera made his first real showing in the Tour. The Colombians were riding for only the second time. Herrera had arrived and, his confidence mounting, won the Alpe d'Huez stage later in that same Tour. Three years later, he won the Mountains Prize itself.

In 1988, Millar's experience of Guzet was not so happy. Well-placed for another win, he approached the car park below the final kilometre in company with Massimo Ghirotto and Philippe Bouvatier. A gendarme stood at the entrance of the car park waving an indicating sign for the following cars to turn in. Whether it was Bouvatier's error or Millar's, they both turned off the road as Ghirotto swung left onto the final hairpin. Millar clocked the mistake almost at once and set off after the Italian at a furious rate. He crossed the line 2 seconds behind him and thumped his handlebars in an access of rage, disappointment and frustration. Bouvatier trailed in 13 seconds down.

The climb has twice featured in the Route du Sud, the only stage race to centre on the south-west of France. Starting in 1977 as the Tour du Tarn, it became the Tour des Midi-Pyrénées in 1982 and the Route du Sud in 1988. Stephen Roche won the climb on this race in 1985.

THE FOUR VALLEYS

Col de la Crouzette 1241m

Southern approach

LENGTH: 8.5 KM

HEIGHT GAIN: 670M

MAXIMUM GRADIENT: 12% (POSSIBLY 19%)

The D18 leaves Biert (590m) in the valley of the Arac and immediately swings up into trees. At 4.9km a bridge across a torrent, and at 5.5km a tiny clot of houses in Encenou (890m) signifying 3 kilometres to go.

A steep pull out of Biert (auberge – not recommended – church, post office) past the school and a hairpin left onto the long approach. Most of the way is shaded. The road follows the right flank of a deep gorge, its sides thickly wooded – a view across to the opposite flank and outcrops of dwellings, single or several together.

Surface pretty good, early gradient steady, road swings easily, serpentine, canopy of trees – oak, beech, poplar, sweet chestnut – km signs.

At just under 2km, a battered old Peugeot car, abandoned, with written on the door: 'Aux mains de l'état, la force s'appelle droit. Aux mains de l'individu, elle se nomme crime… oh chromozome Y' (Force in the hands of the state is called right, in the hands of the individual it is known as crime… oh chromosome Y)[25] and 'Le monde est une vraie porcherie, les hommes se comportent comme porcs' (The world is a real pigsty and human-beings behave like pigs). Good humour is restored at c.2.75km (Loubac) by a laughing horse's head signboard indicating 'Association Cheval Rit Ferme Equestre' (The Laughing Horse Association Equestrian Farm) – 3km-c.4.25km, flat or easy, fast, good warm-up.

From 4.25km, a left-hand hairpin and the gradient stiffens to 6km where the trouble starts: sign indicates 1001m, 12.4%. About 500m of extreme steepness, really demanding, to a shallow right-hand hairpin and a slight easing of the slope, then another shortish stretch to a left-hand hairpin and the extreme gradient returns. 7km shows 1225m and 12%, cuing more very steep climbing as the trees thin on the left-hand verge and the magnificent view south opens up – if you have the inclination to look. Around 600m on to another shallow right-hand hairpin that leads into a relative flat stretch – a terrace from which to take in the panorama, trees all round, no bare rock visible anywhere. The flat rises slightly into the final hundred or so metres to the col. (An independent topographer measured a short stretch – 30 metres or so – of 19.9% on the final extreme slope.)

Three roads on offer at the col: right over Portet towards Tour de Laffont and Col de Péguère, straight on down to Rimont and the main Foix road, left the back way to Saint-Girons.

Western approach:

LENGTH: 17 KM

HEIGHT GAIN: 834M

MAXIMUM GRADIENT: 9%

Turn left off the D3 south from Saint-Girons on the D33 to Rivérenet along a flat valley bottom, river off to the right, well-shaded, a good road surface, no difficulty in the gradient. Into Rivérenert (4km) there's a steep climb and, once more, a gentle slope up the course of the river Nert. Meadows and cordons of trees. Just past the right-hand turn to settlements up the hillside, a house set back from the road with an ornamental pond. A similar sentiment pertains, one imagines, as that expressed in the name of a house on the gentle climb up to the nearby Col de Serailler, *Qui aurait le dit* ('Who'd have thought it?'). The unexpected nest of repose, the dream come true.[26]

This is a lovely road, penetrating the heart of a hidden valley; the gradients undemanding, the surroundings beautiful, lush, close in. A climb with plenty of swing and rhythm, it needs no detailed logging because the climbs it vies with are so much more demanding, but this is a way to be ridden, full of the sheer joy of being on a bike and getting to the top of a ridge.

There's a steep stretch into the small town of Lauch – church and gîtes – and the road winds on, neither hard nor easy, a pleasant detour from the crueller margins of the Pyrenees. A view across the open valley to the hilltop village of Erp, en route to the Col d'Ayens (950m) and the cul-de-sac at Tuc de la Courate. A bonny sight, houses perched atop the thickly afforested slopes of this valley.

Plenty of shade on this ride with sporadic clearings for sun to warm the sweat. A short way from the hamlet of Las Cabesses (around 11km) a 2 kilometre sign, the first noted, to the intermediate Col de Rille, then 1 kilometre and the junction of roads at the col, (938m): up from Rimont, on to the Col de la Crouzette. A metal plaque in the shape of the hexagon of France and a chain – broken – marking the mountain frontier between France and Spain records that this was the site where the 3102 Company FTPF (Francs-tireurs et partisans français – sharp-shooters and French Resistance patriots) and Spanish guerrillas fought the invading

---

25 In mammals, the sex-determining Y chromosome triggers embryonic development.

26 The Serailler (942m) goes up from Biert in the opposite direction and is a lovely ride. Excluded here on grounds of space and the shaky grounds that it doesn't quite make 1000m.

Germans 'for the life of France'. No date given.

A sign indicates 11km. Do not be dismayed: this is the minor road, D18a, which winds up in Biert – the distance to the Col de la Crouzette is a mere 3.5 kilometres. 9km at 1076m promises 9.2% but this is the worst of the climb and from 10km, 7.7%, it's a breeze to the col. Either ride straight down to Biert or enjoy the scenic majesty of the tobogganing ride over the intervening Col de Portel (1432m) and a fine view both north – the plain towards Carcassonne – and south, the first sproutings of the Bas Pyrénées.

Northern approach

LENGTH: 11 KM
HEIGHT GAIN: 720 M
MAXIMUM GRADIENT: 9.6%

The main D117 east from Saint-Girons, direction Foix, is a bit of a pain but 0.5 kilometres past Rimont (525m) take the D18 heading towards Feillet, and where the Feillet road swings left (511m) continue straight on and into the trees – a lovely woodland ride, this. The Col de Vigne (636m) arrives at 4km, and at the Col de Rille (938m) in a forest glade various woodland tracks converge, with the D18 continuing left towards the Crouzette.

A quiet, narrow forest road, a corridor of overhanging deciduous trees, winds out of Rimont – Village Martyre, Abbaye – to the more open side of the valley where, at 3km the climb begins with a kick of 9.3% from a right-hand bend over a bridge. At 4km there is an extremely steep pitch, probably 10%+ before it eases off to accommodate the average of 8.9. The rest of the way to the Col de Rille is as tranquil and delightful a ride as you could wish for, given the dubious appeal of 7.9, 9.4, 7.7, 9.6%. Nearing the top, where the road swings once more into tree cover, a fine view across the valley right where plantations of trees, coniferous and deciduous, in long strips side by side, give the appearance of a chunky sweater, cable and plait stitch, very beautiful.

Eastern approach

LENGTH: 26.6 KM
HEIGHT GAIN: 1000 M
MAXIMUM GRADIENT: 8%

Out of Foix to a roundabout and a sign for Saint-Pierre de Rivière, the road following the course of the Arget River, 11 kilometres of nothing more serious than 4.5%, and for the most part around 1 and 1.5. Just beyond a turn (right) to the hamlet of Sahuc, the gradient thickens to 6.5%, the road crosses a bridge and there are 3 kilometres of 7% average, generally well-shaded, followed by 5 kilometres of around 6% to the Col des Marrous (990m), where the road takes a rest in a broad clearing of pine trees, a centre for research into asthma hidden among them, a friendly little auberge to the left and, usually, a drinks and ice cream van in a clearing to the right. On 7.5 kilometres to the Col des Jouels (1247m) with pitches of between 7.5 and 9%. A tiny road from the north divides just below the ridge: one branch joins at the Marrous, the other just above the Jouels. From the ridge the view is stupendous – way down and across the plain towards Carcassonne, the slopes thickly wooded. (This northern approach, from La Bastide de Serou, is almost identical in profile to that of the eastern approach from Foix; a lovely bucolic road, and a charming ride.)

The final stretch to the Col de Péguère and the Tour Laffont is very easy – 6.5 and 2.5% – and ample reward for what is quite a taxing long haul from Foix. The views across the Massat valley and the Communal Forest of Boussenac are stunning; continue along the ridge for an even finer perspective, north and south, one of the grandest panoramas in the Pyrenees.

Along the ridge, 3 kilometres of pretty-well flat gradients with a few undulations on a broad road, to the Col de Portel (1432m) and on, a twisty, tobogganing route, fairly exposed – hedgerows where locals pick myrtles in late summer – to the top of the Col de la Crouzette.

ROUTE DE SUD 1994

Kelly bows out

In his last season as a pro, 1994, Sean Kelly rode the Route du Sud. World number one from 1984, winner of 3 Tours of Lombardy, 2 Paris-Roubaix/Milan-San Remo/Liège-Bastogne-Liège/Gand Wevelgem and Paris-Tours, 7 Paris-Nice consecutively, 4 points jerseys in the Tour de France and overall winner of the 1988 Vuelta, he had, at last, begun to show signs that the racing was getting to him. Hitherto he was like granite; nothing ever penetrated the mask of apparent indifference to anything that life in the peloton threw at him. The man was impervious. However, as his career moved towards its close, the *King of the Classics* was, maybe, just growing a wee bit tired.

The second stage of the Route du Sud, 149 kilometres from Saint-Gaudens to the mountain-top finish at Guzet Neige, traversed the Crouzette. Nick Flanagan, who lives nearby, describes how, on the climb – and not from the extreme southern approach – Kelly simply got fed up to the teeth with the whole business and dismounted. He wasn't, surely, going to pack it in. For a while it seemed that he was. Bobet on the Col d'Iseran… Anquetil between Chamonix and Saint-Etienne… climbing off in mid-race, removing the number, the face blank, that's it, fellows, I'm out of here, quit for ever.

Well, maybe the brief rest gave the man from Carrick-on-Suir second thoughts. He remounted, finished the race and came tenth. Over the Etang de Lers en route for the Agnès,[27] the road was pretty well blocked by cows – free ranging and not subject to local bye-laws – so next morning in Seix, the riders went on token strike. Racing against each other was one thing, taking on the strolling milkers of the high ranges quite another. They were, eventually, persuaded to get going.

Kelly's last year passed without victories and one of the finest riders ever to have pushed a pedal stopped racing after 16 years as a professional and a glorious range of wins.

---

27 Agnès is pronounced 'Ann-yes'.

Col d'Agnès 1570m

Southern approach

LENGTH:	10.5 KM
HEIGHT GAIN:	820M
MAXIMUM GRADIENT:	10%

The D8 east from Aulus-les-Bains (750m), reaches Agneserre (1100m, 4km), crosses a bridge over a stream (1368m, 7.2km) and another bridge 0.7 kilometres on by the Plateau de Coumebière, leaving just less than 3 kilometres to ride.

Aulus has restaurants, bars, camping facilities and hotels as well as the thermal spa, recently resuscitated. All treatments (mud, massage and much more) have to be booked in advance but the swimming pool and integral jacuzzi are open on demand. The once-favoured Grand Hôtel – dilapidated and for sale – remains grand in name and size only, a relic of the heyday of fashionable Aulus.

The road linking Aulus and the valley of Vicdessos to the north was envisaged in the 1930s but the road over the col was not built until the mid '70s. From Aulus, this is a severe climb, the first half a testing succession of 10.5, 10.6, 10, 8.4, 8.1, 8, 8.9%. However, it is a lovely road, winding up the ravine of the Garbet River as it flows down from the high lake to which it gives its name. There is little shade but the bends are long and at 4km, in the hamlet of Agneserre, where there's a car pull-off but no houses apparent, through the trees there opens an imposing view of the mountain wall looming over the head of the valley, its crest a fretted line of broken rock teeth, then below the bare gums of a smoother bulk of grass-covered slopes.

The valley narrows, the babble of the river coursing over rocks is a treat, flat meadows spread out below the road. Hairpins begin from 5km, where another lay-by gives room for walkers to park cars and set off up the mountain trails to a ring of lakes below the Pic Rouge de Bassiès. An information board shows where the trails go.

At 6km, the road flattens onto a balcony from which you gaze down over the serpentine road you have just ridden, Aulus nestling in a hollow of the mountains and the Col de Latrape and Guzet off to the left. A good spot to pause, if the aesthetic pleasure of getting to altitude supersedes the physical.

Just past 7km, it's 6% where the trees get scrubbier, the terrain more barren and a torrent rushes off the mountain wall to the right and under the road, delivering a welcome breeze of cool air. At 8km, as the road eases onto the Coumebière plateau, another stream courses through flat meadows to the right and finds its way beneath the road. At around 8.5km, the road skirts a protruding bluff of rock onto a ledge from which can be seen the upper reaches of the road and the bastions of the mountain towering above as well as the folded perspective of the mountains bordering on Spain, dominated by the Pic de Certascan at 2840m – layer upon layer in a spectrum of dark and lighter shading, a typical Pyrenean aspect, pleated spines of rock in graduated textures of green and misty grey, like a theatre set, back-lit. Dotted either side of the great ridge are a number of lakes, fed by the mountain sources and the melted snows of winter.

This final section of the climb offers a good illustration of the definition of 'col' – a narrow ridge-like depression between two higher mountain points. The pass is clearly visible from some way off and the mountain itself is revealed as a conglomerate of large bosses of rock rather than a single stone-cast formation. Indeed, this is the general characteristic of these ancient mountains which have settled into position over millennia of earth movement and the moulding of weather.

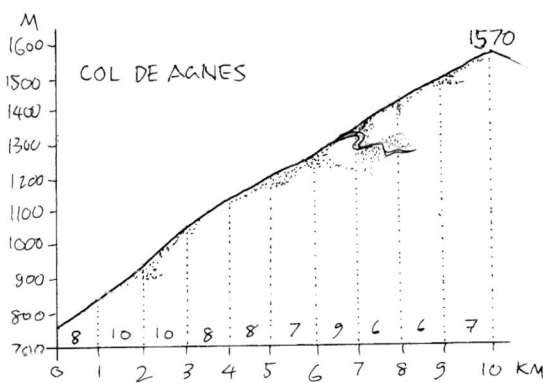

The last slopes are gentler in grade (7.6, 3.7, 4.4%) save for a vengeful 10% from 9km but this makes the run-in an absolute joy, the final bends taking nothing out of legs and lungs which have endured the assault of much worse for most of the way.

From the top, a narrow, windswept buckle in the rock's gaunt bulk, fine views back across to where you have come from and down across the bleak ranges towards the Etang de Lers on the first sector of the descent. Someone has chalked on the road: 'Santé Bonheur' (Health Happiness).

When the Tour de France crossed the col by this route for the first time in 2004, Rasmussen, former Worlds MTB champion, won the prime.

Northern approach

LENGTH: 17.6 KM
HEIGHT GAIN: 940 M
MAXIMUM GRADIENT: 8.5%

From Massat (650m) to Le Port (730m, 3.8km) and Courtal de Bastard (1295m, 12.7km). At the T-junction, turn right on the D18 past the Etang de Lers (1274m), 3.7 kilometres to the Agnès, left to the Port de Lers (1517m), 3.8 kilometres.

A gentle ride out of Massat, original administrative capital of the region, the route taken by the cattle and sheep when the animals are driven up from the winter quarters to the summer pastures, the Transhumance. A short drop and onto the climb and an easy 3.8 kilometres (2.5-3%) to the sleepy hamlet of Le Port – named for the gateway that is the col. A graveyard prominent to the left – ever reassuring – and a turn right to the high estives (summer pasturage) below the Pic des Trois Seigneurs, the humped mountain peaks named after the Three Kings who arrived at the stable in Nazareth on what became the Feast of the Epiphany.

From Le Port the road winds on at a straightforward 5-7.5%, with long stretches where one can see way ahead; houses pop up on either side, but by around 10km the only habitation consists of abandoned drystone cabanes up the hillside – small refuge cabins, conical in form (easy to build without the materials to make a flat roof), used by shepherds during the long summer grazing. At around 4 kilometres from the summit the view of the intermediate col by the Etang de Lers winks from the horizon, the hairpins begin – no great steepness, between 6.5 and 8.2%, long steady ramps in between, a good rhythm in the road – and the climb beckons.

The final 2 kilometres really zip along. Past a refuge at 12.7km called Courtal ('small hut') de Bastard – make of that what you will – and well-munched grass to either side the road: the cows eat it down to about two inches, the sheep nibble it down to razor fineness. A near-flat run into the T junction: right turn to the Etang de Lers and the Col d'Agnès and left to the Port de Lers. Above the Etang de Lers there is a good restaurant with tables at the front for drinks and a balcony overlooking the water for meals. Recommended. A plaque, installed on 12 August 2001, commemorates the passeurs. The gamelan of cattle bells, slung round the throat, is pleasing.

A steep drop to the lakeside and there remain 4 kilometres to the Col d'Agnès. The road stark and steep in view, cuts into the bare rock of the Pic de Cayzardet to the right. 7.5, 5.5, and 2 kilometres of 8.5% to the summit, but no large toil because the rock is up there and when you get this close there is nothing to stop you. This is the moment of crux, between the slog of turning the pedals for so long, so very long, and the realisation that the prize is, finally, within grasp.

At the junction above the Etang, the road left leads 3.8 kilometres round a sharp left hand to a steep up and a right to the Port de Lers, 8.5 to begin and then fairly mild (see page 246).

Col de Port 1249m

Eastern approach

LENGTH: 17.5 KM
HEIGHT GAIN: 774 M
MAXIMUM GRADIENT: 8%

Take the D618 (that road gets everywhere) north-west out of Tarascon-sur-Ariège (475m) to a roundabout and second exit right towards Massat and Saint-Girons. At 4.5km a small town, Bédeilhac (630m) followed by 1.5 kilometres downhill. A bridge over the river Saurat (620m 6.1km) and the village of Saurat itself (680m, 7.8km) on a by-road off to the left. A long flat straight, then more climbing into Prat Communal ('common pasture' – 936m, 11.5km) leaving 6 kilometres to ride.

From the roundabout north-west of Tarascon, across the main road between Foix and Ax-les-Thermes, take the D618 towards Massat and Saint-Girons, a gentle climb of 4.5 kilometres through Surba to Bédeilhac (630m). Restaurant and bar.

The Grotte de Bédeilhac, an immense cavern hollowed out of the limestone by millenia of mineral water seepage, is decorated with prehistoric wall paintings and was later used as a refuge by Cathars on the run from the Catholic armies in the 13th century and by the Germans during the Second World War as an aircraft hangar.

From Bédeilhac, an easy pull with scarcely any gradient to a longish downhill stretch followed by a sharp right-hander, the Le Chalet restaurant and a bridge over the river Saurat, 7.8km, with the village it names (630m) off to the left. A long, flat straight (past a restaurant/bar) to the designated start of the climb at 9.3km from the col (555m) and offering an average of 4.5% with 8% maximum. That average, you quickly discover, is misleading: the climb up into Prat Communal past the church (11.5km) and for a couple of kilometres beyond is genuinely steep before evening out to a gentler 5% or so. A string of houses of venerable date, meadows falling away to the right, tree-lined verges. The trees thin out, and from a more exposed line the far side of the valley comes more boldly into view.

Three kilometres from the summit, the weight of the mountain begins to lower round you and the hairpins kick in; at 2km, the auberge on the col comes into view and the road gradually shakes itself free of the twistier kinks and steadies for a long run in to the top.

The view is beautiful: back the way you've come, a small gathering of big rock peaks, like a civic deputation petrified in time; ahead, the aerial launch-pad into the Massat valley.

Western approach

LENGTH: 12.3 KM
HEIGHT GAIN: 619 M
MAXIMUM GRADIENT: 8%

A sharp drop out of Massat leads to a bridge over the Arac (630m) and a steep pull onto the start of the climb. At 5.9km, the Col de Caougnous and the infernal road leading up to the Péguère.

Through Massat past the church, the road pike-dives almost back on itself down to the bridge over the Arac River and surfaces onto a steepish double bend. Once settled, the gradient is fairly sedate, through the little community at Espies – grocery store and baker – and for some distance beyond. This is a climb where you can hit some speed and flirt with the idea that riding cols is a breeze, after all.

A flash of memento mori follows, the mountain reasserting itself with an injection of contourish pride, but the steep run is brief and the way is pleasant – houses dotted along the roadside, either makers of milk cheese from local ewes, or small holdings that feed up the cows whose meat will appear in the Massat butcher's shop.

The intermediate Col de Four ('oven col') is a non-event and at the Col de Caougnous, (947m) 6.4 kilometres from the col, a road joins to the left, leading to the vicious climb of the Col de Péguère. The Col de Port – in effect 'the pass of the gateway' – can be vaguely discerned now, a large teardrop of sky falling into the forest lining the slopes of the valley ahead.

An easy ride in, long bends, some tighter crimps in the tarmac, and the final 2 kilometres – GPM ('Grand Prix de la Montagne') signs in red paint at regular intervals – are fast.

TOUR DE FRANCE 1937
Charlie Holland

Holland, the first Briton ever to enter the Tour de France, was amazed at the French riders: they habitually spent up to a whole hour on dinner. Imagine. In fact there was little or no time to spare for much else but riding, sleeping, and eating (and that ravenously). In Perpignan they got up at 2am for a scheduled 3am depart (eventually 4am) and tucked into soup, fish, meat, ham, eggs vegetables, fruit, beer, wine, coffee, mineral water. The Roman gladiators were given a sumptuous condemned man's last meal, the saguntum: Holland had just eaten his Tour version.

In the pitch dark, the first miles of the route – another triple-split stage – were hampered by long bottlenecks of farmers' carts and lorries coming to market; riders spilled in the crush. At daybreak, one jumped away, the bunch chased him down and the bosses of the peloton gave him a rollicking for his stupidity. They had to cover 325 kilometres in toto over a giant's mogul field of mountains. Holland had caught a slight cold and was breathing heavily. By the Col de Puymorens, the halfway point, his head felt clearer but on the descent his back wheel started to bump: he'd picked up a large boot stud in his heavy-gauge rear tyre.

From lunch at Ax-les-Thermes, the race moved onto the Col de Port. A short way from the summit, Holland, a bare 30m down on the leaders, punctured. The heat had warped the washer on his pump and he could only half inflate the spare tyre. He rumbled along a short way, begged another pump from an English-speaking journalist and crossed onto the descent. He punctured again: both spare tyres gone now. A third puncture. He had no option but to sit at the side of the road waiting – and hoping – that something or the service lorry would turn up.

Even in that remote Ariège region the roads were commonly lined with locals from the hillside hamlets and tourists on bikes and in cars, all drawn to see the passing of the Tour and its heroes, the giants of the road. A friendly priest gave the lone British racer a bottle of beer, but the sacristy didn't run to bike spares. A cyclist spectator offered him a touring tubular; in the excitement of inflating it, thinking he was saved, Holland broke the rod of the pump. He begged and borrowed yet another pump and set off, but the tyre was too big, it squirmed loose on the rim – impossibly dangerous to ride. He cadged yet another tyre which did fit and went his way down the long Massat valley. It's a lovely ride, but for Holland, anxiety gnawing at him, it must have been grim. Twenty-five miles on, the control in St-Girons was closed: the commissaires (officials) had moved on. Disconsolate, Holland took off his number; his Tour was over. He'd been beaten by punctures.

A Press car rolled up and he asked for a lift to the finish in Luchon. The journos gave him some spare tyres so he could ride on; a lift – even for an injured rider – was against the rules. He said the rules had already eliminated him; he'd pulled out. He fitted a tyre and remounted. The men in the Press car told him, in broken English, there was no reason not to carry on; they even grabbed his jersey to tow him, assuring him that he'd be reinstated, it wasn't his fault. But the Englishman baulked; penalised for missing a control, fined for taking a tow, he wasn't going to infringe regulations again. They insisted this was different. He didn't understand the workings of the race. But for Holland, the workings of the race were as impenetrable as if they'd been in code.

'I think they'd have done anything to keep me in the Tour,' wrote Holland, 'but I did not want to finish this great race unless it was by my own efforts.'

Col de Péguère, 1375m

Southern approach

LENGTH: 3.6 KM

HEIGHT GAIN: 425 M

MAXIMUM GRADIENT: 14%

From the Col de Caougnous halfway up the road to the Col de Port, the narrow road to the Péguère swings off at an acute angle and there follow 3.6 kilometres of one of the nastiest stretches of climbing in the Pyrenees. One year, the Tour de France route incorporated this climb but the organisers cancelled on the eve of the stage: they decided, after all, that the Péguère was too narrow to accommodate the following cars. Local cyclists had a different take: the Tour riders had got wind of what a severe ascent it is and complained.

Whatever the truth of the story, brace yourself for an extremely leg- and lung-sapping 30 to 45 minutes. The gradient does vary but never drops below 10.5%. The road is narrow and shaded to begin with, then exposed.

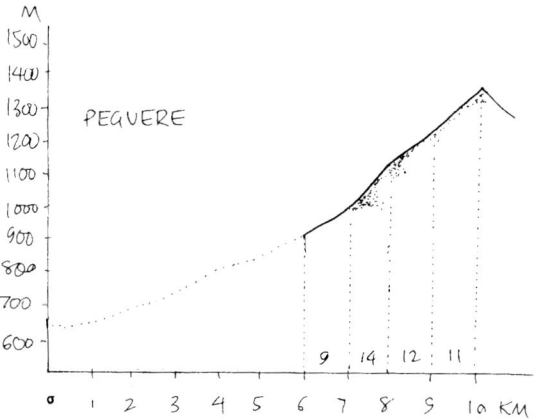

Port de Lers 1517m

Eastern approach [28]

LENGTH: 11.3 KM

HEIGHT GAIN: 807 M

MAXIMUM GRADIENT: 10%

The D18 runs south-west 15 kilometres to Vicdessos off the N20-E9 just outside Tarascon. It continues out of Vicdessos through Suc-et-Sentenac (852m, 1.6km) and up via the hamlets of Berqué (945m, 3.2km) La Prade (1070m, 4km) and Caqueloup (1110m, 4.8km) leaving another 6.5 kilometres to the Port.

For a truly memorable ride pick up D8 outside Tarascon and head for Etang de Lers and Goulier. The access to the Port de Lers and on to the popular little spa at Aulus-les-Bains is well-maintained and wide but fairly exposed, so it is hot. There are great views of the mountains to the side and interesting rock colorations and formations. The road, quite wide, open and flat, follows the river Vicdessos and provides a nice, relaxing tour along it. As you head into the lovely little village of Niaux and in the direction of the prehistoric caves at the Niaux Grotte you pass a restaurant, Le Petit Auberge de Niaux. The village nestles between the rock walls of two converging mountains, the remains of a mediaeval smelting works sits by the river – the Forge de Niaux – and the Musée Pyrénéen is devoted to lost folk traditions of the Ariège. Soon after you enter the village a left turn leads to the Grotte de Niaux – approximately 2 kilometres of a very steep incline and the ride, hugging the cliff wall, offers a spectacular view to the village below – but if you plan to see the caves and the famous wall paintings you must make reservations in advance.

[28] For the northern approach, see the description of Col d'Agnès, from Massat.

The road out of Niaux is quite flat and at Capoulet-et-Junac (7.5km), crosses a bridge over the river. (To the south stand the ruins of the 14th-century castle of Miglos – destroyed in the 17th century by order of Cardinal Richelieu.) A fine prospect of the high Pyrenees loom in the distance as you continue straight through the village on the meandering valley road over the Siguer River at Lamarade. Through the village of Arconac, past the old station, (the railway line is long gone) and into the narrow ravine on the lower threshold of the Port de Lers, a natural gateway through the mountains from ancient times.

Veer right into the village of Vicdessos (710m, 15km) and across the old bridge. At a fork in the heart of town bear left, then take the right onto D18 which is the entry to Port de Lers, distance 11.5km, 7% average, maximum 9.5%. A narrow alleyway guides you through the old section of the picturesque village and stone walls flank the two-lane road. A sharp hairpin to the left signals an increase in gradient as you head up and out of the village. Off to the left an escarpment and the rolling slopes of the mountains, from a cleft of which flows the river which names village and valley. Up here, above the village of Olbier nearby, stand the ruins of a Templar fortress, Montréal de Sos, where, in 1890, was uncovered a mediaeval mural depicting the Holy Grail and the Lance which pierced Christ's side on the Cross. The centrality of the Grail in Templar mythology and Cathar legend has been well-explored[29] and, to the east of the castle's broken walls, a forest trail leads over the Col de Grail (1485m).

After the first kilometre at 8.5%, 790m, the road flattens out a bit and there's a good view back over Vicdessos. After the brusque, initial take-off, this is a nice gentle ride into dense woodland, quite lush and enclosed with little to see beyond the trees. A slab of rock face to the right and a steep kick of gradient up to 10%. The road swings right, there's a sign for Port de Lers, km 2, 7.5%, alt 875 m, and you're in a sort of corridor really tucked into the mountain side, flanks rising sharply to either side. The view is restricted but you are well shaded. At the intersection – a side road to Sentenac – continue straight. A small farmhouse to the right, the road narrows considerably, and you are travelling a secluded forest route with stone houses in clearings, occasional meadows, and the stream coursing its way alongside. Dappled sunlight graces your passage.

The stretch of road between 3km and 4km is fairly easy going, with a gradient of about 5–7%. The corners are broad and easy. 5km, 6.5%, altitude 1045m is – isn't it? – like a friendly wave. Through the tiny hamlet of Caqueloup and you wonder what life must have been like up here in the days before even this narrow road had a surface. The road hears your unspoken query and gives its answer in kind with a sudden sharp turn to the right at km 6, 1110m and an intense incline of 8%, the harder because it is so sudden. It sets the pattern, too, for these final 5 kilometres.

The road meanders, passing over a small waterfall and a stone wall after which it flattens out and bears to the left and begins to criss-cross the same torrent which has been shadowing you up the mountainside – it's like reconnecting with an old friend. km 7, 6%, 1190m, ushers in some great views of the rock formations on the mountainside to the left. The road flattens out and as it takes a right turn and falls away to the left into a field of wildflowers, the formidable landscape of the mountainous outcropping confronts you, a reminder that mountains are rarely, if ever, finished with you. Rivulets join the torrent, a cascade tumbles off the mountainside to the right and a short way along another cascade courses under the road. There is almost no shoulder to speak of on either side and the view of the rock formation to the left looks as if someone once scooped out a section of rock with a giant spoon and the diagonal slashes of the road appear like a scar on its face. At km 9, 7.5%, 1345m, there's a superb view of the craggy mountains to the left, which may take your mind off a succession of harsh switchbacks at an unremittingly severe gradient.

Quit the hairpins onto the open brow of the mountain, its left cheek dropping away dramatically below a great view of interlocked mountains. Boulders pepper the side of the road. A viewpoint offers nearly 360 degrees of breathtaking panorama. The road winds around great twisting turns, slowly gaining altitude, past km 10, 7%, 1420m, and the side of the mountain is awash in summer colour, carpeted with wildflowers. At 11km, 5.2%, 1490m, the gradient eases up again onto the summit and, circling the top ridge of this bowl of mountains, there's a sense, not unusual in the Pyrenees, that you have reached the top of the world.

At the Port de Lers, there are full views in every direction, and paragliders share the air with buzzards. The descent to the Etang de Lers is a fast 3.8 kilometres of big sweeping curves, unparalleled views of your route, scenes of rocky meadows and graffiti from Tours past.

---

29 Graeme Fife, op. cit.

7. Ravines and High Woods

Sault comes from the Latin saltus, a mountain glade or a ravine, and the Pays de Sault, a beautiful, bosky enclave of rural France, riven with narrow valleys and afforested remote uplands, nurses a troubled history.

In 1208, Pope Innocent III called for a crusade against a rival Christian religion which flourished in the Languedoc, that of the Cathars, 'the pure ones'. He castigated them as 'worse than the very Saracens' and the Roman church denounced them as heretics. Their faith, always in conflict with Catholicism, was a dualist doctrine which distinguished between corruptible corporal matter and incorruptible spirit and advocated purity in daily life. So they neither preached or proselytised and practiced a simple, decent, communal existence. However, their perceived challenge to the established ecclesiastical authority went hand-in-hand with the old problem of Languedoc, namely its separateness from the rest of what must, at that time, loosely be called France. Languedoc, for so long autonomous and independent from the dictates of the French king, the neighbouring Catalan king of Navarre and the Pope, wished to remain so.

The Albigensian Crusade became as much a local resistance struggle as a bitter fight for survival on one side and extirpation on the other. It ended in 1244, when the Cathar stronghold at Montségur fell to the holy warriors of Rome. Over 200 heretics were fettered, dragged into an open space close to the foot of the rock on which the citadel stood, and burnt alive. They call this ground the Champs de Cramachts ('crémats'): The Field of the Burnt Ones.[30]

The history need not cling to your wheels unless you so choose, but there is an undeniable poignant force in the prospect of many of these Cathar fortresses, silent

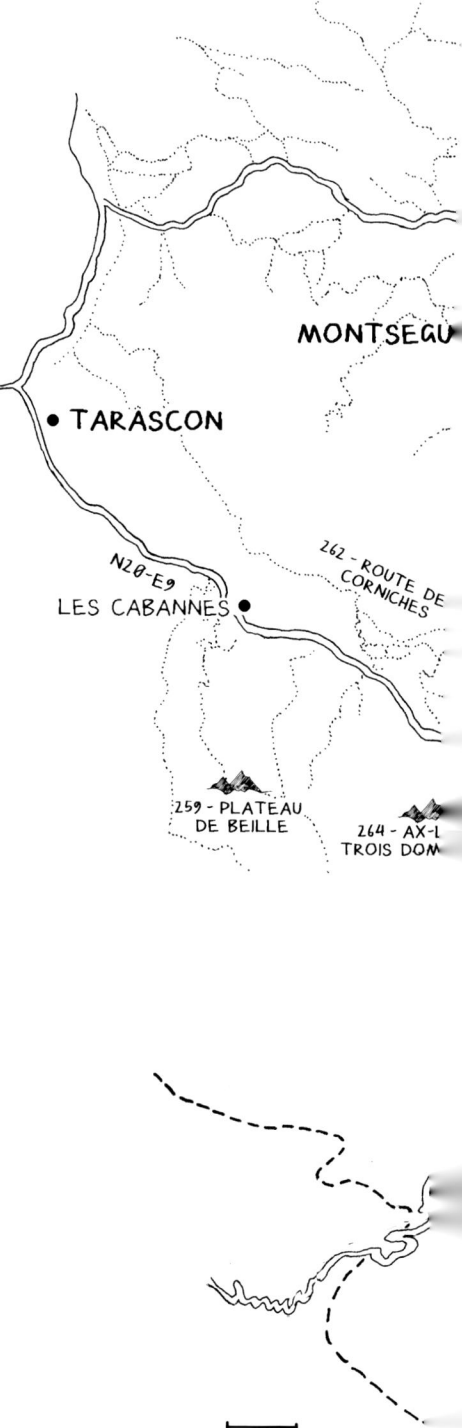

---

30 For the full, harrowing story, see Zoé Oldenbourg's Massacre at Montségur or Jonathan Sumption's The Albigensian Crusade.

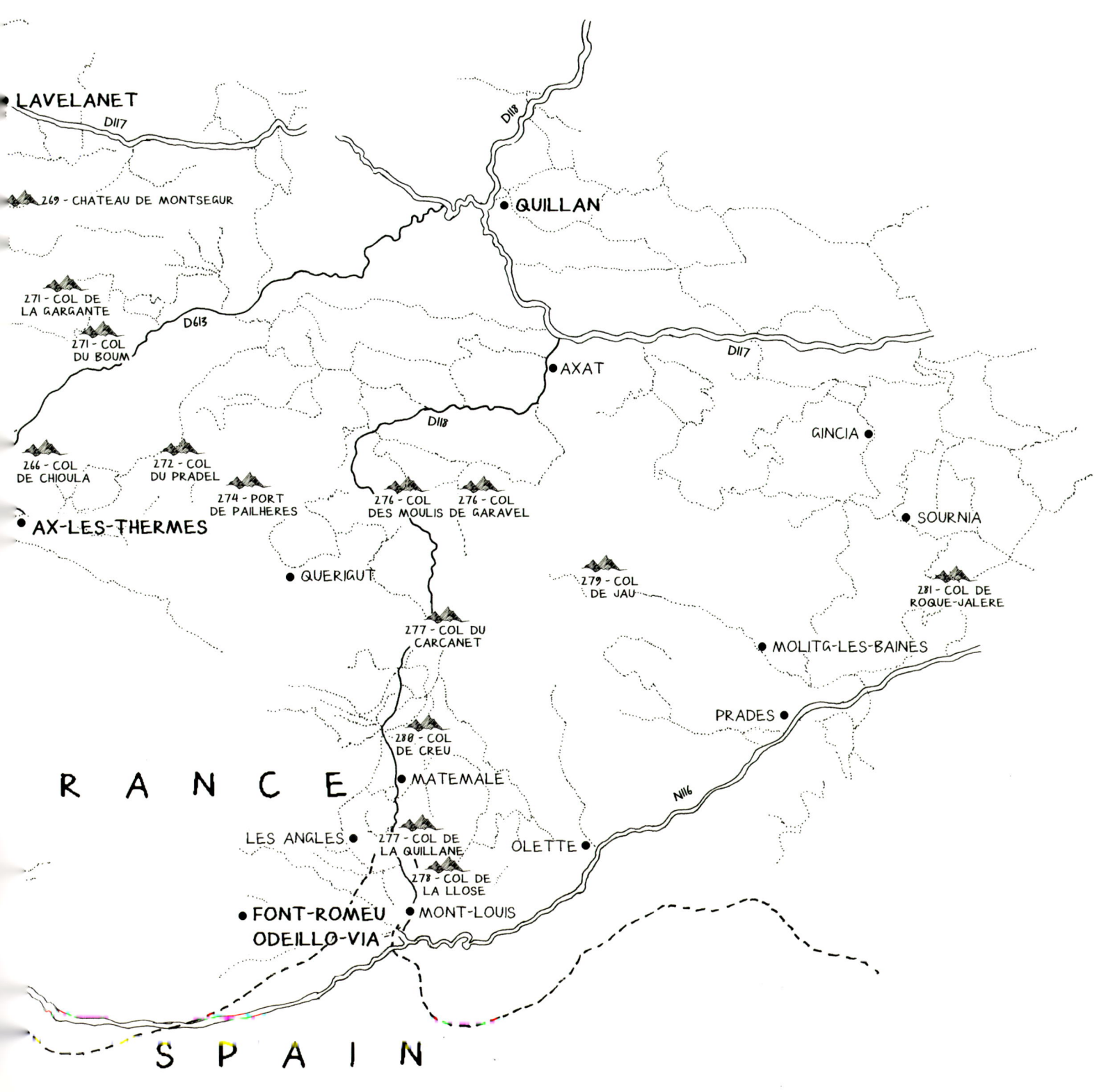

witnesses to a tragedy, whose masonry seems to thrust up out of the living rock, the pinnacle hilltops on which they sit, precarious and inhospitable.

One of this area's climbs will take you close to Montségur. Another, the Route des Corniches, takes you past the ruined Cathar fortress of Lordat, to which a number of Cathars fled for refuge from the Inquisition. Other Cathar castles can be found at Quérigut and Usson, on the far northerly side of the Col de Quillane, Montaillou, north-east of the Col de Marmare,[31] and Roquefixade, a short detour north-west of Montségur. Further west, at the eastern foot of the Col de Port in Bédeilhac and nearby Tarascon-sur-Ariège, are prehistoric caves used as hideouts by Cathars on the run, in one of which they were trapped and immured. Informed estimates suggest that the Albigensian crusade led to the deaths of around 500,000 people, many by mass hanging, drowning or torture.

If ever those fine Revolutionary principles, namely liberty, equality and fraternity, were followed as a living code of ethics, it was by the Cathars. The ravines and high woods were then not so much bandit country as the fastness where a decent, hunted people sought escape from vicious persecution.

Today the area is a delight for cyclists, a glory of quiet country roads and approachable cols, the pitiless and downright ugly inquisition of Beille and Bonascre apart... but you know, don't you, that there is no escape from the totemic stuff and you just have to do them? Here is some of the loveliest Pyrenean terrain, human in scale, full of discoverable secrets, green and shady, the ravines carved by rain and river, the woods of long date, and the promontories, the conical outcrops of rock on which the old châteaux perch, like eagles' eyries, preserving a sad, timeless beauty.

---

31 The French historian Emmanuel Le Roy Ladurie's Montaillou: Village Occitan 1294-1324 offers a classic study of mediaeval village life based on the detailed records compiled by the priest of the Holy Inquisition who interrogated the Cathars of Montaillou. (A UK edition of Montaillou is available in paperback.)

P251 Ruins of a *Cathar* castle near *Axiat* near the eastern end of the *Route des Corniches*

P252 The rustic tranquillity of the *Route des Corniches*

P254 The *col de Port* on a fluent downhill run towards *Tarascon* and the *Ariège* valley

P256 The snow-topped ridges north from the *Plateau de Beille*

P258 Bleak, cold, forbidding... the *Plateau de Beille* in its winter coat

Plateau de Beille 1780m

From Tarascon

LENGTH: 15.9 KM
HEIGHT GAIN: 1265 M
MAXIMUM GRADIENT: 10%

There are French hard men who say that the Plateau de Beille is on a par with Mont Ventoux and very few people who have cycled up it have a nice word to say about the brute. Indeed, there are a number of club cyclists I know who go queasy at the mere mention of the word 'Beille' for the wretched memories it invokes of their participation in the local Ariégois touriste-sportif one-day event for cyclists of all levels. Nerve-shattering souvenirs punctuated with expressions of horror – 'grovelling… parched… dead… horrible…'

Out of Tarascon take the N20 and bear right onto the D522 towards Les Cabannes. The exit ramp from the Nationale is narrow and it leads first into the quiet village of Aulos. The road surface is fairly good and the closed horizon ringed with mountains. Under the railway bridge the road enters Les Cabannes along a wide, tree-lined thoroughfare in good condition with plenty of room for cars and bikes and a view of a plateau hillside off to the left. Bar and restaurant, public loos to the right just before the centre of the village and a Sunday-morning market in the central square.

Immediately after the square bear right, then onto the D522 and the base of Plateau de Beille. A sign at 535m forewarns you: summit at 1780 metres, average 7.8% and the maximum, 10%. The mountain greets you with a respectable incline and graffiti mementoes of past Tours. A sharp hairpin swings you around to the left and starts a visually long uphill climb. The road surface is good with an even amount of shade and sun.

The road levels out for a moment before a brutal left-hand hairpin with a kick-up in gradient and a marker for km 1, altitude 600m, average 8%, followed by more hairpins and an increasing rise in the gradient. If there is one feature which makes the Beille such a hard climb it is the long straight ramps, the deadly slopes which show no movement, the ugly 'up and ahead' sections which, sliced out of the mountain for cars and coaches, show no friendship at all to bikes.

There are beautiful views to the right of the village below, an old church and a jagged escarpment, and here the road is quite wide and offers a fair amount of shade. There's a slight levelling off at km 3, 8.5% altitude 770m. The next kilometre seems very long, with unforgiving stretches of tough inclines connected by 180 degree switchbacks, but the road is quite wide and there are plenty of places to pause if need be. Pause? Why, the very idea. Cyclists do not get off and walk.

At the marker for km 4, 9%, altitude 855m, the mountain dominates your view, the road takes a harsh right and the incline picks up again passing by cascades, followed by tremendous views of the rolling mountains off to the right and more graffiti. The slope falls away sharply and with little vegetation there are great opportunities to gaze out over the valley of the Ariège. At km 5, 8.5%, 945m, the road levels out and there is a gentler stretch which provides some momentary relief to the legs. Be warned, however: try at least to maintain a pace

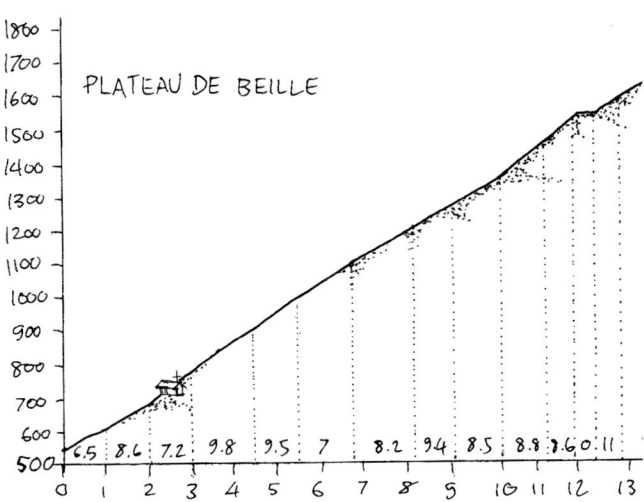

slightly faster than the horseflies because they do not give up and are congenitally vicious.

Traversing lush landscape, the road takes a hard right and the gradient steps up a notch which is noted on the marker for km 6, 7%, 1030m. The 7% is misleading. This is a very difficult stretch of road: the metal runs steep, straight and long, which seems to make it last forever. The views are some recompense: an awesome almost complete panoramic view of the surrounding mountains and the deep valley below.

At the sign 'Fôret Communale des Cabannes et Pech' the road takes a sharp left and the surface improves. The incline eases for a stretch then a tight right-hander signals an increase in gradient and a series of hairpin turns which crank up the gradient at each jink. This is relentless, very demanding. A series of switchbacks follow the Pic Forestière de la Garde – a walking path leading off road. There is momentary relief as the gradient levels off a bit into the forested portion of the mountain.

The road now curves round following a stone parapet wall. In this more heavily forested section, the road surface is good, but the shoulders offer little in the way of refuge with the forested slope to your right and the hillside falling away quite sharply to your left. The gradient barely slackens at all: the briefest of levelling out followed by a sharp hairpin turn and more percentage. km 10, 7.5%, altitude 1370m. Past the Fontaine Henry IV, another straight along a high stone wall and then a veer to the right into another series of sharp hairpin turns. This is a beautiful stretch of road – the rock face to the left is punctuated with wildflowers and to the right the evergreens draw back like curtains to reveal the valley and distant mountains.

A sharp left, Tour de France graffiti and the road is hemmed in by evergreens past the Routes Forestières des Ruis, after which the view opens up and the landscape clears out. A sudden inkling that you are approaching the top. But you have been approaching the top for nearly 12 kilometres. Patience, patience.

A long stretch that levels out towards the sign for km 12, 7.5 %, altitude 1525m. Fabulous views of rolling hills and a picturesque stone cabin, La Cabanne de Pierrefitte, (1606m), but into the thinner air, the immediate landscape becomes more barren. After a slight descent and more graffiti, the view opens up completely. The Basque climber Iban Mayo gets a mention. It didn't help him. He has never done anything on this strip of road. km 13, 7%, 1600m. This is the domain of raptors and there is a definite perception that you, too, are soaring far above everything… the effect of extreme muscular stress and hyperventilation, perhaps.

The plateau lies straight ahead and there are full views back down of the jagged road zigzagging up the side of the mountain. Off to the left, another stone refuge hut and fantastic views across the high peaks of these Pyrénées Orientales and the forested slopes of the adjacent mountains. Up the barren slope sprinkled with low-lying shrubs, more tight hairpins (Km 14, 7.5% 1670m) and then a great winding stretch of road flanked by a rocky escarpment. Lone huts stand like gazebos on the tops of the slopes. At km 15, your eyes check: 5% . 5%? Yes, 5% …altitude 1745m with the road, quite wide at this point, flowing in sweeping turns with a consistent incline onto the plateau, a huge area paved to accommodate crowds of ski traffic. The natural graces of this fine belvedere, high amongst the surrounding mountains, are fine, its human accretions in the shape of buildings – 'coyote ugly' as one Canadian cyclist, of strong legs and capacious lungs, described them. They do furnish a full complement of amenities, however, before you broach the adrenalin-rushed descent.

TOUR DE FRANCE 1998
Ullrich's fatal complacency

On stage 11 in the Pyrenees, the Spanish rider José Xavier Gomez was joined by the Swiss Roland Meier and their break consolidated. On the descent of the first climb of the day, the Portet d'Aspet, Meier crashed over a roadside barrier but recovered, chased Gomez and, with some 90 kilometres of the stage still to ride, went on alone over the Col de la Core and the Col de Port. At the foot of the Plateau de Beille, he had a lead of 3min 53sec on an elite chase group which included Jan Ullrich, the previous year's winner, in yellow, together with his team mate Bjarne Riis, Marco Pantani, Bobby Julich, Michael Boogerd and others. Surely they had left their pursuit too late. Meier was clear and going well.

Ullrich punctured, Riis waited and rode him back onto the group. Suddenly, Pantani attacked and took a hundred metres. Ullrich seemed about to respond but didn't go. He settled into his routine, churning, bum-on-saddle big-gear assault on the gradient. He had 4min 41sec on the Italian with an individual time-trial still to come, so he could afford to limit losses. The year before he had clinched what was to be a winning lead on the climb to the ski station at Arcalis in Andorra, not far to the south across the ranges. For a short while Pantani seemed to linger but then, out of the saddle, he surged ahead. Halfway up the mountain, he flashed past Meier who simply did not have the legs to match his speed.

Ullrich came second, still in yellow. Pantani won the day and, almost certainly, the Tour with that stunning show of force. He had, it seemed, broken something in Ullrich's will and exposed a fatal complacency. Ullrich's failure to answer the Italian's attack was evidence of his crucial lack of explosive speed, both physical and mental. It is a flaw which Armstrong, winner of only the second finish on this climb (in 2002), ruthlessly exploited.

Route des Corniches

South-east from Tarascon

LENGTH: 35.5 KM
HEIGHT GAIN: OVER 800M IN TOTAL
MAXIMUM GRADIENT: 8%

The Route des Corniches is a fabulous ride that follows the Arnave River from just outside Tarascon-sur-Ariège, either to Ax-les-Thermes or further to the D613 and the Col de Marmare. A right turn at the junction leads to the Col de Chioula. The Corniches road crosses one named col en route at about 9km, the minor Pas de Souloumbrie, included here principally because it offers one of the finest stretches of cycling road in the area. No easy detour, either: there are some deeply unpleasant gradients, which is, of course, what you want to hear. As an alternative to the main road into Ax, the N20-E9 arterial with its constant flood of heavyweight vehicles heading for Andorra and Spain, it is perfect. The Raid Pyrénéen eschews the offer however, because it would add significantly to the distance and the labour of an already taxing fourth day.

Picking up the D618 northwards out of Tarascon, it's 3 kilometres to the village of Bompas. The road is fairly flat yet surrounded by low peaks lest you forget that you are, indeed, in the Pyrenees. One of the distinctive features of these most beautiful mountains is the sense that you can ride into their very heart by way of the valleys, re-entrants, long defiles and winding ridges that make the lesser and greater cols so accessible. Where the major valley of the river Ariège, which gives the département its name, is less friendly to the cyclist, the lesser Arnave, its tributary, is most welcoming.

At the village of Bompas (c.700m), take a hairpin right onto the D20, signed as the Route des Corniches. The ride begins as a slow and gentle meandering course along the valley and the line of the river, graced by farmlands, hayfields, stone walls and terraced hillsides on either side. At the village of Arnave bear right over the bridge across the river – a generous display of hanging baskets bedeck the stone parapets of the stream. A fairly gentle incline leads you out of the village onto a long straight, traversing idyllic pastoral scenery. Lush vegetation. A series of switchbacks hoist you through the outer limits of the village, some of them quite steep, after which there is an extended incline for about 7 kilometres. The road is quite narrow so beware approaching cars, but the surface here is good, with a little loose gravel washed down by streams of water off the land.
The region is exceptionally well irrigated.

Cross the river and pass a cascade before the incline kicks up a notch as it leads you round the hillside in a series of sharp turns towards a tiny village which makes much of itself in a grandly oversized name: Cazenave-Serres-et-Allens (838m, 5.5km). A restaurant on the right, Le Manoir de la Mouline, occupies what was originally a forge, converted into a flour mill in the 19th century. About 500 metres past it the road takes a hard right with a noticeable incline, providing a great view both of the valley and the neighbouring peaks – Pic de Saint Barthélemy to the north, the bulk of the massif along the frontier with Andorra and Spain to the south.

Cazenave (838m) – casa nova i.e. 'new house' – gave shelter to Cathars fleeing persecution in 1243. As you head into it, there is a sharp left-hander followed by beautiful stone structures and a view of the hillside village. At this point the road narrows and you will see a sign for Col de Marmare. Cross over the Ruisseau de la Secaille onto a gentle incline leaving the village followed by a brief descent. Here the road falls away sharply on the right shoulder and the gradient flattens out, giving you the opportunity to look for caves carved out of the rock face on your right. Shortly before the Pas de Saloumbrie (911m) there's a strange-looking house to the right, a motley collection of garishly painted sculptural objects on the front lawn and a house sign: VITRIOLUM. Here live the local alchemists. They weren't at home when we called. Perhaps it's just as well.

VITRIOLUM is an acronym from a process described in the Opus Magnum or Great Work towards inner enlightenment, the elixir of life and transmutation of base metal into gold. Visita Interiora Terrae Rectificando Invenies Occultum Lapidem Veram Medicinam. (Search the inner places of the earth and by rectification you will find the hidden stone which is the true medicine.) The inner places are the subconscious mind; rectification means putting things right in the moral sense, namely reinstating true nature and purifying negative emotions. The hidden stone is the precious substance which you will find by opening up the hitherto unexplored mines of your subconscious. It also delivers redemptive powers.

At this stage the ride is very easy, either flat or downhill; along its undulating path are incredible views of monoliths, rock walls, hillside villages and a view of the high peaks of the Pyrenees directly in front of you. At the 'Y' intersection continue straight on, following the signs for Route des Corniches/Col de Marmare. (Thus, temper the advice of the famous baseball ace Yogi Berra who said: 'When you come to a fork in the road, take it.') Turning right offers a quick side trip into the villages of Verdun and les Cabannes, the latter with a Roman church. At the D20/D120 intersection, the road narrows and flattens, then changes to a steep downhill into the valley. There is a view of a village in the distance followed by a gentle turn that guides you over the bridge crossing the Ruisseau des Moulins, after which some fairly well-shaded sections offer numerous opportunities to stop and rest.

As this now-meandering forest road emerges from the woods out onto the hillside there will be a sign for Senconac. Here the surface is pitted and a bit uneven but offers good views of the terraced hillside. A descent with gentle curves leads you down the fern-covered hillside and as you pass over the Ruisseau de Senconac you will arrive onto a flat, exposed section of road. To the left are fields and a beautiful wrought-iron cross. When entering the small village of Caychax notice the war memorial on the corner, a sobering and familiar sight in most of these small Pyrenean villages. The serpentine road now runs along the valley and ahead is the village of Appy, at the foot of a terraced hillside with a good view of the high Pyrenees in the distance. The exit from Appy is gentle, although the road is more exposed to sun here with the right side falling away sharply as it descends. After you pass another bridge you will enter into a small patch of forest where there are stone walls and great views of the mountains. As you emerge, the distant view transforms into a layered hillside with stone outcroppings contrasting with the forested foreground. In the distance you can catch a glimpse of a Cathar stronghold perched on a rocky outcropping. After crossing a bridge and another tributary of the Ariège you enter the village of Axiat. If you have a hankering for pâté seek out the vendor of fresh foie gras du canard; there is also a public phone and a memorial to those who fell in the Second World War. A Romanesque church commands the corner as you descend out of the village and then cross the river Gerul, the road here picking up slightly in gradient and becoming much wider, offering good views on the right of the village, the terraced hillside beyond and the Cathar ruin which comes into full view as you round the bend. At the four-way intersection, which affords stunning vistas of the Pyrenees straight ahead, a couple of detours are on offer: left to the Carrières de Talc (talc mines), right on the D55 to the picturesque village of Lordat, home to the Châteaux de Cathar, a Roman church, and a First World War memorial as well as a café, Le Relais Cathar, with public loo and telephone.

Leaving Lordat you'll relish the sweeping view of the valley down to the industrial town of Luzenac. The descent, with lines of buckets from the talc mines heading down on overhead cables, is beautiful; there are views of numerous peaks and cols and a vista of an impressive rock escarpment, the road meandering round wide sweeping turns through the lovely hillside village of Bestiac with its watering trough to the right, a reminder of an era gone by.

Ax-les-Trois Domaines 1372m

From Ax-les-Thermes

LENGTH: 9.1KM
HEIGHT GAIN: 602M
MAXIMUM GRADIENT: 7.2%

A classic example of how misleading an average gradient for a whole climb can be. Barry Hoban often scoffed at the day's Tour profile because it omitted mention of sections of the route which were far steeper than the outline suggested. For this climb, also known as the Plateau de Bonascre, you need the lowest gearing you've got. It's brutal. Accounts of the gradients vary but French television coverage of the 2005 Tour showed two pitches where the steepness touched 11.5% and one of around 12%. I am inclined to believe this over the roadside signs which are more conservative. Besides, averaging out ignores intervening extremes.

Ax-les-Thermes is famous for its carbonated and sulphurated thermal springs – some 80 all-told – with temperatures varying from 45° (the Bleue du Teich, 'Blue of the Mountain Top') to 65° (the Pyramide) and 78° (the Rossignol, 'Nightingale'). The healing waters gave some relief to those suffering from skin diseases, prevalent when clothing material was rough and washing, especially in winter, infrequent. Scabies, ringworm, erysipelas (severe skin inflammation, often caused by eating noisome rye or wheat), and eczema were common. A military hospital was built here in 1260 for soldiers returning from the Holy Land with leprosy; it's dedicated to Saint Louis (Louis IX), leader of the Eighth (and last) Crusade, who died of the plague in Tunis in 1270 having taken a wrong turn for Jerusalem. All that remains of it is the Bassin de Ladres in the centre of town, used by locals and peregrinating cyclists for cooling and soothing their feet.

Barely out of Ax, head north-west on the N20-E9 and turn left onto the D820, then over the river and left again towards the climb, which announces itself at a sharp right turn and the first ramp. The kilometre and altitude signs are sporadic lower down but this is steep, around 8.5 or 9%, to a big left-hand hairpin by a rock face ahead of you with a white-paint graffito '100 Ans d'Histoire' daubed there in 2003 for the centenary Tour de France.

The road is characteristic of ski stations approaches, mostly an unforgiving, charmless series of cranking hairpins (16 in all) and short and long straights – a reinforced concrete and tarmac chain of cycling duress. There are occasional slips in the tension, but not many. It is thoroughly relentless and gruelling.

Just before the 3 kilometre mark, the road snaps right onto a long, savagely steep, sinuous stretch, the parapet wall to the right is quite exposed and gives a fine panorama of the thermal station down below. At 3km, altitude 940m, the gradient slackens from between 9 and 10 to 6.5% and, for several hundred metres, you feel as if you are riding on the flat. At 4km the illusion is crushed: 10.5%. Very taxing. Shade is sparse, views reduced. 5km at 1110m tells you 8.5%, 6km at 1195m (the arithmetic of the official kilometre signs is generally spot on) says 6% and, after a big left-hander, a straight to a right-hand hairpin and around 2–300 metres of flattish slope until the road recalls its main duty – giving you a hard time – and lifts to 7km, 1255m, 8.5%. Round a shallow left hairpin and on the skyline ahead and to the right, the blockhouse of the teleski terminal – open in summer for walkers and, if you've had enough of this road, even for a white-knuckle descent, cyclists.

The final 2 kilometres of ramps do not slacken until you are 500 metres from where the Tour stages finish in the centre of the resort, when the road drops for about 300 metres before kicking up again to the last thrust. There are, of course, bars and restaurants and the prospect of a giddy ride down the hill back to the valley of the Ariège.

TOUR DE FRANCE 2001

Under the Ax

The Tour has finished here three times: 2001, 2003, 2005.

In 2001, 2 kilometres from the top, Armstrong turned to stare impassively, coolly, into the face of Ullrich who, till then, had been doing most of the work in a vain effort to drop the American. One hard look and Armstrong was gone. Never was the phrase 'putting the hammer down' so expressive. Ullrich's exertions had been punishing, he had no answer, and the American, apparently not at all fatigued, cruised away and very nearly reeled in the two breakaways – Felix Cardenas, the winner by 13 seconds, and Roberto Laiseka, 30 years old and in his first Tour, who held off Armstrong by a mere 2 seconds.

Two years later, Carlos Sastre survived another long escape to take the win when he left his fellow breakaways 7 kilometres from the finish, an all-or-nothing attack. Back down the climb, Armstrong, in a small group of six riders, was suffering. The heat was intense, the speed of the chase high. When the Basque climber Haimar Zubeldia attacked, Ullrich of Bianchi and Vinokourov of Telekom were swiftly onto his wheel but Armstrong didn't react. Another kilometre on, Vinokourov went away, Ullrich answered and the two of them accelerated, ticking off precious seconds of their deficit on the yellow jersey. Zubeldia recovered and overhauled them, Vinokourov faltered and could only watch as Armstrong, mustering a desperate effort, went past. They all finished quite spent but Ullrich had gained 19 seconds on the American and was now only 15 seconds adrift.

In 2005, the wasting punishment of the Ax-Bonascre all but did for the winner, Georg Totschnig, who rode his first Tour in 1995. No sooner across the line than he crumpled and fell off his bike in a gasping heap. The photographers pounced as if on a bargain at a Harrod's sale. A woman peering over the barrier lit a cigarette. I fumed.

Col de Chioula 1431m

Western approach

LENGTH: 10.4 KM
HEIGHT GAIN: 720 M
MAXIMUM GRADIENT: 8%

From Ax (720m) follow a long hairpinned stretch of the D613 east to Ascou for 3.7 kilometres and a junction with the D25. (This leads to the Port de Pailhères – included in two recent Tours but previously avoided – and via a narrow side road, the D22, to the Col du Pradel.) The D613 passes the village of Sorgeat (1040m) on a slip road to the right, and at 7.8km, 1246m, a turning left to Vaychis. The Col de Chioula lies 2.6 kilometres further on.

The Chioula has featured in four Tours: 1955, '65, '97 and 2001. The word chioula appears to be linked with chioulet, referring to the local Pyrenean practice of communicating across the silent wide space of the valleys by a range of piercing whistle calls. Thus shepherds could flute various messages to companions on the far side of the mountain, this not so dissimilar to a shrill bosun's call.[32]

Begin with a gruelling climb out of Ax-les-Thermes on the D613 following signs towards Col de Pradel. The story of the statistics is misleading – 7% average? Don't be fooled. This is one of those climbs that sneaks up on your wheel rims and squirts lead into them. The views back across the valley to the heights of the Ax-Trois-Domaines ski station and the villages below are breathtaking but beware such distractions here. The climb is intense, challenging and demands your full attention, with no shoulder to speak of, sharp hairpin turns, and a narrow road that affords barely enough room for cyclists and vehicles to share it. On the other hand, the surface is excellent and there is a good balance of sun and shade. As you head towards Col de Chioula you will make a sharp hairpin turn to the left after which the road levels out, widens, gets straighter, and the good surface continues. Grafitti for the Tour de France, the tarmac Visitors' Book, greet you as you arrive at an intersection (road left to Vaychis) where there is a sign for the Col de Chioula. Ignore all turnings, this is the strait and narrow to cyclists' satisfaction, so head straight through and follow the broad sweeping curve which propels you towards the mountain.

The road surface changes and gets grumpy, worn and uneven. There is an intoxicating view of the mountain ridge and, way off to the left, a captivating view of the peak at Ax-Trois-Domaines. Further up the hillside the road veers right and the gradient steepens to a blackguardly 8% which feels rather worse just before a viewpoint from which there is a sparklingly detailed panorama of the valley below. From here you can look down at the rail line – that fine alternative mode of transit across the mountains from Spain – and a full study of the complexity of the ranges westwards. You can also watch the teeming activity of the lorry-clogged N20 and rejoice that you are not on it.

Up to this point there have been no gradient markers – at least none that is easily noticed. After a sharp turn the gradient eases off a bit as the road turns inward heading into the folds of the peaks. Here you will see a gradient marker for km 7 at 7.5%, altitude 1200m. A series of hairpins follow and grafitti for the Tour decorate the rock wall flanking the road. There is a furtive increase in gradient, another series of hairpin turns, followed by another kick up in the gradient and a sign for km 9 at 8%, altitude 1350m. However, there is not much relief

---

[32] This ancient form of simple language, rather more complex than it may sound, is still going strong in the small Canarian island of Gomer.

– it's one of those climbs – iron fist in velvet glove – but the road does widen as you approach the main area of Col de Chioula (1431m). The ascent rounds off with generous sweeping curves and the road is flanked by grazing land, so beware of cows in the middle of the road. Or milk them. There's a place to rest, sit, and eat. Straight ahead are breathtaking views of the lofty peaks of the Montagne de Tabe and the Montagne de la Frau.

Eastern approach

LENGTH:	20 KM[33]
HEIGHT GAIN:	OVER 500M IN TOTAL
MAXIMUM GRADIENT:	8.5%

The Col des Sept Frères and de Marmare (1361m) are intermediate lifts on the way to the Chioula, making the long eastern approach along the D613 from the Col du Portel, above Quillan a long but rewarding excursion.

From the Col of the Seven Brothers, a 3-kilometre descent brings you past Camurac (1224m, 0.6km) onto a short flat from which a gentle rise to Prades (1220m, 4.5km) in the Fôret Dominiale de Pays Daillou. At the time of the writing, sections of the descent were being repaved. Initially there is a nice gentle slope down from the top, then the gradient steepens and you hit a sharp hairpin. The road opens up and widens out with great sweeping turns that allow you to develop a good rhythm. From Prades, the road rises gently for 3.5 kilometres until a sudden jolt of around 6 and 7% for a kilometre over the Marmare (1361m, 8.3km) before easing off again for the run-in to the Chioula. A junction with the D2 on the Marmare leads off to the Routes des Corniches.

Another 1.8 kilometres and 70 metres of climbing lead to the Chioula and on into logging territory, so pay attention. Lorries laden with huge baulks of timber frequent the area.

It's a fun 10-kilometre descent into Ax-les-Thermes, with many sharp turns and a good, steady and fast gradient, maximum 8.5%, usually 8–6%. Good chance to let rip. The col sign at the base of the climb shows Col de Chioula altitude 1450m, mildly confusing, but what's an extra 19 metres when you're having fun? This is a great workout, very challenging and blessed with spectacular views as you descend.

The Tour has crossed the Col des Sept Frères but once, in 2001, en route to the Bonascre.

---

[33] The Seven Brothers of the col may be those celebrated in the Catholic hagiography, sons of the martyr Saint Felicity, put to death circa 165–150 AD in Rome for refusing to acknowledge the civic gods. However, the link with Felicity is tenuous and their story may well be a fictional adaptation of that of the seven faithful Jewish brothers and their mother. Captive in Egypt, they are hideously tortured and put to death for refusing to eat 'unlawful swine's flesh'. (II Maccabees, chapter vii.)

TOUR DE FRANCE 1955

Brian Robinson arrives

In the 1955 Tour which passed, he says, in something of a blur, Robinson came up alongside the ace Swiss rider Ferdi Kubler (winner in 1950) on the Ventoux. Kubler had attacked far too hard, far too soon. He'd cracked and was in a dreadful state, weaving from side to side. When Robinson went past – prudently limiting his efforts to staying in the race without any pyrotechnics – Kubler moaned and gasped: 'Pushez Ferdi. Ferdi a mal. Pushez Ferdi.' (Push Ferdi. Ferdi's ill. Push Ferdi). Robinson delivered a short speech in demotic Yorkshire and pushed on – not Ferdi – alone.

By the time they reached the Pyrenees, Robinson had ridden himself in and on the stage over the Tourmalet he finished only 2mins 45secs down on the Belgian Jean Brankart.[34]

When the Tour left the Pyrenees and arrived in Pau, André Leduc (winner in 1930 and '32) was there to greet the riders. For the tiro Englishman he had special praise: 'Well done, you climbed splendidly and descended like a devil. With your class and a good team to support you, you could finish in the top 15 next year.' Robinson, so tired he could hardly speak, commented dourly: 'I've learnt to descend in this race.' The kind of descending he refers to takes balls, balance and bike-handling. On occasions, you just have to switch the brain off and let it roll.

Robinson finished 29th overall and, in 1956, honouring Leduc's prediction, 14th. Chapeau, as they say in France, 'hats off'.

---

[34] Brankart, in excellent shape, might well have taken the overall from Louison Bobet, riding to a third victory in spite of being haggard, tired, nervous, but for want of boldness and self-confidence. He came second and won two stages but, despite a win in the Grand Prix du Midi Libre in 1959, his career never lifted off.

Chateau de Montségur 1059m

Western approach

LENGTH: 10.9 KM

HEIGHT GAIN: 550M

MAXIMUM GRADIENT: 10%

From Lavelanet (530m) sitting athwart the river Touyre, go 2 kilometres south on the D117, direction Foix, and turn left onto the D109 at Chaubet (576m). At Villeneuve d'Olmes (4.4km) take the D9, (a continuation of the D109) to Montferrier (6.5km) and Montségur. The gradient begins to snarl, up to 9.5 and 10%. After 1.2 kilometres, the D909 leads off at 799m right to les Monts d'Olmes (1480m), 14.5 kilometres distant.[35]

The Château de Montségur (from the Latin mons securus –'safe mountain') betrayed its name in 1244 when the Cathar defenders capitulated to their besiegers [see Introduction]. The final 3.2 kilometres are very hard, as befits the approach to such a stronghold.

Eastern approach

LENGTH: 15 KM

HEIGHT GAIN: 570M

MAXIMUM GRADIENT: 10%

From Bélesta (493m) on the D117, take the D5 for 4.5 kilometres to Fougax-et-Barrineuf. Gentle gradients for another 3 kilometres. Across a stream at 598m and a big left-hand bend, followed by three relatively easy kilometres to around 750m whence a final four at varying degrees of nastiness.[36]

Alternative from Bélestra

LENGTH: 15 KM

HEIGHT GAIN: OVER 500M IN TOTAL

MAXIMUM GRADIENT: 10%

About 1.5 kilometres out of Bélesta, the D29 passes a natural curiosity, the Fontestorbes, an artesian spring which suffers from hiccups in summertime. Spurting water continuously through the winter, in the hot months it spews for 6 minutes at a time then rests for a gap of 32 minutes. This is a gentle spin along the banks of the river Hers, gradients all but indiscernible, nothing more than 2.5%. So on into Fougax-et-Barrineuf (549m), one of those double villages which probably result from a bitter feud years back: violent row, storm out of house, resettle within sight of the hated former lover/wife/husband/brother – no more than a couple of hundred metres upstream – and gather your supporters across the

---

[35] The ride to this ski station gives a height gain of 1100m on a well-surfaced road, through stretches of woods interspersed with gaps. The climbing is fairly steady and mild in steepness to around 1190m at 7.5km; then a drop of 2 kilometres to 1140m and a final 5 kilometres of harder work.

[36] A southern approach from east of Belcaire, left on the D29, a 14-kilometre ride, crosses the Col de la Croix des Morts 898m, on a nice wide road with a good surface and sweeping curves. Almost no climbing from this direction and a flying descent for 8 kilometres into Bélesta.

divide. (Perhaps we know who was the victor, there being no river His to rival the Hers.)

From here you catch a glimpse of the imposing crag of Montségur in the distance. A sharp left turn through the village and an arbour of trees marking the centre of the split community. The church is beautiful, there's a noted restaurant, Les Cinq Fours (The Five Ovens – testimony to the building's original purpose as a factory producing combs made of bone), a logging mill and, as you leave the village, a fine perspective ahead of the mountains.

Bear right at the fork with the small side road (D5 for Comus) towards Montségur. Here the road is quite wide with a double yellow line and the surface quite even. The road starts to twist and turn, like the criss-crossing streams, as it traverses farmlands and vineyards with small bridges. The gradient begins to wake up as the pinnacle of Montségur looms, dominating the landscape. The Cathar castles share a singular characteristic, being constructed out of the living rock on seemingly inaccessible precipitous ledges. The puig, (an Oc and Catalan word, pronounced 'putsch') or pinnacle, an enormous, rounded boss of bare rock to which the keep of Montségur clings, like an eagle gripping a bollard, is some 1207m high. The very improbability of simply getting up there, let alone building a castle on top, reinforces the grandeur, the mystic inaccessibility of the site.

Approaching Montségur, the road enters a deep chasm sliced through the side of the mountain, bare rock on either side, like a natural funnel. It breeds foreboding and, sure enough, after a sharp right turn, the incline increases dramatically. The challenge of the gradient is heightened by hairpin turns, which crank up the pressure to an 8–10% incline. After some time the road flattens out a touch (probably illusory but that is the effect of getting used to extremes of steepness) and the turns evolve into gradual sweeping arcs. There it stands ahead, the imposing fortress of Montségur, the sacred crag, drawing you on. Just before the village, a memorial records the death of the Cathars who were captured when the castle fell by auto da fé on the 'burning field'. The final 2 kilometres are harsh, aptly so.

A sharp left into the village is followed by a sign signalling the Col de Montségur. Proceed on D9 which affords incredible vistas of the surrounding peaks. It is a challenging climb with sharp turns and steep ascents, but worth every moment for the views. The climb levels off at the parking lot at Montségur. If you wish to ascend the steep flanks of the puig to the ruins of Montségur itself, you must continue by foot – a good 20–25 minute climb.

The ride back to Lavelanet on the southwest side of Montségur is superb. What an American informant calls the blacktop (tarmac) is new and the sharp slopes of even gradient, 8%, give an initial 2 kilometres of good rhythm descending on long smooth stretches of flying road. Rein in as some serious switchbacks kick into gear a couple of kilometres from the top at which point the decline stiffens to as much as 10% in some places. At 4.5 kilometres, you enter the village of Montferrier (680m) and head on in the direction of Foix. The hill dwindles to nothing, 3.5% the norm, but it's always a joy to turn the big ring on such slopes, time-trial mode, fast as you please, 6.5 kilometres into the nondescript village of Lavelanet. There are plenty of gîtes and hotels in the vicinity, a good enough base for the exploration of this Pays Cathare.

Col de la Gargante 1352m and Col du Boum 1298m

A detour 'off-piste'

LENGTH: OVER 20KM
HEIGHT GAIN: OVER 800M IN TOTAL
MAXIMUM GRADIENT: 9%

Like the Route des Corniches, this adventurous loop into the Fôret de la Plaine and the Pas de l'Ours (Bear's Footprint) is included as a foray into the interior of the lonely sylvan wilds of the Pays de Sault. It's a taxing, roughneck ride on not very good roads, but worth every dance of the back wheel.

Both cols straddle the D20, branching off the D613 between Ax-les-Thermes and Quillan north of the Col de Marmare.

The descent into the village of Prades (1220m) from the Col de Marmare is enjoyable. Although the road tends to carry a lot of traffic it is wide, with some sharp but negotiable turns, an average to good surface and pleasant views of the valley of the Hers to the right. Prades, for many years the home of the cellist Pablo Casals who inaugurated the music festival that bears the village's name, boasts the well-preserved remains of a 14th-century fortress and a restaurant/bar, La Bexanne.

Emerging from its shimmy through the cluster of stone buildings which comprise Prades, the road straightens out again into the countryside, verdant fields and a riot of wildflowers. This is a great place to open up, turn the pedals faster and get the adrenalin flowing. Heading towards the village of Camurac, the road starts to incline slightly with a few twists. There are long meandering sweeps of road before you meet the intersection of D105 which will take you some 2 kilometres up to the ancient village and ruined chateau of Montaillou. Also public lavatories. The D613 continues towards Camurac (1220m) the Fôret de la Plaine and the Col de Gargante, the pastoral landscape affording a gentle ride on a pleasant road, wide with a good surface but fully exposed, so if the sun is out in force expect it to be hot. (The D5 to Camurac just out of Prades will bypass the village itself.) Camurac extends welcome refreshment and/or accommodation at the Auberge du Pays de Sault, a general store, charcuterie, and various other shops. It also offers a choice: a tricky ride up into the kind of country in which the Cathars hid and communed with those beautiful compounds of nature which made their refuge such a seeming paradise, or just to keep going straight through along the valley to Belcaire and the Plateau de Sault.

If you chose the first option above, the road to the Col de Gargante out of Camurac is easily missed. Enter the village outskirts and cross over a small bridge. A road to the left, signed D20 Comus, leads you to the auberge on a meandering route through the village. The surface is not particularly good – bumpy, narrow and generously smeared with cow dung from the daily passage of the herds. As you leave Camurac the road bears sharply to left, followed by a slight decline. The landscape of this Fôret de la Plaine might seem rather inhospitable, and as you descend into the valley on a gentle slope, the road surface deteriorates somewhat and becomes increasingly gravelly. But take heart. As you ride up the steepening incline into Comus (1166m), past a scatter of houses that comprise the hamlet's last vestiges there opens a great vista of the valley and farmlands teeming with livestock below. The road remains narrow and the surface improves, although it is still the rougher macadam not the smoother asphalt. You will now see the sign for Col du Boum (1305m). Straight ahead continues the Route des Sapins and the Sentier Cathare, one of the ancient tracks well trodden by the Cathars who lived in this hidden corner of the Ariège.

The road up to the Col du Boum is fairly tight but surfaced, veering towards mountain bike territory but accessible to the intrepid road cyclist. From the Boum (3.5km) take the road left towards Col de la Gargante, but prepare for a rougher ride as the road becomes rather gravelly and narrow, its many twists and turns offering little or no visibility and no verge to speak of. There are, however, some wonderful views of the impressive expanse of valley below where cows and horses can be seen grazing. The road surface is now hard-packed dirt with scattered potholes, not an ideal ride on a thin-tyred bike, but the views as you move in and out of the forest and skirt the Gorges de la Frau (uninvitingly called so, the Gorges of Fraud, Deception) are spectacular.

At the Col de la Gargante (1352m, 7km) take the right for Belcaire, 9 kilometres distant, and cross the Cols de Lancise (1307m) and Perrucel (wooden sign, satisfyingly rustic) at 1064m. The road surface gets more tenuous but, come on… still manageable and the last section into Belcaire is not bad.

Col du Pradel 1673m

Western approach

LENGTH: 14.9 KM
HEIGHT GAIN: 960 M
MAXIMUM GRADIENT: 11%

The climb begins in earnest on the D22 (left turn) out of Lavail. There is a good long view of the road ahead as you thread past some old buildings in the village. At l'Eychergue, 1.9 kilometres along, the gradient delivers some vicious kicks which make the overall of a constant 8% feel a lot tougher – three double chevron sections.

The incline nestles tight between the flanking hillsides and is another of those roads which characterise the remote and wild – *sauvage* – nature of the Pays de Sault. The longish straight sections add to the toil. The road is narrow, well-surfaced and very exposed, so the ride can be hot. Another sharp S-turn is followed by an incline of around 7% into the charming hamlet of Pujal, (1200m, 9km) the road getting even narrower as the incline levels off.

Pujal itself may be all smiles, but the road out is a bilious creature, very steep, though you have a nice sloping view of the pastoral landscape to the right. The road has no verge to speak of, falling away abruptly on the right while the left embankment rises sharply from the edge of the road. The road is so pinched, the edges so impinging – there isn't sufficient room for two cars and there are few passing places – that you need to stay focussed. It is an exhilarating ride, however, to the accompaniment of an ever-present tinkling of cowbells. Sudden glimpses of mules emerging from the forest laden with firewood will transport you to a time when life was much simpler. Inspiration to feel rugged.

Through the riverside village of l'Eycherque (1260m, 9.5km) and another brief interlude of flat meandering as you follow the ridge round the basin wall of the valley. This is a beautiful, heavily wooded and well-shaded road, a cooling stream off to the right, real backwoods country, picturesque and tranquil. The intimate nature of the road and the sensation of moving in and out of the forest glen provide a counterpoint to the spectacular panoramic views of the Pyrenees typically experienced on many of the more celebrated climbs, but this is the particular attraction of these most lovely mountains: their contrast and variety.

Out of l'Eycherque comes a series of sharp hairpin turns and the incline increases in severity, too. The road and the river below part company quite soon and you are on the climb proper of the Pradel. Across several streams, a double chevron's worth of real toil, some very sharp switchbacks, gradients which talk 8–9% and echo rather more, you reckon, and the extreme narrowness of the road... all this makes for a tough ride. By the way, *chevron* is French for 'rafter' and in heraldry signifies protection and a mark of loyal service. Be cheered.

The road establishes its pattern: the middling relief of sweeping stretches that seem flattish only because they lead onto sharp gradients and hairpins. What begins as a bucolic byway wandering in and out of the troughs between the mountains slowly transmutes into a high-rock ledge of a road with superb views of the valley below.

Closer to the top as you clear the treeline, the road sheds all cover and follows the cirque. The vista from all round the bowl of the mountainside is wide open with views of the rock-laden hillside and the line of the road that cuts a serpentine figure in the landscape. A small farm with a paddock perches high up on a bluff while to the right is a stunning view of the layered peaks of the high Pyrenees. This ascent of the Pradel epitomizes the ying and yang of cycling: the extreme character of the ride, long and demanding, in contrast with the sheer exuberance of close acquaintance with the beauties of nature. It's a gruelling climb, amply rewarded with a multiplicity of views and, at the top, a field carpeted with wildflowers, ('pradel' means 'small meadow'), the air ringing with the stridulation of crickets. Good bear country, too.

Northern approach

LENGTH: 20.9 KM

HEIGHT GAIN: 950M

MAXIMUM GRADIENT: 11%

From Espezel (895m) take the D29 south from the D613 to a junction, right, onto the D20. Soon another fork right onto the D107 and, after 2.5km, through a defile into Niort-de-Sault (840m, 8km) and left at a fork on the continuation of the D120. Through Mérial (936m, 10.8km) where the climb proper begins, on stiff gradients, never less than 7%, to La Fajolle (1090m, 13.3km) and the Pont de Rouby (1172m, 14.5km). The final 6.4 kilometres rise 501m... 'do the math' as George Clooney might say. Another bridge, the Pont sur le Rébenty (1467m, 18.5km) underlines just how much water – thermal, curative and rock-filtered – these mountains pump out.

Between Espezel and the junction with the D20, the road goes from flat for 2 kilometres to a 3 kilometre descent, thence onto a steady and fairly easy 6 kilometre ascent to Mérial – nothing more onerous than 4.5–5%. Stay loose.

Above the ravine where Niort is sited once stood the castle of the lords of Niort, two of whom were prominent Catharist sympathisers, openly entertaining fugitive heretics. The castle itself, a veritable eagle's nest, is gone, but the natural ramparts of rock, the steep-sided walls of the gorge, made it a formidable stronghold. Beyond Mérial, the road enters another of the ravines celebrated in the regional name, Sault: the spectacular Défile d'Adouxes, a dramatic entrance to the upper reaches of the mountain where the road tunnels through a large cave-filled chasm dominated by a massive overhang.

At the end of the gorge over a stone bridge you enter La Fajolle, a captivating village snuggled against the rocky walls of the chasm long ago carved by the river. The road continues to follow the river, entering the Fôret Domaniale de la Fajolle past the intersection with a forest track to the right. The forest soon engulfs you, which may take your mind off the unrelenting drag of the gradient, a steady 7–8.5%. Numerous streams replenish the main flow of the Rébenty and the road widens somewhat. The surface on this side is, on the whole, not nearly as sound or as even as on the western approach: there tends to be a lot of debris washed and broken off the cliff face onto the road, plus the usual hazards – out of sight round the bend, straggly herds of cows and solitary grazers lolloping into your path. You cross two small bridges at 1432m and 1467m, and enjoy terrific views through the forest across the valley to the adjacent ridges via a fairly relaxed gradient of between 6 and 8%.

About 2 kilometres from the top, the road gets horribly steep – 10% and more – and, to compound the affront to your growing faith in and affection for this most lovely of climbs, the surface gets more uneven and broken up (frost damage) with patches of loose gravel but this is the Pradel – you are traversing beautiful, verdant fields of wildflowers and the reward of the col is sweet indeed.

Port de Pailhères 2001m

Western approach

LENGTH: 18 KM
HEIGHT GAIN: 1281M
MAXIMUM GRADIENT: 12%

Take the D613 east out of Ax, fork right at Ascou (3.5km) onto the D25. 3.5 kilometres to Lavail, then through the Fôret d'Ascou along the course of the Lauze, 11 kilometres to the Port. Numerous shops and a supermarket in Ax-les-Thermes. An auberge between Ascou and Lavail on the right side of the road. Public water source at Lavail on the left side of road just after the turning left to the Col du Pradel. A ski centre at Ascou-Pailhères 5.5 kilometres from the Port.

The road is open on the lower and upper sections, forested between Lavail and Ascou-Pailhères, exposed again higher up, frequently two cars wide, occasionally wider, narrowing on hairpin bends. A generally good surface which can break up in very hot weather from the pounding it gets in the winter.

This 18 kilometre climb, like all climbs in the most bicycle-friendly département of the Ariège, has kilometre markings with average gradient markings for the next kilometre. You may find these comforting. You may, however, on the ascent of a real unforgiving steep and vindictive pig like the Pailhères, find them to be a sort of running sore, an intermittent jab of truculent unkindness, like a malicious arbiter holding up a sign reading 'Nul Points' as a judgement on your progress, even on your fitness ever to be doing the climb at all. Right then.

The climb begins at Ax-les-Thermes on the D613 with gentle switchbacks winding up along the river valley through the trees. A succession of relatively mild 6–6.5% gradients for the first few kilometres to Ascou where this most attractive valley road straightens and kicks up slightly, seemingly tossing its head as it goes past the village. The centre of this pleasant little mountain community, a higgledy-piggledy collection of stone houses, is set back off the road to the left. Ignore the roadside water fountain also on the left – not drinkable. To the right of the main road an auberge, with outside seating at the back.

There are a number of dwellings on either side of the road, houses for the hill pasteurs (shepherds), and at the hamlet of Lavail (1100m, 7km) a small turning on the left reveals the first steep ramp of the D22 leading to the Col du Pradel.

Through Lavail and on, the road keeping company with the river Lauze to the right, its waters

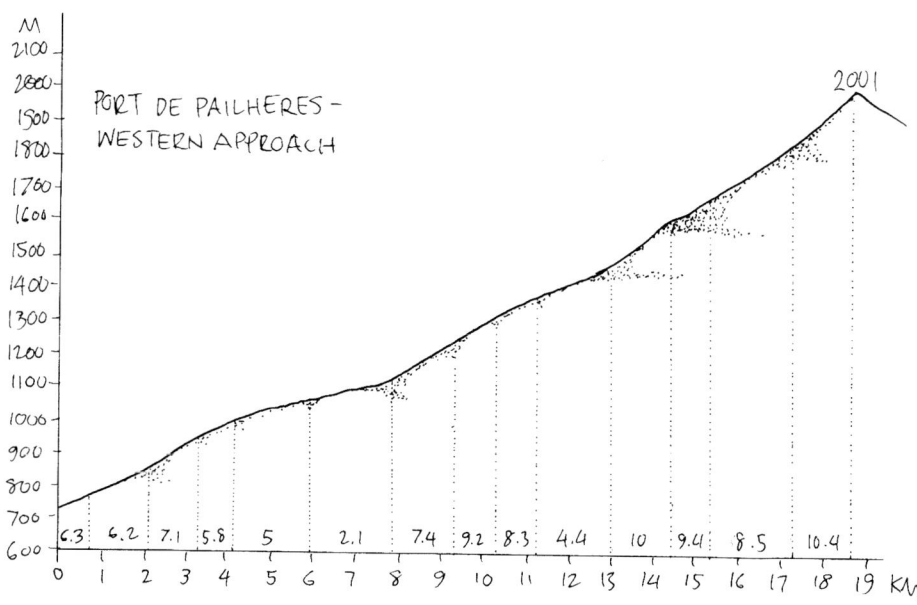

274 THE RAPHA GUIDE

tumbling fast along a boulder-strewn bed amongst the trees. A short way beyond the hamlet, the gradient suddenly increases to upwards of 10% and after this rarely drops much lower as wide bends in the road veer left, away from the river and onto the hard sides of the rock.

Moving away from the river, the road straightens and widens. The gantries of a ski station at Ascou-Pailhères loom like giant metal scarecrows stranded on the hillside up to the right on the slopes of the Pic de Tarbezou. Now a swing left into the first of a series of hairpin switchbacks which crank up the height in sizeable increments of between 9 and 10.5%. But, there is a reward in the wild prospect of dramatic views back down the valley.

Towards the top of the col, the road opens out and tiptoes along the contours round the ridge, past a group of small holiday chalets to the left and on to a small hut, perhaps an old hermitage, symbol of triumph, relief, welcome... the col and the delicious reminder that this is what you have come for.

The summit is exposed. A col sign and altitude marker. A sizeable area for car parking on what is a magnificent belvedere that rewards the efforts made on the ascent by offering panoramic views of pasture meadows and surrounding peaks - the Pic Madre to the east and the High Pyrenees to the west and south, the Plateau de Sault to the north. Also visible is the road which descends the col, snaking down on the opposite side. Even in mid July when the sun was blazing, hot enough to melt the tarmac on the road surface, there remained small areas of unmelted snow on the north facing slopes.

Eastern approach

LENGTH:	15.1 KM
HEIGHT GAIN:	1216 M
MAXIMUM GRADIENT:	12 %

For the approach to Usson, see overleaf

From Usson-les-Bains turn off towards Rouze (2km), on another 2 kilometres to Mijanès (1130m) with a small shop and café bar, thence 11 kilometres to the Port.

The route is mainly open with some lightly wooded sections around 1000m. Exposed high up, it can get very cold in bad weather conditions.

The descent from the col on the D25 is fast and exhilarating. After negotiating a set of tightly packed hairpin bends down through grassy slopes, the road straightens and passes through the edge of the Forêt des Hares into Mijanès.

From here, the descent continues on either side of the river Bruyante down, left onto the D116 through the village of Rouze and on towards the junction with the D118. Alternatively, after leaving Mijanès, continue on the D25 towards Quérigut for a sight of the ruined Château de Donezan, final refuge of the Cathar leaders after the fall of Montségur.

At the junction with the D118, the options are:

- turn right and either continue to Mont Louis via the Col de la Quillane (1713m), or take a turn on the left for Roquefort-de-Sault via the Col de Moulis (1099m) and the Col de Garavel past the turning for the Col de Jau, and on into Axat,

- turn left and rapidly descend to the starting point of the loop at Gesse, or beyond past a turning on the right for the Col de Jau, or, straight on for a dramatic descent through the rock walls of the Gorges de St-Georges down to Axat and the D117.

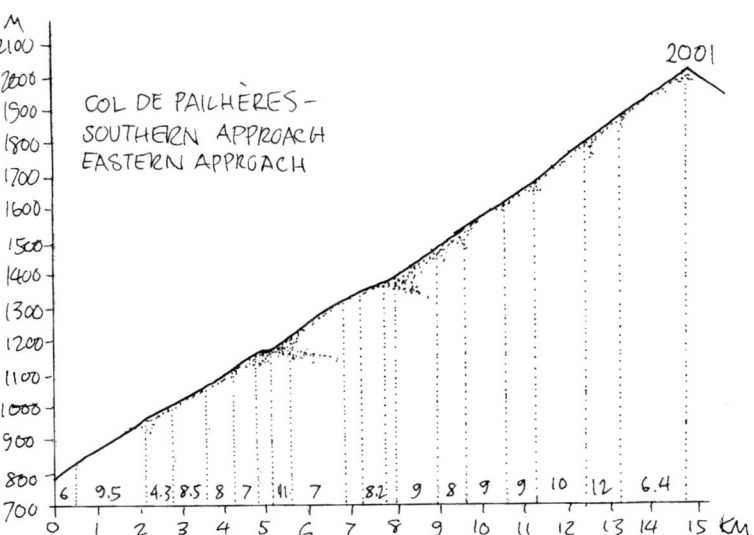

Col de Garavel 1256m and Col des Moulis 1099m

Round trip from Axat, scenic counter-clockwise direction

LENGTH: 51.7 KM
HEIGHT GAIN: 855 M
MAXIMUM GRADIENT: 6 %

This is a crackerjack of a ride, a perfect day out through picturesque, wooded scenery – rolling hills that skirt the sides of the Aude valley, forest and ravine, the signature features of the Sault.

The road north from Axat to Quillan passes through the narrow Défile-de-Pierre-Lys, its exposed slabs much favoured by rock climbers. Six kilometres to the east of Axat, atop a 695m ridge stands the Château de Puilaurens, another Cathar fortress but well preserved and in course of restoration. (That 'pui' is a form of puig and the Laurens may be that saint whose emblem is a gridiron, souvenir of his martyrdom.) Built on the site of an earlier Visigothic stronghold, Puilaurens has a remarkable defence system: the approach through a long fissure of rock winds up a zigzag stairway of stone chicanes formed of hah-ha walls and made any intruder highly vulnerable to attack. Having given shelter to Cathar refugees after the fall of Montségur in 1241, it eventually surrendered in the last grisly round-up of the remnants of the Cathar resistance some 11 years later. The feelings aroused by the church-backed Albigensian crusade against these reviled heretics were, it is almost otiose to say, exceedingly bitter. In the Chanson de la Croisade, 'The Song of the Crusade', an epic poem about the tragic episode, the Count of Foix, voicing the acrimonious sentiments of his fellow Languedociens, calls the sanctimonious Catholic thugs, the so-called crusaders jobbed in to slaughter the innocents, 'traitors without faith of honour' and then: 'All those whom I slew or destroyed filled my heart with joy; those who fled or escaped gave me great agony of mind.' The Crusade planted an implacable hatred of the French – the northerners – in the Provençals, the people of the south. Leave Axat (small shop and café bar) south on the D118 heading into the Gorges de Saint-Georges, the narrowest defile in the upper valley of the Aude. The road snakes through the close gauntlet of high cliffs to either side of the chasm. Gorge, remember, means 'throat' and gorgeous here applies. It's a beautiful ride, gradients of no consequence, 3% tops (there are no kilometre signs) but possibly a bit cold at the beginning and end of the day.

After around 6.5 kilometres, you enter the Fôret de Gesse, through the eponymous village, and the gorge becomes the more generalised Gorges de l'Aude. (The river gives its name to the département established during the revolution in 1790; the Romans named it Atax, classical Greek for 'disorderly'.) At 663m the D84 to the left leads to Escouloubre – an alternative approach to the Col des Moulis on this very narrow road up a smaller valley.

Whereas the ride through the gorge is wonderfully scenic, the ride up to Escouloubre on the D84, dramatic enough in its challenge, is in sharp contrast: suddenly there is little to look at and nothing to focus on but the climb. The thick, high vegetation makes it difficult to fix reference points as you continue up the mountain. So, a long 8-9 kilometres to Escouloubre, near which an auberge and farm with a café serves light snacks and drinks: to get them bear left through the village and ascend the hill. The village square has a First World War monument commemorating the lost sons of the village. Turn your back on it and take one of the alleys before you, all of which lead down to the village recreation hall which has a small café that serves sandwiches, ice cream and beer. The ascent to the Garavel continues out of the village, and, as you approach the top of the climb, a good view opens out. Take a left at the three-way juncture towards Le Bousquet and Roquefort de Sault on the D17. The surface is hard-packed gravel, which suggests it may be repaved soon, the gradient gentle and the road fairly exposed, meandering up the hillside with gentle curves.

A short way further on you pass the Grotte de l'Aguzou, a complex of caves; the whole area is honeycombed with caverns, many formerly Cathar hideouts. Between here and the side road to the two cols, there are no fewer than three small spas: Usson-les-Bains, (closed and for sale, another Cathar castle nearby), Carcanières-les-Bains and Escouloubre-les-Bains, (895m) whose hot spring in the Maison Roquelaire (B&B and evening meals) has always been rated sovereign for the relief of rheumatism. This isn't a valley, it's an ailing, near-defunct health farm. The Tour de France swept through in the early afternoon of 16 July 2005.

The D17 turns off left and there are 3.7 kilometres of easy climbing, no worse than 6% to the Col des Moulis (1099m). Views across towards Mijanès and beyond to the high Pyrenees. Col sign with altitude marker. Large silo with attendant pigs.

A bit less than a kilometre of descent jettisons sixty of the metres you have bagged and leads to the foot of the 4 kilometre climb to the Garavel, steady all the way, gradients no worse than 6%. At the Col de Garavel (1256m) there are open panoramic views to the north, the high Pyrenees to the west and back down the valley to the east, some trees and shrubs to the south. Pasture land. A private house. Col sign with altitude marker, numerous interesting geological formations and generally a good gathering of horses and cows.

Col du Carcanet 1400m and Col de la Quillane 1713m

Tougher, clockwise direction

MAXIMUM GRADIENT 10%

The worst difficulty is posed by three double-chevron sections between Sainte-Colombe-sur-Guette and Roquefort de Sault on the clockwise route. The surface is generally good except between Axat and Sainte-Colombe-sur-Guette because of stone-carrying lorries serving an active quarry.

Take the left fork onto the D17 on the far side of the Gorges de Saint Georges and a moderate 3.5 kilometre climb to Sainte-Colombe-sur-Guette where the going gets seriously tough: 4 kilometres of around 9% into the village of Roquefort-de-Sault where the country opens out into pasture land with flower meadows exposed to the sun. There follow 3 kilometres of no great difficulty at around 4% before a final big push through the forest up a 1 kilometre, 7–8% slope to the Col de Garavel.

Considered as a 25.4km extension of the anti-clockwise approach to the Garavel

LENGTH: 25.4 KM
HEIGHT GAIN: 800M
MAXIMUM GRADIENT: 7%

At the junction with the D17 in Escouloubre (940m), continue south along the D118 into the Fôret du Carcanet. (A carcanet is an ornamental collar or necklace, usually of gold, set with jewels.) This is a great touring road, wide and quite busy in terms of traffic. A steady gradient for most of the way, save for a belt of 6–7% between the bridges which bracket km 5 and the final 4 kilometres which wind up to 5–6%. The main attraction is the scenery: the ski-slopes of the Pic de Ginèvre above Puyvalador (13.4km, 1445m) up to the right and the barrage and lake to the left, another barrage and the enormous Lac de Matemale (a reservoir) and long views south of the Pyrenean ranges. Indeed, our American informant writes: 'The landscape is just breathtaking here.'

Formiguères (1505m, 17.1km) is a lively little place – cafés and crêperies – and rather more attractive than most ski station villages.

On the descent from the Col de la Quillane (1714m) the road is a bit more pitted and older, but it's invitingly wide and shallow and there are numerous places in which to eat, drink, relax and drink in the terrific views. Into Mont Louis (1580m), 5.4 kilometres from the col, the highest fortified town in France and. rated one of the finest citadels designed by Louis XIV's great military engineer, Vauban. Constructed between 1679 and 1682, the massive, low walls were all but impervious to artillery bombardment and, dominating the approach road up from the coast, posed a considerable deterrent to invading forces. It now garrisons French commando units.

Col de la Llose 1866m

Eastern approach

LENGTH: 24.5 KM
HEIGHT GAIN: 1239 M
MAXIMUM GRADIENT: 8%

From Olette on the main N116 20 kilometres east of Mont Louis, take the D4 north towards Oreilla then left at the fork onto the D4c via Ayguatebia and on to the summit.

Small shops and café bar in Olette. A roadside pipe on the left between Tourol and Ayguatebia on the D4c. Public water source in Ayguatebia.

Forested to begin with as it climbs out of the gorge, the road opens out in the middle then finishes in forest. Exposed to the sun for much of the ride. Can be warm to ascend and therefore comfortable to descend. Always more than one vehicle wide. Road surface generally good. Few vehicles.

At Olette, leave the N116 on the D4 signposted Ayguatebia. The climb is fairly steep to begin with, oscillating between 5 and 7-7.5%, under the cover of trees. The road opens out and curves around the edge of the mountain with a castellated stone wall on the left. Just after Tourol (1048m, 8.3km) take the left fork D4c which descends around 50 metres before ascending again through fairly dense vegetation to Ayguatebia (1325m, 15.2km), a picturesque village of small stone houses, with fish-scale shaped slates on their roofs. There is an eau de source (a spring) near the pristine village school to your right before leaving the village.

The road opens out into pasture land further up where cattle graze lazily while the bells around their necks clang gently. You will pass occasional farm buildings before arriving at the col at 1866 metres. There is a car park, and a visitor centre with a snack bar but it only opens during the summer months. There is also a map showing starting points for several VTT routes if you should be so inclined. The actual col is amongst trees but you are rewarded with good views over the plateau during the quick descent on a wide road with immaculate tarmac to the junction with the D118.

Turn right and continue to descend to the Col de la Quillane passing a small airfield on the right. Here are views over to the left of the skiing pistes of Les Angles and the Lac de Matemale nestling in the valley floor. Descend towards Matemale and at the beginning of the village, turn right to rejoin the D4 signposted Col de Creu.

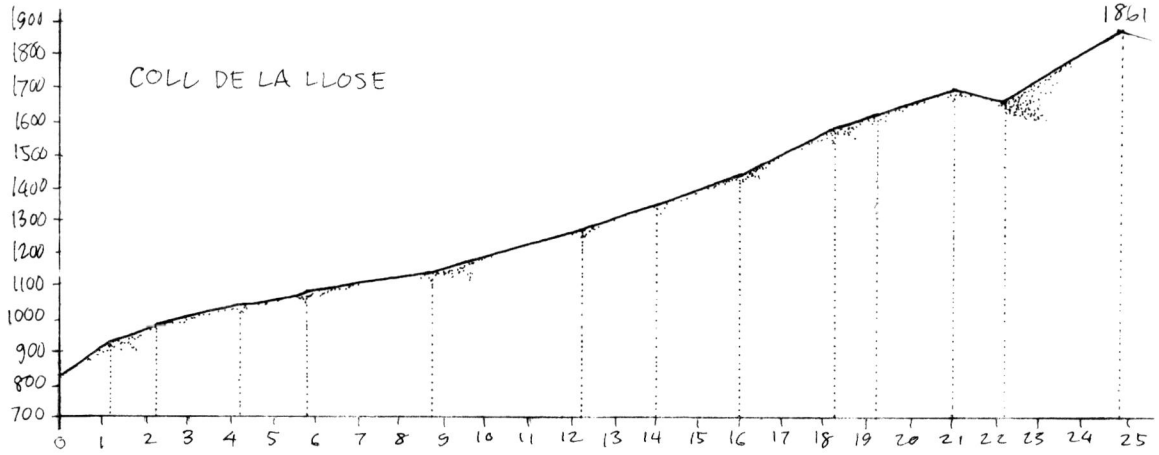

Col de Jau 1506m

Northern approach

LENGTH: 22 KM
HEIGHT GAIN: 1111 M
MAXIMUM GRADIENT: 9%

Follow the D118 from Axat, turn left onto the D17 towards Sainte-Colombe-sur-Guette, then turn left again onto the D84 climbing steadily into the deep Gorges de Saint-Georges cut by the river Aude, then via densely forested slopes for long stretches beside the Aiguette, with occasional flower-spread meadows, to the col.

Southern approach

LENGTH: 25.5 KM
HEIGHT GAIN: 1156 M
MAXIMUM GRADIENT: 10%

Take the D619 out of Prades (a good place to stop overnight) for 2.8 kilometres to Catllar (330m, 2.8km). After Molitg-les-Bains (510m, 7km) it's the D14 towards Mosset (700m, 12km) and the summit. The road is always more than one vehicle wide, the surface generally good with not much traffic, though watch out for the occasional lorry transporting felled trees.

Numerous shops and supermarkets in Prades, a bike shop next to the 'Super U' supermarché on the N116 roundabout in Prades. Small shop and café bar at Molitg-les-Bains. Small shops and café bar at Mosset.

Leaving Prades on the D619 the climb begins at the village of Catllar on a gradient quite gentle at first as the road hugs the contours of the mountain following the Castellane valley. Approximately 2 kilometres from Catllar, the road crosses the river Castellane on a beautiful old stone bridge. The main body of Molitg-les-Bains is situated off the main road up on the right and down in the gorge on the left you pass a magnificent – very expensive – spa hotel complete with thermal baths, supplied by mountain springs. Through Moltig-les-Bains there are a few short traffic-calming sections of cobbles which may temporarily affect your peddling rhythm, but congratulate yourself: think Paris-Roubaix. Thereafter the road surface is generally smooth. Take the D14 out of Molitg all the way to the summit. (The D14a loops to the left and rejoins at Mosset.)

The climb is a steady pull of around 4.5% with flatter sections here and there. Up the valley just south of Mosset, stands an impressive architectural pile dating from the 13th century, formerly the Monastère de Corbiac, now a private house, set back a little from the road. It commands majestic views across to the complex summit of the Pic du Canigou, an impressive geological pile jutting out of the long range of the Massif du Canigou, strikingly on its own.

The mediaeval walled village of Mosset was built in 1135 by the king of Majorca as a fortress on what was then the frontier between the kingdoms of France and Aragón. It's still an imposing sight and reckoned to be one of the 'plus belles villages de France'. The approach enhances your first view; round a bend in the road and there it appears ahead atop the steep buttress slopes, swifts and martins wheeling and soaring above it during the summer months. The road climbs up stone-paved narrow streets to the centre of the village where there is a café bar with incredible views back down the valley towards the Pic de Canigou. Out of a fissure of masonry in the bell tower grows a dwarf woodland pine, two metres high, that reputedly sprouted on the eve of the French Revolution. The revolutionaries had a thing about symbolic trees of liberty, planes mostly.

Above Mosset sprawl cultivated meadows set in trees on the left, the slopes to the far left heavily forested. Perfumes of rock rose, beech trees and conifers. For 3 kilometres out of Mosset, the gradient plods on lazily, around 3–4%, but at 790m the road swings round past the Tour de Mascara, a stone watchtower perched on a rocky outcrop on the left, and suddenly wakes up. Right, it's col time. An immediate hike to 7% and nothing much below that for the next 10 kilometres.

Beyond the tower the valley opens out into grassy meadows. In spring and early summer there is an abundance of wild alpine flowers including orchids, which in turn attract an array of different species of insect and butterfly. The road gets steeper and a series of hairpin bends take you up through the meadows and eventually, at approx 1070m, into the forest of mixed pine and deciduous trees. Snow poles can be found at this altitude and on the left you will pass a small ski station hidden in the trees.

Eight kilometres up the valley above Mosset, the former Cistercian abbey of Sainte-Marie-de-Jau gave succour and rest to pilgrims on the long trek across France to the shrine of Jesus' brother James in Santiago de Compostella.

The col sports a sign, 1506m. Here the road briefly quits the forest and opens out into pasture. There is a car park and fantastic views to the right and back down the long valley. Horses and cattle snack on the summit and the surround. Take pleasure in the natural sonata for birdsong and cowbells.

It's a 22 kilometre descent from the col through the spectacular rock funnel of the Gorges de Saint-Georges to Axat. The D14 becomes the D84 at the col and the gradient on this northern approach is markedly steeper than on the southern side. The first 5 kilometres to around 1000m are steep, double chevron, single chevron, on a fairly narrow but well-surfaced road passing through dense woodland, predominantly pine. Periodically, the trees thin and

Col de Creu 1712m

stand round small grassy clearings overflowing with wild flowers, like tall, mute spectators gathered round a horticultural display. The Aiguette River accompanies the road on its passage downhill. If you choose to cycle up this side of the mountain first thing in the morning, wrap up well – it will be in deep shade and frost may well linger until late into the day. The road passes a small junction on the right signposted Counozols, a village which you can see from the road, built on a rock buttress jutting out from the mountain wall, nestling among trees. Take the right fork at the junction signposted Axat onto the D17 (the left fork connects up to Roquefort de Sault, the Cols Garavel and Moulis, and eventually the Port de Pailhères). You will descend a steep section, 2 kilometres of 9–10%, over a stone bridge through the narrow streets of Sainte-Colombe-sur-Guette and down to the D118 where the rivers Aiguette and Aude meet to form a torrent, cascading through the high-walled gorge. Just before the junction of the rivers stands a hydro electric power station.

After joining with the D118 the route continues to descend all the way into Axat. Beware of frequent, large quarry trucks carrying stone on this section of road, rendering the surface poor in places as a consequence. However, this does not detract from the stunning and dramatic scenery of the gorge itself. The road passes beneath some huge overhanging limestone rock faces with the gorge sides towering many metres above in places forming enormous rocky buttresses. Just past the bibliotech (library) to the right on entering Axat, there is a bridge over the river. Cross the water by way of some stone steps and a small wooden walkway to an island with grass and benches. A nice spot for lunch.

Western approach

LENGTH: 2.6 KM
HEIGHT GAIN: 180 M
MAXIMUM GRADIENT: 9%

From Matemale on D118 north of Col de la Quillane, then D4 in the direction of Railleu:

Ride along past chalet-style houses for a short distance until the road rears up sharply into a snorter of 8% and ascends steeply through pine woods. The road is marked with snow poles, but in summer, if the pines have been baked by a generous sun, the air is heady with the wonderful fragrance of resin. This is a cheery climb, steep and short. The col is encircled by pine trees at a height. There's a picnic site but no open views and two col signs with different altitudes, one a rustic slice of wood and the other a more official-looking metal version.

Eastern approach

LENGTH: 13.5 KM
HEIGHT GAIN: 629 M
MAXIMUM GRADIENT: 8%

A small road, at times only one vehicle width, road surface generally quite good with some rough sections. Plenty of afforested shade.

At the fork of the D4/D4d, continue on the D4 to another fork, at a big right-hand hairpin, with the D4e. A steady 4–5%. Swing left on the D4 to Railleu – good backward views of the road just travelled snaking for several kilometres down the valley, flanked by its stone wall. (If descending into Railleu from the Creu, the first sight of the slate roofs and the village church is picturesque.) There is an attractive pump supplying drinking water built into the wall on the right, a good view of the village of Sansa high up on the flanks below the Puig d'Escotou. Two kilometres out of Railleu, there's another junction: left towards Caudiès-de-Conflent and the Llose, right to the Creu and the serious stuff: 4.3 kilometres of around 8%, leaving the open pastureland for the forest.

This is a tranquil route – it's not on the way to anywhere and the only cars normally belonging to riverains – local inhabitants.

Col de Roque-Jalère 976m

Southern approach

LENGTH:	11KM
HEIGHT GAIN:	611M
MAXIMUM GRADIENT:	10%

The col lies on the D619 between Catllar, south, and Sournia to the north. It marks the passage from the two regions of Conflent to Fenouillèdes.

From Catllar (365m) take the D14 towards Molitg-les-Bains and the Col de Jau. After less than a kilometre turn right onto the D19, signposted Sournia.

From Sournia (530m) – a public water source and a small shop – 8.7 kilometres with a height gained of 486m at a maximum 10%, take the D619 signed Prades and follow this to the summit. A small, quiet road all the way without distance markers, remote and peaceful, although steep from the start, three sections of triple chevron. (Don't always believe the statistics, the chevrons do not fib.)

Afforested low down and at the very top. Otherwise open hillside covered in flowering shrubs, the road climbing up gullies and valleys onto open slopes via short sections of forest.

From Catllar, the road winds up through the gulley for approximately 2 kilometres with the Castellane River below to the left beyond a stone wall. After the right turn onto the D619 signposted Sournia, the road immediately climbs steeply around a series of bends which help to break up the road into manageable sections. There is not a lot of shelter from the sun – the vegetation consists mainly of low shrubs and the exposed rocks and boulders soak up the sun and radiate heat so the climbing is hot work. In the spring and early summer the air is pungent with the scent of wild thyme, lavender, roses and gorse bushes. Roughly two thirds of the way up towards the col, the road leaves the gully and the terrain opens out. Excellent views back down towards Prades, particularly when descending this side of the col; Prades then becomes a valley El Dorado – cool drinks, pavement cafés, nutritious provender.

The road remains steep, marked with double arrows on the map. To the right a small piste or track leads down to the abandoned village of Comes, a sad reminder of just how tough and isolated life must have been in these hills. Near the top of the col the road passes through a short stretch of mixed beech and deciduous forest and the high point of the road is around here. No col sign to greet you, but there is an altitude marker by the road. The actual Roque-Jalère, a minor peak at 1104m, lies further up the grassy slope behind to the north-west. There are two large antennae near the col which can be seen from miles away in both directions and give a fair idea of how far you still are from the col as you climb. The summit offers views to the south into the Têt valley and across to the might Pic du Canigou beyond.

The other side of the col towards Sournia is very open with sweeping views out over grassy slopes dotted with rocks and boulders, consequently the road is rather exposed to the wind. There are some interesting rock formations including one called Roc Cornut which, in the opinion of one informant, resembles a duck. (Cornuto is Catalan for 'horned', also 'cuckold'… who knows what local overspill of illicit passions this may record?)

There is a small turning towards the village of Campoussey but this apart there are really no other dwellings between Roque-Jalère and Sournia. The final descent into Sournia is steep and fast, across a small bridge into the sizeable village. There is a fair small shop but this is lonely-ville territory, the opening hours tend to be erratic, so it's best to carry plenty of fluid and food supplies.

8. Judgement Mountains

The Sierra del Cadí in northern Catalunya, a spectacular group of summits at the eastern end of the Spanish Pyrenees, is part of a national park. A cadí was a Moorish judge, hence this section's title. Dominating the Cadí stands the Pedraforca, a summit with twin peaks, Pollegó Superior (2498m) and Pollegó Inferior (2407m) – the Higher and Lower Spur – yoked by the Enforcadura (2348m), a tree fork. Pedraforca means 'fork of rock' like the pitchfork the Devil uses to prod sinners into the eternal bonfires of Hell, or else like his cloven goat's hoof. Mediaeval witches used to gather for sabbaths on the bare mountain and the local wiccans assemble to celebrate the solstice every feast of Sant Joan (Saint John) on Midsummer Eve.

To the west, the landscape of Judgement Mountains is riven with ravines; further east, it becomes greener as the Pyrenees make a lengthy descent to the vineyards of the Roussillon and the Vermilion Coast by the peacock-blue waters of the Mediterranean.

The refugee route across the passes is well trodden. Professed Jews were expelled by the Spanish Inquisition in 1492, after the conquest of the Moorish kingdom of Granada by Ferdinand II of Aragón and Isabella of Castile whose marriage united Spain. Then it was the turn of the Mudéjares (Muslims) in 1502, tramping northwards across the stern mountain barrier to markets less picky about a trader's religion. When Franco's Falangists took Barcelona during the Spanish Civil War, many Republicans left Spain in the wretched, footsore exodus, including the cellist Pablo Casals who took up residence in Prades, the father of Luis Ocaña, Tour winner in 1973 and the poet Antonio Machado, who died in Collioure in 1939. 'I have walked many roads,' Machado wrote, 'and opened many new paths… everywhere I have seen caravans of

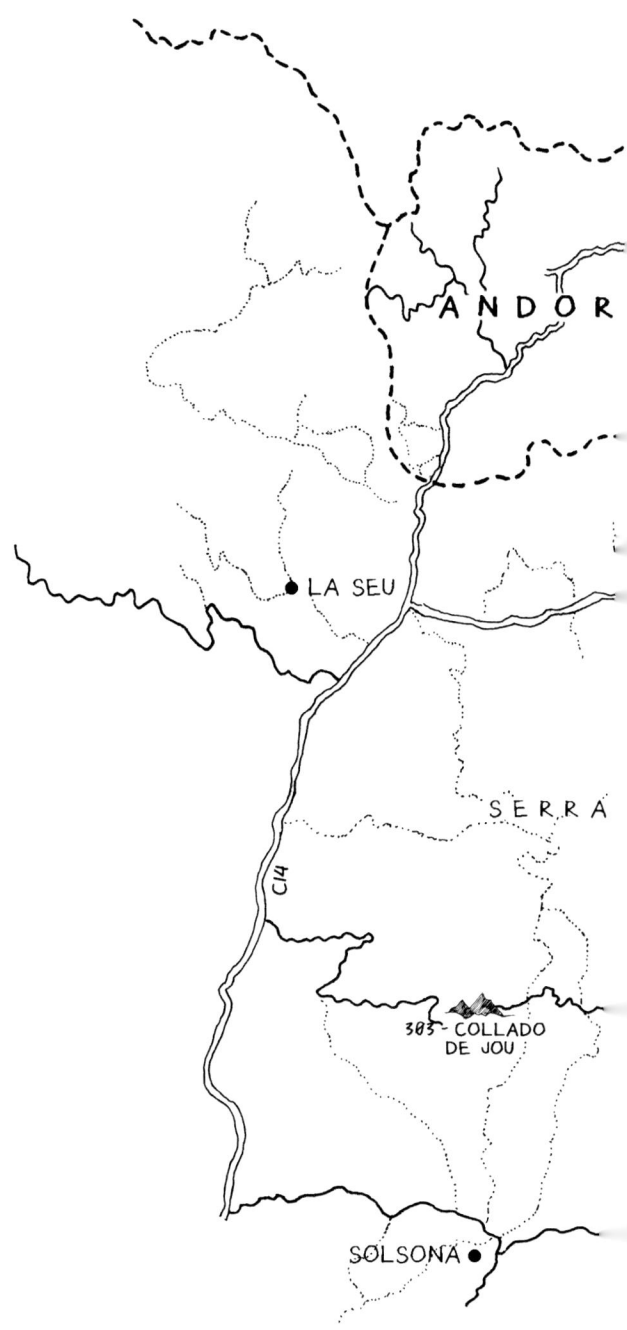

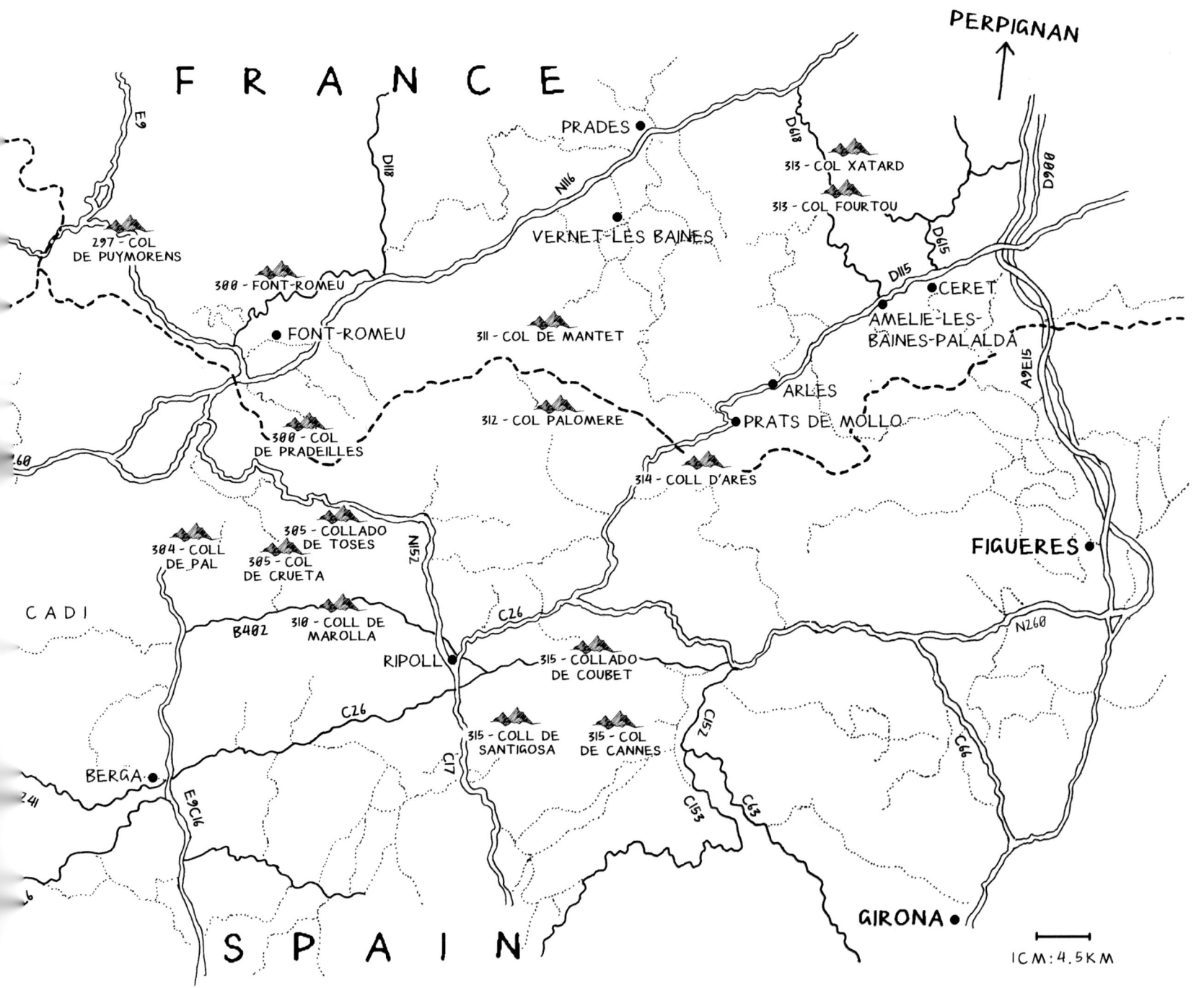

sadness, proud men, beaten men, in the dark shadows, bewildered.'

The culture changes eastwards, too, from proud Basques with their pelota, tugs-o'-war, fandango, dried red peppers and unfathomable language, to the gentler dances, songs and 'demà, demain'[37] attitudes of southern and south-western France, from Provence across Languedoc to the Pyrenees, an area known (in French) as Occitanie.[38]

The Occitanes said 'oc' for 'yes' in their language of Occitan, closely related to the lyric tongue of the Provençal troubadours and also to Catalan, banned by Franco for being threateningly non-conformist. Similarly, the sun-kissed southern French, ever despised and mistrusted by the frosty northerners, the powerbrokers in Paris who said 'oy, oui', lost out. But, along the eastern Pyrenees, you'll hear Oc on market days, in bars, town squares and at village fêtes when they sing.

Sample the famous sobrassada and botifarró sausages. Sobrassada (which originated in Mallorca), a raw cured sausage made with ground pork, paprika – which lends it a distinctive flame red colour – salt and other spices can be grilled or spread on bread and is an ingredient in the famous Catalan dish llom amb col (pork loin with cabbage). Botifarró is a pork intestine filled with coarsely ground pork of various cuts, including the liver, flavoured with pepper and *anis* (aniseed). It is usually boiled and eaten fresh.

---

37 With 'demain' pronounced as 'domaing'

38 Occitan was also known as the Langue d'Oc (the 'language of the Oc' – hence modern 'Languedoc') and Provençal.

P285 A Spanish cow ponders the advisability of wandering out into the road

P286 The road leads onto the ridge on which sits the *collado de Pal*

P288 From the *Creueta*, south, a whiplash of fast descending

P290 The *Creueta* gives onto high moors and fine perspectives south

P292 The mountains give judgement… the rocks blush

P294 Riding into the sunset, warmth, peace, fine high road

P296 Night falls and day's end, weary cyclists heading for home, talk, food and drink

Col de Puymorens 1920m

From Bourg-Madame

LENGTH: 26.6 KM

HEIGHT GAIN: 900M

MAXIMUM GRADIENT: 8%

In neither direction is negotiating the Puymorens particularly difficult, except as regards distance and the aggravated annoyance of traffic. Let's not putz about: lorries. Indeed, I had originally decided against the inclusion of what is, *force des choses*, necessarily an iconic col in the legend of the Tour de France. So too the Envalira in Andorra, excluded because it's in Andorra and there is nothing good to be said about Andorra except as a ski resort.

However, the decision to reinstate being made, the Puymorens is in. With grave reservations, albeit. I have ridden it on three occasions (both ways), the last time on the Raid Pyrénéen and it's not a pleasant experience, though some quite like it. De gustibus nil disputandum… chacun a son goût.

The col was first included in the Tour de France in 1913, when the race traversed the entire Pyrenean chain in two massive stages, and every year after that till 1937; since then, only a handful of times… for those with an extra finger.

The N20 north leads to the village of Ur (1200m – of later date than the ancient Ur of the Chaldees, the first recorded city) where it swings left along the valley of the Carol. An easy, serpentine road into the cleft of the re-entrant, through Enveitg (1255m, 6km). This border village is linked across the railway line with Latour-de-Carol, where the Hôtel Transpyrénéen was well-known during the War as an assembly point for allied airmen and Frenchmen escaping forced labour and their guides. Latour is also the terminus for the Train Jaune, mainly for tourists but still a necessary link for the villages between here and its other terminus in Villefranche-de-Conflent through the mountains to the east.

Further on, the Tours de Carol mark the ruins of a castle built to defend the Cerdanya, a county of Catalunya, from the hostile encroachment of the Count of Foix's scallywags. Alongside them runs the viaduct carrying the railway line from Barcelona to Foix.

Through the small village of Porta (1520m, 17.5km) with a café, Burton's Gare, (Burton unidentified, but probably not he of 'gone for a…') in the small station building and a right turn on the approach to the tunnel. Porté-Puymorens (1640m, 20.6km) is an ugly little ski station – war memorial, bars – from which the road ahead appears slaloming down the hillside. The sight of the final zigzags – long slashes of concrete across the rocky slopes below the col, like razor cuts – is impressive, even intimidating, but the gradients are not taxing, with nothing worse than 5%. The pay-off is a pleasing sense of cracking a big climb without excessive exertion. The downside is the col, without question one of the most unattractive in the region, a scrubland of rocks and stones. Perhaps it wears a permanent petrified scowl at the proximity of Andorra, a giant's boulder throw across the neighbouring range. The view – perhaps from the terrasse panoramique in the hotel on the col – is, unsurprisingly, of mountains.

From Ax-les-Thermes

LENGTH: 27.6 KM

HEIGHT GAIN: 1200M

MAXIMUM GRADIENT: 8%

The road linking Ax with Pas de la Casa, a tax-free, charm-free zone across the border, follows the course of the Ariège River at an easy stroll. The juggernauts thundering into your slipstream will make it seem neither easy nor a stroll. Best to go at lunchtime when most of the drivers are safely off-road, lunching.

From Hospitalet (1430m, 18.1km – bar, post office, railway station, a mess of buildings) a steep side road off to the left cuts out the first big corner of the climb proper. After a further 3.4km the tunnel approach turns off right and the long hairpins begin. The surface is newly repaired and excellent, the terrain bleak, the sense of clambering out of France in the direction of Spain powerful.

TOUR DE FRANCE STAGE 14, 6 JULY 1964

Unstoppable Anquetil

Before the start of the Tour, a journalist writing in France-Soir had predicted that Jacques Anquetil, four-times winner, would abandon after an accident on the fourteenth stage, that is after the Rest Day in Andorra. He repeated this in a private letter to Anquetil himself. Anquetil had won that year's Giro d'Italia but victory, his second, had drained him and he was clearly rattled and out of sorts.

Radio-Andorra issued a general invitation to the journalists and other Tour followers to a barbecue on the Rest Day, and, for form, extended it to the riders. Only one responded: Anquetil. He was a notorious bon viveur, quite disinclined to abstinence, even for a bike race, even when he wasn't on top of his game.

News that he was pitching up to the pig-out soon got round the peloton. One of Raymond Poulidor's team mates spat: 'He really takes us for mugs, playing at tourists.' When Henri Anglade and his team mate Georges Groussard, in yellow, heard, Anglade was furious. 'He's taking the piss. He's going to find out what we think of his vagaries. Tomorrow, boys, everybody off the front, we attack from the off.' Anquetil always hated fast starts.

While the Norman was tucking into copious quantities of barbecued lamb and sangria – photo-journalists snapped up pictures of him and his directeur, Raphaël Géminiani tearing chunks off the same roasted leg – the other riders were back in their hotels, preparing for bed.

Was Anquetil bluffing? Pushing his doubts into a cul-de-sac of endgame risk? Sure it is that he didn't sleep a wink and in the morning looked haggard and ill, his face the colour of papier mâché. Antonin Magne, Poulidor's directeur, told him: 'Raymond, today you have to attack at the foot of the Envalira, right from the start.'

So, while Poulidor, Bahamontes, Anglade and his team shot off up the climb of the highest col in the Pyrenees (2048m), the entire Saint-Raphaël team gathered round their ailing leader to coax him up the slopes. He was in a dire state, wanting to vomit, haunted by the prediction that this would be his last day in the Tour, his legs powerless.

As he finally neared the top, already more than 4 minutes down on Poulidor and Bahamontes, Géminiani drove up and handed him a bidon half full of champagne.

'Either that finishes him off or he takes off,' he said.

Anquetil took off.

The descent of the Envalira leads onto the northern slopes and the tight hairpins of the Puymorens. This day they were thick with fog, but Anquetil hit the downhill like a suicidal maniac, following the tail light of one of the motorbikes. He clipped parapet walls, nearly came off a dozen times but, in the fury of throwing off the jinx and the ravages of his gourmandising, he was unstoppable. When he caught the yellow jersey group, Anglade asked him if he was going to work with them or not.

'I'll let you know in 10 kilometres,' Anquetil replied.

Along the valley of the Ariège, Anquetil steadily cranked up the speed to 50kph, catching Poulidor and the lead group in Tarascon. His Tour was back on track. Twenty-five kilometres from the finish in Toulouse, Poulidor's back wheel collapsed. The mechanic fitted a new wheel, but when relaunching him pushed so hard that Poulidor fell. By the time he got going, the Anquetil group was away up the road. Poulidor lost 2min 36sec that day. The legend of his misfortune was born.

Col de Pradeilles 1983m

From Bourg-Madame

LENGTH: 14.7 KM
HEIGHT GAIN: 1300 M
MAXIMUM GRADIENT: 10%

From Bourg-Madame, the D70 runs south-east to Osséja – a picturesque village of narrow hillside streets and plenty of places for stocking up – and continues as the D30. Head on through and to the right at a crossroads, over the river Llavanera, and continue round sharp hairpins for 0.5 kilometres to a camp site. There follows a steep climb – as bad as 10% – for 5 kilometres, the road becoming very exposed, to a fork (1660m, 10km) in the Route Forestière, as this road is designated. Turn right and the Pradeilles is 9.2 kilometres further on; turn left and it's steeper although only 5 kilometres. Both routes run through the woods of the Fôret de Palau.

The longer route is much easier, with intermediate difficulty at around halfway and nearer the top. The shorter route has a distinct snarl in it: a pretty-well constant 8–8.5% most of the way.

The Col de Pradeilles straddles the meeting of the two approaches and the single road continues up to the Cime de Coma Morera (2205m) 4 kilometres further. But this is mountain bike territory and from the Cime, the intrepid VTT enthusiast can ride the frontier ridge.

The poor quality of the road overall is the sole detraction from a quiet and very pleasant ride with spectacular views – for instance, at the Fontaine Monnier (1510m, 8km) a windy ledge on a narrow, bumpy stretch of road, and the open plateau at Les Couronnes (1850m, 11.2km).

Font-Romeu 1800m

Western approach

LENGTH: 15.1 KM
HEIGHT GAIN: 1150 M
MAXIMUM GRADIENT: 8%

Probably best approached from Bourg-Madame, a slightly unkempt border town originally known as La Guingette ('pleasure garden') after a local hostelry which enjoyed great popularity and was renamed in 1815.[39] The Duc d'Angoulême, last dauphin of France, later Louis XIX, and his wife, Louis XVI's daughter, spent the long years of the Empire in exile in Poland and England. The Duke returned to France in 1814, took possession of Bordeaux and organised an attempt to resist Napoléon after his escape from Elba. It failed. He was captured, transported to Barcelona and came north once more after Napoléon's defeat at Waterloo, taking up brief residence in La Guingette. The townsfolk proposed Bourg-Angoulême in his honour (and their advantage). He, however, gracefully turned the compliment in honour of his Duchesse, Marie-Thérèse-Charlotte.

From Bourg-Madame (1140m) 17.6km east along the D618, mostly not much worse than 3% through Ur, with a steeper kilometre leading into Villeneuve. Beyond Angoustrine, at 7.5km, the road traverses the distinctive Chaos de Targassonne, 3 kilometres of 5.5 out of Egat leading to a flattish 4.6 kilometre stretch of no more than 2%.

The Chaos ('confusion, jumble') has become famous to 'boulderers' worldwide. Scattered across a plateau at 1500m, a vast number of coarse-grained granite boulders of varying size and shape – large and small, smooth and angular – borne down by glaciers, offer the enthusiast a choice of some 900 climbs, from very easy to severe.

Also near Angoustrine stands the Four Solaire – 'solar oven', a huge gold screen, like a royal Aztec mirror, at 3000 sq. m. larger than the Arc de Triomphe. Built in 1969, it no longer generates solar power but the adjacent buildings house an institute for research into ceramic materials and their conduct under intense heat. There is a Visitor Centre which, through the summer, puts on shows powered by the full moon.

Font-Romeu is Catalan for 'pilgrim's spring' named (legend has it) for a clear source of mountain water discovered by a cowherd who saw a bull sipping from the spring. The town itself, another station climatique, once famous for its treatment of tuberculosis and now for asthmatic children, offers the usual tourist clutter of pancake emporia, beauty parlours, Locasports, service du ski'surfs, scandichalets, ice-rink, souvenir shops, eateries and drinkeries etc. The through road forks to offer more climbing: either 5.6 kilometres to the Col del Pam (2005m) via the Col du Calvaire (1830m) or 6.4 kilometres to the Mollera dels Clots (2040m). Neither ascent demands much more than 6–7%. On the way, a grand view of the ranges which flank the Massif du Canigou opens up southwards. The Canigou is as iconic in this part of France, the Roussillon, as the Pedraforca is in Catalunya.

---

[39] There's an excellent bike shop, Esports Iris, on the main road between Puigcerda and Bourg-Madame, close to the French border.

TOUR DE FRANCE 1968, 1973, AND 1976

The Curse of Font-Romeu

The Tour first came to Font-Romeu in 1968. After the 14th stage which ended in Perpignan, the peloton spent the Rest Day here and departed hence at the start of stage 15. There had been some doubt in that year of violent political turmoil in France – two governments fell – whether the race would go ahead. Poulidor was the great favourite and in superb form, relaxed and strong: this really did promise to be his winning year, at last.

But on that stage out of Font-Romeu, one of the press drivers lost control of his motorbike and smashed Poulidor's rear wheel; he came off headfirst and was out of the race with a broken nose. He bled and so did France. He would never win the Tour or wear the yellow jersey.

'With that fall,' wrote Antoine Blondin 'came the annual calvary. We saw the architecture of his handsome head, obstinate and enigmatic, composed, impassive, ardent, on a stretcher, an image at once bloody and confused. The ambulance discharged Poulidor on the threshold of a hostelry which promised every sort of luxury and he was carried in between two lines of neatly-dressed maids and waiters in short skirts and short horizons who yet gave him a spontaneous ovation, welling out of an unexpected source of delicacy and feeling. The more permanent and familiar glory of Alain Delon, (the film star) also in attendance, was, for a short time, relegated to the partial shadow where large armchairs serve as the stretchers for matinee idols.'

Roger Pingeon won the stage that day (Jan Janssen the Tour). The race ended that year on the municipal cycle track in the Bois de Vincennes, to the east of Paris. A month after Pingeon's own triumphant arrival in the capital the year before, the demolition teams arrived at the Tour's traditional final destination, the pink track of the Parc des Princes, and proceeded with their picks to destroy a little of the Tour's history.

In 1973, after another Rest Day in Font-Romeu, the riders went from Bourg-Madame to Luchon. On the descent of the Portet d'Aspet, Poulidor overcooked a bend, his wheel hit the parapet and he came a purler into a thorn bush, although his wounds were more spectacular than serious.

'What happened to me? Can I get back on? Tell me,' he said when the journalist Louis Caput came over to attend to him.

Caput shook his head. 'Come on Raymond, better to stop.' Once again Poulidor was out.

In 1976, the only other time the Tour has visited Font-Romeu, the stage was taken by Raymond Delisle, after a bold attack. Lucien Van Impe, playing the cautious hand, tamely let the break go despite an offer from Zoetemelk for a shared chase, and thus surrendered his yellow jersey by nearly 5 minutes. An unthinkable dereliction. He did regain it and took the Tour but had to be prodded all the way.

Collado de Jou 1480m

Western approach

LENGTH: 41KM
HEIGHT GAIN: 860M
MAXIMUM GRADIENT: 7%

This col lies on the road that links Lost Mountain to Judgement Mountains.

From the foot of the Collado de Bóixols turn left at Coll de Nargó – a good bar/restaurant with a menu del dia – and follow the main Andorra road north for a couple of kilometres to the right turn (620m) for Sant Llorenç de Morunys. The bed of the river to the right is a mixture of shingle, mud and ribbons of stone, lined with rivulets of water. The road dips and rolls at no great gradient past savagely pollarded poplars that resemble lumpish tree chandeliers for 5 kilometres (760m) where the slope begins that long, tiresome business of moving away from the course of the stream up into the fastness of the rock from which it springs. These Spanish trajectories rarely offer much in the way of sustenance – a tiny community called Perles (860m, 7km) has no bar, but the Spanish are kind and a knock at a door will usually yield a filled bidon.

The interlocking folds of the mountains on either side make what looks like a chicane. A series of short tunnels give shelter from rock falling off the big overhang of cliff to the left – at the end of one 100-metre tunnel, the bollard shows 8km – and the surrounding crags begin to shrug off the shawls of vegetation for serious sunbathing.

Through Alinyá the road flattens through to a bridge (1010m, 10km) followed by another village, Les Sorts (1060m, 11km) from which opens a fabulous plummeting view down into the gorge. There is very little shade. Ahead appears to be a yoke between the opposed mountainsides – a col, surely, to which the road is picking its way up the rock face on a long traverse. Glance back and the height you have won is laid out in a long scrawl of tarmac. At 14km, 1230m the gap you saw proves not to be a col, after all, but no more than a cleft in the stone, very exposed and with scant vegetation. Pylons stride across country parallel with the road, keeping pace with the 7% to 15km where the road begins to fall away gently into El Solsones and the Collado de la Travessa (1300m, 17km). The sign is down. But now you click: this is an up-and-over-several-times col journey.

The descent begins, a steady 5%, good riding, to a bar/fonda (inn), Casanova, at Cambrils (1200m, 19km) and on through hills which are rounded and kneaded like lumps of plasticine heading for more defined shapes to 22km, 1130m, where the climbing inches in again. The road becomes a ledge round a cirque, through another tunnel, and on round the pleats of the re-entrant.

At 30.5km, 1320m, a natural spring affords more bottle-filling. Locals line up with demijohns to take advantage of the pure font water. Big haunches of rock jut from the landscape, the road courses a ridge, the relief map of Catalunya spreads out to the south. On one tunnel, a graffito proclaims 'Som una nación' (we are one nation), though whether this is for or against Catalunyan separate (not separatist) identity, is not certain.

Bare-faced, beetling cliffs dominate, a kilometre of around 7% at 34km leads to a flattish section and the last 5 kilometres are mild, to a crossroads. The Collado tops the road to the right, a narrow lane leading down to Solsona.

Straight on for 9 kilometres down tight bends at 5–7%, with a long view of the blue water reservoirs outside Berga, to Sant Llorenç (1000m) a nondescript town with no discernible attraction, though it does offer a beer to the parched ciclista.

After courting a sterner, more rugged identity with very little movement in it for 15 kilometres, the route becomes an undulating country road, settling into 4.5km of swinging hairpins at a gentle 5% to 1280m through trees offering sylvan views. At this summit, an unlit tunnel, 100 metres long but the far end visible, and a descent of some 11 kilometres into the industrialised zone of Berga – where this end of the Pyrenean ranges rear up on the Spanish side – and the C149 on to Ripoll.

Coll de Pal 2080m

From Baga

LENGTH: 19.3 KM
HEIGHT GAIN: 1235 M
MAXIMUM GRADIENT: 10%

The Coll de Pal is a dead-end as I and my photographer, Pete Drinkell, discovered one dark October Sunday night. We left the humped neck of the col in a chilli-red sunset on a broad, curvaceous, smooth band of tarmac, pale beige-pink in the dying light, towards a far-off inky chasm of space, speckled with a growing array of town lights. The road was fast, the day's work done, hotel, food, drink lay ahead of us, where exactly we neither knew nor really cared – an itinerant author and photographer racing to a tight schedule and an inflexible itinerary. After 2 kilometres of easy descent, me at the wheel, a-chirrup about how this day's end was a slam dunk on such a fine highway, we crossed the Torrent de Comabella, signs for the Estació d'Esqui de Coll de Pal off to the right, whereupon the fine highway ran out, transmogrified into a wide scree of loose pale stones. A recent landslide? The torrent in fearsome spate depositing a rubbish of mountainside debris? Surely no more than a minor obstacle.

We motored on, gingerly, steadily, in search of the soon-to-be-recovered tarmac. Six or seven kilometres on, no tarmac. The track we were following was only marginally more amenable than what lay to either side of it, only just distinguishable from it and little better, in truth, than a faintly defined dry gulch coursing through a watershed of boulders. The doughty hire car inched, nosed and picked its careful way over the loose and lumpy obstacles strewn in its incautious path, its headlights carving out a spectral corridor in the besetting pitch dark. We humped and bumped past a gantry ringed with arc-lights round the shadowy bulk of a building: possibly a border post housing guards armed to the teeth, infra-red binoculars at the ready, on the alert for smugglers and drug-runners – the area was once thick with them – which we were not but whom, given the circumstances they might reasonably argue, we closely resembled and might well be.

We emerged, at last, onto a flat rectangle of asphalt in the spread of woods above Masella. A municipal carpark. Since the municipality had in effect been pissing on us for the last 45 minutes or, I strolled over to the girding hedge and, so to speak, pissed on the municipality.

We got back into the car. Thereafter hangs another tale, but take it as proven: some of the information in this book was hard won, very hard won.

Baga lies on a minor road which runs parallel to the thundering major highway through the Tunel del Cadi, north and south under the massif of the Serra de Moixeró. Just to the west runs the G107, a twisting green route known as 'El Camí dels Bons Homes' (the path of good men) reputedly used by Cathars fleeing the religious persecution in south-west France during the early years of the 13th century.

Baga offers a number of hostels, an old arcaded central plaça, a campsite and restaurants serving local specialities.

The first kilometres of the approach, an up-and-down of mild climb and flattish in betweens, drifts through a rocky gorge, a couple of tunnels cut in the overhangs, the tarmac quite good, a sense of penetrating a mountain fastness way up ahead in the unseen heights. Bandit country. Ambush waiting round the next projecting bluff. Arid stream bed to the left. Forested hillside flanks above.

There's a picnic area and campsite at 2.4km and, on a cliff above, a belvedere, the Mirador de Bac de Divi, ('shady viewpoint of the gods') – possibly those gods of the high places who sit on outcrops or cruise past on the wings of the storm and deliver judgement of bad weather, fogs and roads going nowhere, on mortals intrepid and foolish enough to sally forth into their realm.

The gradient is easy until 6km where it hits 9%, then tightens to a maximum 10 over the next 3 kilometres. There is a real sense, now, of clambering up towards a remote ridge reinforced by long views over the yawning valley re-entrant to the left where the carretera (highway/road) at the floor drives on towards the tunnel mouth. Around 6.9km, the road swings round a big right-hand hairpin at a junction with a small rutted and rock-strewn camino (track) to the left. Cattle lounge or lollop vacantly about. The forest track is not strictly a ride for a racing bike, but the views from the mirador (viewing point) some kilometres along are stupendous. It was on this track that we'd seen the chilli red sunset beginning to sink over the far ranges, leaving them in stark purplish black silhouette.

The final kilometres to the Pal even out after the fiercer rack of the middle section. The woodlands thin too as the road hoists itself up into the thinner air and the incumbent rock forces itself clear of any significant cloak of soil. A viewing point at 11.2km is a gallery of wonder – a fabulous panorama – loose stone chippings from intermittent falls lie across the road and, at around 12km, as the gradient slackens somewhat, you pass the intervening Coll de la Canal Mala and, 200 metres or so further on, the Coll del Forn, the two slight peaks making a sort of yoke where one section of the range abuts another.

The road is very exposed from now on, up to the Xalet-refugi (chalet-refuge) de Coll de Pal (17km) beside the Font Canaleta. Open moorland either side, grazing kine, a kindlier slope for the final 2 kilometres to the windy top of the Coll. It has taken a lot to win this one, but the welcome, in the form of a deep, deep satisfaction, is full-hearted. A fine, taxing climb.

Coll de Creueta 1900m

Southern approach

LENGTH: 21 KM
HEIGHT GAIN: 1035 M
MAXIMUM GRADIENT: 12%

Pobla de Lillet is a pleasant little town with a very helpful tourist office, near the old bridge over the Llobregat River in which swim trout served up at the Hostal Pericas, a no-nonsense hostelry, recommended to me by locals as the best place to eat. Fifteen rooms, cyclists and bikes welcome, a menu in Catalan, 10€ for a three-course lunch with wine and bread. The café con leche at the Bar Nuria in the main town square, Plaça del Fort, is, our informant insists, the best in the region.

A bright green, old-fashioned diesel train – a Carrilet – links Pobla with Castellar de N'Hug, 3.5 kilometres up the valley towards the Creueta. Two open wagons carry 25 passengers and a train leaves every hour.

From the centre of town, ride east for 500 metres or so and turn left towards Castellar de N'Hug. The road is wide and clean-surfaced for a short distance of 5.5% and 3.5% onto a flatter stretch which suddenly revolts and slams you with a 9% average, masking the 12% maximum. On the left is the old cement factory, El Clot de Moro, designed by Rafael Guastavino. It opened in 1904, closed a hundred years later and is now once again a cement factory, although only from July to September. Alongside it stands a queer Gaudi-esque house, once a habitation, now derelict, like a disused lot on a Gothic movie set, described by our informant as resembling an armadillo. Guastavino emigrated to the USA from Barcelona in 1881 and reinvented an ancient method of embedding tiles in layers of mortar to achieve large curved surfaces.

There follow 2 kilometres of relatively easy gradient, overhanging rocks to the left and spacious views of the valley down to the right. The road narrows, the

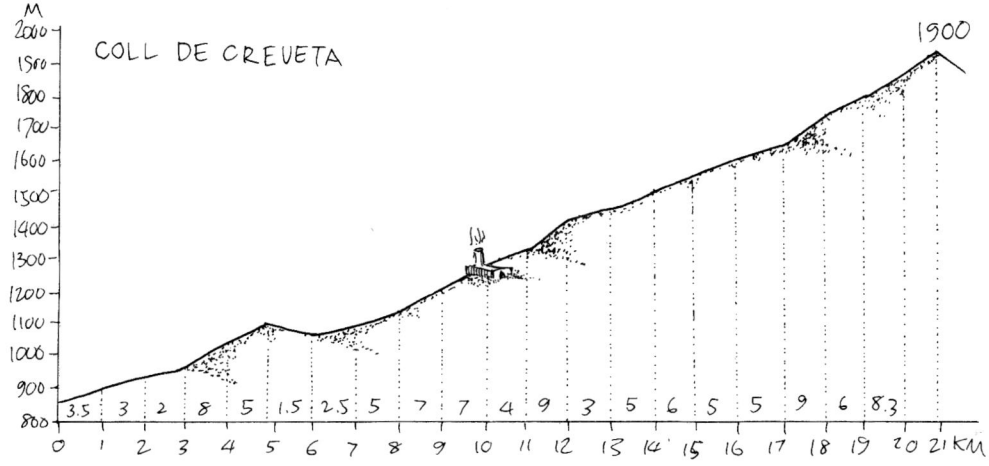

riding is pleasant. At 4.4km there's a picnic area – in summer the traffic will be more intrusive because of various tourist lures in the vicinity. At 7.8km the Hostal les Fonts stands close to the Fonts del Llobregat, the springs from which rises the River Llobregat: it flows down through the middle of Catalunya to debouch into the sea at Barcelona. A cool place to stop, water spouting from the rocks in the ravine, a handsome waterfall, a watermill nearby, food, rooms and gift shop in the Hostal.

The gradient now makes a clear statement of intent: a steady 6% or so, a kick of 7.5+ at 15km, with more than 6 kilometres still to go, but bear in mind that two Dutch cyclists whom I met in Campan reckoned that the climb of the Creueta from this direction is as hard as that of the Tourmalet from the west, which they'd just done. It's largely due to the relentless pitch of the slopes and, higher up, the exposed nature of the road and the yawning mountainscape through which it sneaks.

At 11.4km, 1400m Castellar de N'Hug is a small mountain town atop a dead-end off to the left of the main road, visited by mushroom hunters in the autumn and skiers in winter – a needless detour unless you lack provisions or water.

The final 10.4 kilometres deliver the weight of the Creueta's punishment: the road winds itself out of the valley re-entrant onto the bare mountainside and the awe-inspiring exposure of the landscape exerts itself. The steepness isn't extreme, the continuing stress of a hard, characterless, empty, seemingly eternal road, is. On the other hand, there is a large aspect to this climb, a heroic scale, most pleasing to the ardent adventurer on two wheels; in other words, when you get to the summit, you know you've been in a fight and the contentment at not giving in, of coming through, is considerable.

The final run-in offers a gentle easing down to around 4 and 3% average, the col is windswept and barren but blessed with fabulous views. Ahead, at the foot of the descent – a flying ramp worth the sweat of the climb – lies La Molina, in summer a flaking-paint, concrete and composite shanty town of battened-down snow-gear and souvenir shops, garish hoardings, unstocked bars and restaurants, stubby blocks of apartments, largely deserted in summer (apart from an all-year bowling alley and… well, some tacky stuff here and there).

VUELTA A ESPAÑA 2001, SABADELL-MOLINA

Decimation on the Creueta

This was the third mountain stage of the Vuelta, the third finish at altitude and the decisive move came on the Creueta. Tauler and Cioni broke early and, at 33km Santiago Blanco joined them in company with Elli, Vicioso and Moller. They were no threat to the overall. The peloton, Joseba Beloki in the leader's gold jersey, let them go. At the foot of the penultimate climb of the day, the Creueta, 53 kilometres from the finish, the six escapees had a 5-minute lead on the peloton. On the first slopes Cioni fell away, the pace simply too hot. The peloton was upping the ante too, and breaking up. Marco Pantani was one of the first to shell out and he eventually trailed in 20min 45sec down on the day.

Four kilometres up the climb, Elli and Vicioso were dropped and 6 kilometres from the col, on the long sweeps of the road cut into the bare mountain, Blanco launched a strong attack. By the top of the Creueta he had an advance of 47 seconds on Moller, 4min 50sec on the peloton, now reduced to a mere 30 riders, and was dropping down into the valley. 34 kilometres to go. He rode the punishing climb up to the ski station at La Molina with apparent ease and assurance, the breath of victory flaring his lungs, to take the first Vuelta stage win of his career.

Collado de Toses 1865m

Southern approach

LENGTH: 24 KM
HEIGHT GAIN: 450 M
MAXIMUM GRADIENT: 6%

1865m on N152, the main route north from Barcelona into France. The best way to approach the Toses from the south is by rail from Barcelona [see 'How to Get There'].

Just across the border in France lies a historical oddity: Llivia, a tiny enclave of Spanish sovereign territory on French soil. During the first half of the 17th century, Spanish power waned as that of France waxed. By the Peace of the Pyrenees in 1659, Spain ceded the plateau and valley of the Upper Cerdagne with all its 33 villages to France. (The Cerdagne runs north-west/south-east from the Puymorens to the Spanish border. 'Puigcerda' is Catalan for 'Puy Cerdan', Cerdagne Peak.) The people of Llivia protested: although but a few hundred in number, they were decidedly not the inhabitants of a village. The Romans had fortified it as Julia Libia. Known as the principle town of the region, it lay on the arterial Via Domitia, which traversed the Col de la Perche, a route taken by Hannibal and the elephants. The Visigoths subsequently built a fort here, sure testimony of its strategic importance, as later did the Moors. Not a village, therefore, but a town. France had to concede and Llivia remains Spanish, more strictly Catalan, part of the ancient kingdom of Aragón which means that if you are too late for lunch in nearby Bourg-Madame, Llivia's restaurants will only just be opening for the menu del dia. Most convenient.

The train ride from Barcelona is a pleasure, but leave the train at Ribes, 121 kilometres north, and the Toses offers 24 kilometres of steady climbing, never much more than 5% and mostly a gentle 3 or 4%. The road south of Ribes, a large highway, is not recommended. After Ribes it shrinks to the width of two cars and winds and undulates round the side of the high Reserva Nacional de Freser Setcases, the slopes falling away to the left.

Planoles (127km) lies mostly below the path of the road but a kilometre on there is a bar/restaurant and the overlooking heights to the right stand lower as the road moves gradually up. Around 138km and 1600m the bends begin to get tighter and more frequent and at 1700m, the ridge appears, fenced with trees, where the col must lie. This was the main route taken by successive refugees fleeing various persecutions north out of Spain.

From the Collado a fine panorama of the French Pyrenees opens ahead, the frontier wall. There is a bar/restaurant, a big car turn round and the first metres of tarmac leading to a fast, joyous 21-kilometre descent into the valley and a choice of routes north into High Woods and Ravines.

Climbing from this direction, the Toses offers no great difficulty: 7 kilometres of around 5% and the rest vacillating between 1 and 3.5.

The Tour de France has thrice crossed the Toses. In 1957, stage 17 took the riders 220 kilometres from Barcelona to Ax-les-Thermes, won by Jean Bourlès, first of only two major wins in his career.[40] The

---

40 The other was the Grand Prix de l'Ouest, 1964.

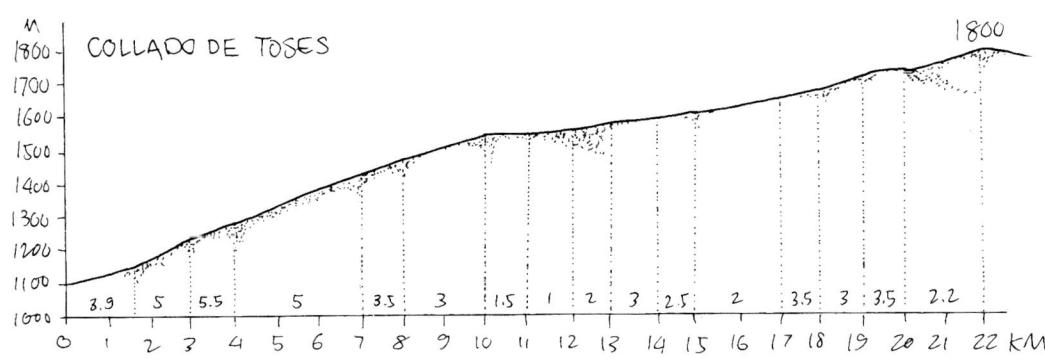

308   THE RAPHA GUIDE

day was horribly marred by the death of the Radio Luxemburg reporter, Alex Virot (the first man to report the Tour on radio, 1933) and his motorbike driver, René Wagner. The machine plunged off the road into a ravine on the road into Ax: both were killed instantly.

In 1965, the route was reversed and José Perez-Frances made a heroic lone escape of 223 kilometres to win. The 1968 race crossed the border into Spain once more and the Toses featured in the 14th stage, 231.5 kilometres from Seu d'Urgell, at the south-western tip of Andorra, by way of the Envalira to Perpignan. Jan Janssen, the first Dutchman to win the Tour, took the stage, but Herman Van Springel kept the yellow jersey and held it all the way to the final time trial in Paris, where he led Janssen by 16 seconds and the world hour record-holder since the previous autumn, Ferdinand Bracke, by 1 minute 56 seconds. Both Springel and Bracke were specialists against the clock; Janssen was given third-best chance but, in the event, over 54.7 kilometres, he beat Van Springel by a healthy 22 seconds and Bracke by 1min 23sec to win the Tour by 33 seconds. Janssen is on record as saying, before the '68 Tour, that since Merckx had now muscled onto the scene – he won that year's Giro – the rest of them had only one chance left to win the French tour.

Coll de Marolla 1090m

Eastern approach

LENGTH: 17.6 KM

HEIGHT GAIN: 350M

MAXIMUM GRADIENT: 7%

This is a hidden jewel of a climb, a delightful escape route from the main highway north, a rustically hidden minor throughway nosing into the heart of upper Catalunya.

Campdevánol sits on the N152 a couple of kilometres north of Ripoll and is the next stop on the railway line between Barcelona and Puigcerda. Turn left onto the G1-401 in the direction of Gombrén. Away from the traffic, you breathe more lightly; the road is in reasonable condition as the town's thinning outskirts give way to juicy meadowland and fields, cultivated and fallow, as you head for the distant hills. There's no toll of gradient to speak of, a bit of a lift from 5.5km, until a bridge over the Llobregat, to whose course the road runs parallel, at 8.5km. Crossing over the stream is a small rite of passage: enough dawdling, the road seems to say, now we face our responsibility, and the climbing begins. The gradient is not hard, but that depends as much on morale as on the spryness of the legs. At 10km a flatter section and the road winds round the flank of the hill and drops into the hamlet of Gombrén, 10.9km, a picturesque hillside village. Bar/restaurant El Portal del Comte. The Count in question, Comte Arnau, (11th century) is celebrated in local legend as an infamous combination of Scrooge and Don Juan, a miserable son of a bitch who treated his serfs like dogs and, more colourfully, seduced a succession of the sisters in the convent of Sant Joan de les Abadesses 15 kilometres away. The story goes that he penetrated the nunnery's defences by a secret tunnel dug all the way from Gombrén, and (one presumes) the nuns' defences by his rakish charm and a threat to spill the not inconsiderable beans if they didn't put out.

Gombrén is overlooked by the eastern end of the massif designated the Cadí-Moxeró National Park and some 3 kilometres out of town a small road up to the right leads to the Santuario de Montgrony. If you are feeling frisky, it's an added 5.5 kilometres and the setting is breathtaking.

The road to the col narrows and begins to twist more markedly. Gradients of around 6–7%, an umbrageous leafy arras to the right, a wide sight of valley to the left, the road dipping and springing with bucolic merriment. The surface is pretty good and the straitness of the road here doesn't stop it being twisty, adding to the perfect charm of the ride. Across a bridge at 13.6km and there remain 4 kilometres of moderate climbing to the Coll de Marolla (alternatively Puerto Marolla) at 17.6km. This marks the border between Girona Province to the east and Barcelona Province to the west. A Refuge with barometer, altimeter and temperature gauges outside the door, handy restaurant inside and great views westwards over the neighbouring valley.

The beginning of the descent is a bit hairy – poorly maintained tarmac, tight hairpins, blind corners and a dramatic switchback leading onto the bridge over the l'Arija torrent. The hamlet El Bergueda (19.2km) announces a far better surface and a substantial widening of the road which makes the descent much more secure. At 22.7km there is a sharp closure of the gradient – to note if you are plotting an west-east crossing of the Marolla – but the drop soon eases and flattens out past a fine stone building at 24.5km and on into the first outcrops of Pobla de Lillet (26.4km).

Col de Mantet 1761m

From Villefranche-de-Conflent

LENGTH: 21KM
HEIGHT GAIN: 1320M
MAXIMUM GRADIENT: 10%

This climb finishes in a dead-end but worth the ride for the stunning views from this vantage of the Massif du Canigou.

The local Vélo Club Vallespir organize a number of uphill time trials in this region every year and the Mantet is the destination for one, in mid-August, from the foot of the climb at Villefranche-de-Conflent. Etrangers (outsiders) – are made very welcome and our guide informants (who have a house in Vinça) entered the less difficult Ria to Nohedes race – a 500m height gain over 13km – and were each awarded small trophies and a bottle of wine as best overseas entrants. Toujours la politesse.

North from Prades on the D116, along the Têt valley, lies the old fortified town of Villefranche de Conflent. Defensible enough from ground level, the town was extremely vulnerable to attack from the cliffs above and the great military engineer Vauban added a number of bastions as well as the castle, known as Fort Liberia perched up high up on the valley rim. Like many such fortresses – the Bastille for one – Fort Liberia did double service as a prison. Odd name, Liberia, for a lock-up. Four women convicted of an infamous poisoning were banged up here for the rest of their life during the 18th century, while the most recent inmates were German prisoners-of-war.

From the roundabout at Villefranche turn right towards Mont Louis and after approximately 1 kilometre turn left onto the D6 (445m) opposite an old bridge over the river Têt.

The Tour de Goa, a mediaeval look-out tower, which stands at 1300m on the ridge, halfway up the climb to the Mantet, is plainly visible.

Once on the D6 the road begins to climb gradually and therefore comfortably as it meanders up through pasture land with the river Rotja to the right. 3% melds with 4% which merges seamlessly with 5… 5.5… 6% for some 12 kilometres. You will pass through a few small villages, Fuilla and then Sahorre (675m, 6.7km) with their attractive, traditional Catalan-style churches, the bells in their open towers faithfully chiming out the hours. In the village of Py (1023m, 12.8km) a fountain supplies eau potable and a café/bar, Café des Mines, more flavoursome drinking. The road rears up sharply through the village and at the junction take the right-hand fork for the Col de Mantet.

Here the trouble starts: 738 metres in a little over 8 kilometres. From Py the road climbs relentlessly up to the col. Expect to spend a lot of time working hard out of the saddle and hearing the desperate cry echo in your head, 'Oh for a triple chain ring'. On the final approach to the col a long, very steep and straight section is worth a triple Michelin arrow. These arrows, unlike the restaurant stars, once awarded can never be lost. The punishment of the Mantet and other zones of excruciation is for ever. But the reward for the killing efforts is stunning: open views back over to the slopes of Canigou. It stands in France but the Catalunyans claimed it as a symbol of their independence, its solitary splendour like a beacon of their own sense of self and separateness. Look across, left, to the Tour de Goa and a few kilometres directly south to the line of peaks along the Spanish border – Pic de la Dona, Pic du Géant, Pic de Coma Armada. Draw breath and wonder.

The immediately surrounding slopes are grassy and carpeted with a vast array of species of wild flowers. The area around the col sign is open with woodland over to the left in which, according to a local French fungus hunter, excellent cèpes, known here as 'penny-bun mushrooms', can be found. A little way up the slope to the right there is a memorial stone in memory of Georges Bassouls, a well-known French Naturalist who dedicated his life to the protection of the fauna and flora of the Pyrénées Orientales.

The tarmac road ends at a car park on the col but a track continues beyond the col sign down a short, steep descent, some 200 metres, to the village of Mantet. Locals call this 'the end of the world' and it is the last village at this end of the French Pyrenees. On an established escape route into Spain during the War, Mantet was a centre of Maquis resistance to the Germans who marched in, expelled all its inhabitants and razed the village to the ground in 1944. It wasn't rebuilt and resettled again until the 1960s. The famous GR10 high walking path leads to the Réserve Naturelle de Mantet, founded by Bassouls, a haven for walkers and nature lovers, and the Pyrenean mountain goat, the isard, which gives its name to a local event for Espoir (under-23) riders, the Ronde de l'Isard.

The descent from the Col de Mantet is obviously steep and therefore rapid but the road surface is pretty good. It is possible to take a right turn in Sahorre and descend down into Vernet.

Col Palomère 1036m

From Vinça

LENGTH: 22 KM
HEIGHT GAIN: 776 M
MAXIMUM GRADIENT: 7%

From the centre of Vinça, take the D13 road climbing at a gentle gradient through abundant fruit orchards – pendulous branches of peaches, nectarines, apricots, grapes and cherries. Umpteen different varieties of finch flit in their dipping between the laden trees. At a roundabout approximately 1 kilometre outside Vinça, turn right and shortly after turn left, continuing for a little way before taking the right-hand fork in the road signposted Baillestavy and Valmanya. As the D13 leaves the fruit trees behind in the Tet valley it quickly gains height climbing towards Baillestavy (586m, 11.5km). The gradient is manageable and comfortable and the road is partially shaded by small trees and shrubs. The river Lentilla flows through the gulley below to the right. The road winds up round some fairly sharp, blind bends, and although it's usually fairly quiet, there will be some occasional passing local traffic.

Signs on the way up to the col ask drivers to watch out for – and avoid – fir salamanders, amazing and very striking little newt-like creatures which stray onto the roads, particularly when it's been raining, to bask in the sun. Mottled black and yellow – a warning livery, as with wasps – these salamanders secrete a poison which makes them inedible. According to the Roman naturalist Pliny the Elder, the mythic salamander was supposed to be able to live in fire which it quenched by the chill of its body. The alchemist Paracelsus used the name for the elemental being that inhabited fire and Francis I, king of France, adopted the salamander as his badge with the motto Nutrisco et extinguo (I nourish and extinguish) as fire purifies good metal but consumes dross. Compared to the darting, slippery lizards they resemble, the salamander is a sluggish, laid-back breed of reptile, much given to sunbathing for the fiery heat that legend bids it crave.

Baillestavy (585m, 11.5km), historically an old iron-mining village, is the first place you pass through on the way to the col, There is a café bar on the right just before a picturesque stone bridge over the Lentilla which is fairly fast flowing at this point. From the bridge, the main village and church are visible to the left further up the valley side by way of a small, steep road a little past the bridge on the right.

The road becomes steeper after Baillestavy, marked in places with single arrows on the map with one very steep but mercifully short section as you enter Valmanya (865m, 16.5km), a small village with stone houses, many of which I believe are now holiday gîtes. Many residents of Valmanya, a Resistance stronghold, were killed by the Germans in 1944 and much of the village was torched or bulldozed flat. On the road out of Valmanya a poignant memorial – a brass plate inside a small stone arch – commemorates those victims of the reprisal.

Having crossed the Lentilla again just outside Valmanya, the road drops for 1 kilometre and around 50m before climbing steadily, mainly through trees before you emerge into the open just before arriving at the Col Palomère at 1036m. The col is marked by a sign at the high point in the road. There are fantastic views from here back over to Pic du Canigou to the left and down towards the Tech valley from the opposite side of the road.

From the Palomère, there is a choice: the D13 descends around a series of bends to the village of La Bastide. On a clear day it is possible to see right over to the Mediterranean coast and if you stop the bike for a moment it will be completely silent, no noise pollution from nearby roads. The road surface is a little rough in places, sending vibrations up through the handlebars at times. The terrain consists of grassy meadows and woodland. La Bastide stands alone in the middle of nowhere. It has a small campsite and a good eau de source coming from a running pipe under a stone arch at the side of the road. A nice spot in which to cool down on a hot day. There are some basic toilets along from the eau de source by the road which may belong to the campsite although they appear to be open for public use. There is also a small café at the side of the road reached by climbing a flight of steps.

After La Bastide, the road continues to descend through trees providing a little shade before climbing fairly gradually to the Col Xatard.

The alternative is to turn right at the col along a poor forest trail south for 9 kilometres towards the Col de la Descargue (1393m) on the D43 below the ancient iron mine at La Batère and so on down a reasonable road to Arles-sur-Tech. From Arles-sur-Tech, north to the Descargue, is 19.5 kilometres, a height gain of 1098m and some stretches of around 10% in the first 7.4 kilometres to Corsavy, really very steep indeed with a breathing space at 3km. From Corsavy (790m) the road flattens for 3 kilometres and then begins a steady trudge of around 6–8% to the col.

Col Xatard 752m via Col Fourtou 646m

From Vinça

LENGTH: 21.3 KM
HEIGHT GAIN: 400 M
MAXIMUM GRADIENT: 7%

Named for Senyor Xatard, a botanist and pharmacist of Prats de Molló who also gave his name to a plant found uniquely on the high pass between the Val d'Eynes and Catalunya at the east of the region. A member of the Apiaceae family (which includes celery, anis and hemlock), the Parsley of Isard, as it is commonly known, is a weird-looking, emerald green, leguminous triffid of a plant which sprouts in clefts of rock.

The passage of the Col Xatard links the east-west valleys of the Têt and the Tech and offers one of the most attractive ways of approaching the Spanish climbs of the Judgement Mountains from France.

At Bouleternère, 6 kilometres east of Vinça on the main N116, turn right onto the D618 to Amélie-les-Bains, 21.3km, height gained 550m, maximum 6%. The D618 follows the old coaching route across the mountains, twisting in and out of the lower folds, nosing into the gullies and canyons which gave easier access, and this section of the route is a fine example of such a canyon in the rolling hills of the Aspres. The vegetation is sparse – stunted dwarf oaks, broom and scrub – the road surface a bit rough, houses scarce, but the winding trace of the old coaching thoroughfare round the wriggles of the Gorges du Boulès is a beauty, wild and remote. The low bluffs lining the rim of the gorge might be a-wink with heliograph mirrors, Rapha scouts signalling your approach to the Campagnolo ambush party up ahead, alert to the alien incursion of Shimano… Our guide informants nicknamed this route – exposed, with not much shelter from tree cover – The Valley of Death because the warm wind and arid air blowing through means it can get incredibly hot.

The gradients are never very demanding. From the dusty little village of Bouleternère the road dawdles into the valley for a 3 kilometre lift of 50m or so, drops over a series of three small bridges and then lifts its heels for the rest of the way to the intermediate Fourtou, at 17km.

At 7.4km, a steep turn right onto a series of tight hairpin bends leads up to the 11th-century Romanesque Prieuré de Serrabone – well worth a visit to see the columnar gallery in pink marble decorated with bas-reliefs of the Apocalypse like a crypt in Christian churches, but a marked Mozarabic feature mimicking the pillared interior of a mosque. There is a botanical garden round the old priory. Serra bone is Catalan for 'good hill' and the frame of the chapel, its walls and bell tower built of irregular-sized flat stones in mottled shades of grey, sits well on the mound of its rock base, stark against the sky. Wonderful views, too.

Opposite the turn to Serrabonne on the left there is a small shop with a couple of tables outside where refreshments and local artisan products are available.

Between Boule d'Amont (12.8km) and the Col Fourtou (17.2km) the gradient does kick up somewhat but at the col the road flattens onto a ridge. Views open out and, 4 kilometres on, past the chapel of La Trinité, a steeper section of around 5–6% tops out at the Xatard.

The road surface from the southerly direction and Amélie-les-Bains (21.3km) is much better and the gradients no tenser; on both sides the real difficulty of the climb is its length. However the road is quiet and very attractive, tree cover on the south side for much of the way lower down.

There are plenty of bars, restaurants and hotels at the old spa and casino town of Amélie-les-Bains and the road west towards Prats-de-Mollo and the Col d'Ares is a lovely riverine ride.

Coll / Collado d'Ares 1513m

Eastern approach

LENGTH:	32 KM
HEIGHT GAIN:	1250 M
MAXIMUM GRADIENT:	9%

A good port between the eastern French end of the chain and the main Spanish ranges of Judgement Mountains.

Arles-sur-Tech, famous for its 11th-century abbey and the annual Bear Fest in February, stands on the D115 linking the French Mediterranean coast to Ripoll on the main northerly route to the Pyrenees from Barcelona. The road from Arles is twisty, relatively easy to Prats-de-Mollo (18.5km), following the former course of a railway line, washed away in floods in October 1940. Old railway buildings en route. Steeper gradients through woodland to the more exposed intermediate Col de la Seille (1185m, 25.7km) and Col de la Guille (1194m, 26.5km). Big panoramic views from this intervening plateau: north to the Pic de Canigou, east over what the French call the Côte Vermeille, because of the soft red of the sunsets. From here the climb gets harder again, around 8% for 3 kilometres, until it flattens out for the final kilometre run-in. The road surface is not particularly good. The col marks the French-Spanish border: height on the French side given as 1513m, on the Spanish, 1610m. No Customs Post but a bar/restaurant.

The descent is tricky to begin with, because of the sorry condition of the tarmac. A large number of derelict dwellings lend the area an abandoned air, but this adds to the sense of passing from the fatter, greener region of the Mediterranean littoral to the stonier acres of northern Catalunya. A sign warns against falling rocks. What, one asks, is one supposed to do? Dodge, just in case? Or is this merely civic foresight, an implicit insurance policy, a sort of 'we told you so, don't say you weren't warned' if you do get hit by a chunk of mountain?

Lower down, the road surface improves dramatically, and the long drop into Camprodon (18 kilometres from the col), on steady, undemanding gradients down the valley of the Riu Ter, is fast and most pleasurable.

Camprodon, at the confluence of the rivers Ter and Ritort, sits to the side of the main road. An agreeable little mountain town, its centre (away from lines of modern apartments lining the outer limits), is good for a ramble: a collection of old buildings, a small antique square, cafés and bars. Famous son: the Catalan composer Isaac Albéniz.

The Ruta del Ferro, an 18 kilometre cycle track, follows the path of the old railway line from Sant Pau de Seguries, 6 kilometres further on from Camprodon, all the way to Ripoll. Ripoll as a whole is a bit of a mess, its centre lost in the wider sprawl of urban development. It does boast two good bike shops, however: Casa Vilia (Trek specialists) and Technobici. The Benedictine Monestir de Santa Maria, founded in 888, a short step to the south, is well worth a visit. The Hostal des Ripolles is recommended.

Collado de Coubet 1010m, Coll de Canes 1120m, Coll de Santigosa 1064m

Eastern approach

LENGTH: 11 KM
HEIGHT GAIN: OVER 600M IN TOTAL
MAXIMUM GRADIENT: 8%

Girona is used as a base by many professional racing cyclists – latterly Armstrong, Hamilton and Landis, now David Millar – so, humming with that kind of vibe, it makes a good place to start from. A Green Lane, the Ruta del Carritet, runs 57 easy kilometres along the old railway line north-west to the former terminus at Olot. The outskirts of Olot are grim: industrial estate squares fists at urban sprawl and the resulting scrap is dirty. The old town at the heart is very different: a fine, antique Catalan town, full of life and grace. (The mediaeval town was largely destroyed in two earthquakes in the 15th century.) Olot is capital of the Garrotxa region, known as 'the city of volcanoes' from the three dormant volcanic cones nearby. The Coubet straddles the route along the D260 further on towards Ripoll and the main foothills of Judgement Mountains. An alternative is to turn right off the D260 after Blanya onto the C153A, from where it's 12.5 kilometres towards Sant Salvador de Blanya and thence over the lesser Collado de Capsacosta (870m): a beautiful, leafy, tranquil ride on a narrow road, no great stress of gradient, 10 kilometres into the far valley of the Ter and the C26 south of Camprodon.

The climb to the Coubet is intermittently quite hard, made tougher by long stretches of road without any bends to speak of. Always rather demoralising, these long straights of hard-boiled road, but the surface is excellent. At the col the road forks: right towards Sant Joan (on the C26) over the Collado de Santigosa, 1064m at 4.3km, on first-rate tarmac with some narrow barriered sections, the road generally in tree cover with occasional glimpses of the spectacular vista beyond. A pleasant scoot down into Sant Joan. The left fork continues along the ridge, then into undulations which take in the intermediate Collado de Canes, 1120m after 3.8km. The road is generally very quiet – most of the traffic opts for the main C26 running parallel to the north – and the views are glorious all the way into the valley at Ripoll (19km).

Essential repair vocabulary

Note: Don't forget that, although it is better to be able to ask for exactly what you need, you can always point and rely on the international language of bike shops. Mechanics in most small garages in France are happy to help out with running repairs on bikes.

English	French	Spanish
Adjustable spanner	clef (clé) anglaise	alicates
Allen key	clef hexagonale or à six pans	llave allen
Bag	sacoche or musette	bolsa
Battery	pile	pila
Bike	vélo	bicicleta
Brake	frein	freno
Brake block	patin de frein	zapata de freno
Brake cable	câble de frein	cablero de freno
Brake lever	poignée de frein	palanca de freno
Brake hood	cocotte	gomas palanca freno
Broken	cassé (-ée)	roto (rota)
Cap	casquette	casquete
Cassette	roue-libre à cassette	piñones
Chain	chaîne	cadena
Chain rivet extractor	dérive-chaîne	troncha cadenas
Chainwheel	plateau de pédalier	platos
Cleat	cale-chaussure	pedales automáticos
Crossbar	tube horizontal	tubo horizontal
Down tube	tube diagonal	tubo diagonal
Forks	fourche	horquillas
Frame	cadre	cuadro
Front	avant	de delante
Gear cable	câble de dérailleur	el cable de los cambios
Handlebar	guidon	manillar
Handlebar tape	tresse pour guidon	cinta de manillar
Headlamp	phare	faro delantero
Headset	jeu de direction	dirección
Head tube	tube de direction	pipa de dirección
Helmet	casque	casco

With thanks to Josep Bort Grau and Leticia Nova Parareda who helped with the Spanish vocabulary.

English	French	Spanish
Hub	moyeu	cubo
Inner tube	cambre à air	cámara de aire
Jersey	maillot	maillot
Nut	écrou	tuerca
Oil	huile	aceite
Pedal	pédale	pedal
Pump	pompe	bomba
Pump up	gonfler	inflar
Puncture	crevaison (verb: crever)	pinchazo (tener un p.)
Quick-release hub	moyeu à blocage rapide	cierre rápido
Rear	arrière	de cola
Rear lamp	feu arrière	faro trasero
Rim	jante	llanta
Rim tape	fond de jante	cinta de llanta
Saddle	selle	sillín
Saddle post	tige de selle	tija de sillín
Screwdriver	tournevis	destornillador
Shoe	chaussure	zapato
Shorts	cuissard	coulotte
Socks	chaussettes	calceta
Spoke	rayon	rayo
Sprocket	couronne	dienta de rueda de cadena
Stem (of handlebar)	potence	potencia
Tights (bib tights)	collant (collant à bretelles amovibles)	mono
Tyre	boyau / pneu	neumático
Valve	valve	válvula
Washer	rondelle	arandela
Water bottle	bidon	bidón
Wheel	roue	rueda

Acknowledgements

To Simon Mottram, the inspirational founder of Rapha, who asked me to write this book, I owe an enormous debt of gratitude. Not only has it been a unique privilege to work on such an absorbing, challenging and exciting project, but the chance to spend so much time, on and off the bike, in the mountains where I feel so at home, has been a rare treat. I hope that, in knowing them now much better than I did, I have imparted some of the unalloyed pleasure that the voyages of discovery have been.

To Nick Flanagan, who has given me time, help and transport as well as hospitality in the Massat valley in the Ariège, on so many occasions my base of work, a huge thank you.

Brit Steen Beedenbender came to the Pyrenees for the first time and produced some really outstanding reports on the climbs she did there. It was a tall order – riding and writing about them in the short stay she had, but she delivered excellent material to deadline.

Michelle Sayell and her partner Timothy Leonard Jordan supplied me with first-rate accounts of the climbs in the vicinity of their house in the Pyrénées Orientales. Their enthusiasm and keen observation were of great help.

For the wholehearted support of the amazing and devoted Rapha team I am deeply grateful. Their sense of style and their belief in the highest ideals of workmanship as well as the loftiest calls of cycling are a constant source of delight.

On a number of occasions, not least when I was riding up cols one-handed as I gasped notes into the recording machine, I have returned from the mountains in a rickety state. Thanks, therefore, to Gillian Allsop for her kindly and efficient way with the acupuncture needles in restoring me to something like poise.

To Dr Corinna Abesser, many thanks for expert help in explaining the intricacies of geology and asymptotic valley formation.

Pete Drinkell was not only a perfect companion in the two weeks of the photography shoot – never a cross word and total complicity of work and purpose – but has, in my view, produced a truly astonishing portfolio of landscape studies, both broad and intimate, from mountains which he had never before visited.

David Duffield, whose generosity has cost him a number of irreplaceable books loaned to ne'er-do-wells and fly-by-nights, kindly gave me long-term use of a rare volume on trust from his extensive library.

Andrew Maxwell-Hyslop is that rara avis, an editor whose interventions are always astute, thoughtful and, above all, mannerly. The final shaping of the text owes much to his deft analysis, amiable good humour and lively intelligence.

Finally, to all the friends and pals, men and women, with whom I have, over a number of years, ridden in the Pyrenees, and Susanne, with whom I walked in them for the first time, hearty thanks for their company, their cheery disposition and, most particularly, their sharing in that love of those mountains which underpins every sentence in this book.

Graeme Fife 2008

Index of Climbs

Climb	Page
Abaurrea Alta 995m	48
Col d'Agnès 1570m	241
Alto de Remendia 1047m	48
Alto Laza 1129m	50
Coll/Collado d'Ares 1513m	314
Col d'Aspin 1489m	169
Col d'Aubisque 1709m	149
Ax-les-Trois Domaines 1372m	264
Col d'Azet 1580m	202
Col de Bagargui 1327m	46
Port de Bales 1755m	205
Puerto de Beret 1860m	112
Col de Beyrède 1417m	173
Puerto de la Bonaigua 2072m	115
Puerto de Bonansa 1380m	110
Collado de Bóixols 1380m	117
Col des Bordères 1156m	157
Port de Boucharo 2270m	194
Col de Bouézou 1009m	78
Col du Boum 1298m	271
Col de Burdincurutcheta 1135m	45
Coll de Canes 1120m	315
Collado del Canto 1725m	116
Col du Carcanet 1400m	277
Cauterets 934m	191
Chateau de Monségur 1059m	269
Col de Chioula 1431m	266
Cirque de Troumouse 2100m	196
Col de la Core 1395m	233
Puerto de Cotefablo 1423m	103
Collado de Coubet 1010m	315
Col de la Couraduque 1367m	155
Coll de Creueta 1900m	305
Col de Creu 1712m	280
Col de la Crouzette 1241m	238
Piau Engaly 1870m	197
Col d'Erroimendy 1362m	49
Collado de Espina 1407m	109
Collado de Fadas 1470m	109
Collado de Faidella 1250m	117
Font-Romeu 1800m	300
Col Fourtou 646m	313
Col de Garavel 1256m	276
Col de la Gargante 1352m	271
Gavarnie 1365m	194
Guzet-Neige 1520m	236
Hourquette d'Ancizan 1560m	174
Col d'Ispeguy 672m	40
Col d'Issarbe 1450m	75
Col de Jau 1506m	279
Collado de Jou 1480m	303
Col de Labays 1351m	78
Port de Larrau 1585m	49
Col de Latrape 1111m	236
Port de Lers 1517m	246
Col de la Llose 1866m	278
Lourdes-Hautacam 1535m	158
Luz-Ardiden 1720m	162
Col de Mantet 1761m	311
Col de Marie Blanque 1035m	145
Coll de Marolla 1090m	310
Col de Menté 1349m	225
Col des Moulis 1099m	276
Puerto de Oroel 1090m	83
Port de Pailhères 2001m	274
Coll de Pal 2080m	304
Col Palomère 1036m	312
Col de Péguère 1375m	246
Collado de Perves 1350m	111
Col de Peyresourde 1569m	203
Pico Gorromakil 1090m	39
Col de la Pierre Saint-Martin 1760m	73
Pla d'Adet 1680m	200
Collado del Plano 1380m	110
Plateau de Beille 1780m	259
Pont d'Espagne 1496m	191
Col de Port 1249m	243
Col de Portet d'Aspet 1069m	229
Col du Portillon 1293m	207
Col du Pourtalet 1794m	189
Puyarron 1240m	82
Puyeta 1201m	72
Col de Pradeilles 1983m	300
Col du Pradel 1673m	272
Col de Puymorens 1920m	297
Col de la Quillane 1713m	277
Col de Roque-Jalère 976m	281
Route des Corniches	262
Saint-Jean-Pied-de-Port	41
Coll de Santigosa 1064m	315
Puerto de Sarrablo 1291m	106
Señor Banos 1400m	105
Col de Soudet 1540m	76
Col de Spandelles 1378m	156
Superbagnères 1804m	208
Paso Tapia 1340m	48
Collado de Toses	308
Col du Tourmalet 2114m	164
Col de Tramassel 1615m	158
Val Louron 1580m	202
Vilas de Turbón 1300m	108
Col Xatard 752m	313
Zuriza 1290m	71